A Handbook of Qualitative Methodologies for Mass Communication Research

A Handbook of Qualitative Methodologies for Mass Communication Research

Edited by

Klaus Bruhn Jensen
and
Nicholas W. Jankowski

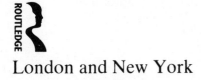

London and New York

First published 1991
by Routledge
11 New Fetter Lane, London EC4P 4EE

Simultaneously published in the USA and Canada
by Routledge
29 West 35th Street, New York, NY 10001

Reprinted in 1993 (twice)

Printed in Great Britain by
Redwood Books, Trowbridge, Wiltshire

British Library Cataloguing in Publication Data
A handbook of qualitative methodologies for mass communication
research
  1. Mass media. Research. Methods
  I. Jensen, Klaus Bruhn   II. Jankowski, Nicholas W.
  302.23011

Library of Congress Cataloging in Publication Data
A Handbook of qualitative methodologies for mass communication
  research / edited by Klaus Bruhn Jensen and
  Nicholas W. Jankowski.
    p. cm.
  Includes bibliographical references and index.
  1. Mass media—Research—Methodology. 2. Humanities—
  Methodology. 3. Social sciences—Methodology.
  I. Jensen, Klaus. II. Jankowski, Nick.
  P91.3.H35 1991
  302.23′072—dc20   91–3686

ISBN 0–415–05404–4
ISBN 0–415–05405–2 pbk

Contents

Tables

Contributors

Teun A. van Dijk is Professor of Discourse Studies, University of Amsterdam, The Netherlands. After early work in poetics, text linguistics, and the psychology of text processing, his recent work focuses on the social psychology of discourse, especially news discourse and the reproduction of racism through discourse. He is the author of several volumes in each of these domains, and is current editor of *TEXT* and founding editor of the new journal *Discourse and Society*.

Michael Green is Senior Lecturer in the Department of Cultural Studies (formerly Centre for Contemporary Cultural Studies), University of Birmingham, UK. He has written extensively on media, cultural policy, and education (for example, *Unpopular Education* from CCCS); he also works actively with media teachers at different educational levels and with an arts and media center.

Nicholas W. Jankowski is Associate Professor at the Institute of Mass Communication, University of Nijmegen, The Netherlands. Author of *Community Television in Amsterdam*, he has been conducting qualitative research of small-scale media since 1975. He is also involved in the study of cable television services and is research director of the Centre for Telematics Research in Amsterdam.

Klaus Bruhn Jensen is Associate Professor in the Department of Film, TV, and Communication, University of Copenhagen, Denmark. He is the author of *Making Sense of the News* and of many articles on reception analysis, qualitative methodology, and news. During 1988–9 he was a Fellow of the American Council of Learned Societies affiliated with the Annenberg School of Communications, University of Southern California, USA.

Kurt Lang and **Gladys Engel Lang** are sociologists on the faculty of the University of Washington in Seattle, USA, where both of them are Professors. Previous joint publications include *Collective Dynamics* (1961), *The Battle for Public Opinion* (1983), and most recently *Etched in Memory: the Building and Survival of Artistic Reputation* (1990). The American Association for Public Opinion Research honored them with its award for a lifetime of exceptionally distinguished achievement in the field.

Peter Larsen is Professor in the Department of Mass Communication, University of Bergen, Norway. He is the editor of the recent UNESCO study, *Import/Export: International Flow of Television Fiction*, and has written extensively on mass communication research and semiotics.

David Morley is Lecturer in Communications at Goldsmith's College, London University, UK. He is the author of *The Nationwide Audience* and *Family Television* and of numerous articles on qualitative audience research, cultural theory, and other aspects of mass communication research.

Horace M. Newcomb is Professor of Communication in the Department of Radio–Television–Film at the University of Texas in Austin, USA. He is the author of *TV: the Most Popular Art*, editor of *Television: the Critical View* (now in its fourth edition), co-author, with Robert S. Alley, of *The Producer's Medium: Conversations with America's Leading Television Producers*, and has written extensively on television and other aspects of mass communication.

Michael Schudson is Professor in the Departments of Communication and Sociology at the University of California, San Diego, USA. He is the author of *Discovering the News: a Social History of American Newspapers* and other works, including as co-editor, with Chandra Mukerji, of the forthcoming *Rethinking Popular Culture*.

Roger Silverstone is Director of the Centre for Research into Innovation, Culture, and Technology, and Reader in Sociology, both positions at Brunel University, London, UK. He is the author of *The Message of Television* and other works on various aspects of mass media, and is currently preparing a new volume, *Television and Everyday Life*.

Gaye Tuchman is Professor of Sociology at the University of Connecticut, Storrs, USA. She is the author of *Making News: a Study in the Construction of Reality* and many articles about news. Her most recent book is *Edging Women Out: Victorian Novelists, Publishers, and Social Change*.

Fred Wester is Associate Professor of Research Methodology in the Faculty of Social Sciences at the University of Nijmegen, The Netherlands. He is the author of several books and articles on interpretive sociology and qualitative research methods. A recent work of which he is co-author, *Qualitative Analysis in Practice*, examines uses of the computer in qualitative research.

Preface

The publication of this Handbook marks the culmination of several professional and personal itineraries. The chapters of the volume suggest that the field of mass communication research has been undergoing two interrelated developments in recent decades: the rise of qualitative approaches as methodologies with an explanatory value in their own right, and the convergence of humanistic and social-scientific disciplines around this "qualitative turn." As editors, we offer the Handbook as a resource for the further development and social use of qualitative methodologies in different cultural and institutional contexts.

The personal itineraries have taken one editor from Europe to the United States, the other from the United States to Europe, and both to India, where the idea for the Handbook was first conceived during the 1986 meeting of the International Association for Mass Communication Research. As participants in this conference, we were reminded repeatedly that while qualitative research represented an important (and frequently the most inspiring) part of the scholarship presented at that and similar events, there were as yet hardly any journals, conference sessions, or handbooks available which could serve to institutionalize this area of inquiry and to introduce students and young researchers to its methodologies. The cultural setting of the 1986 conference also contributed to our awareness that for the study of communication in its varied social and cultural contexts to become valid or meaningful, methods of qualitative and "thick" description (Geertz, 1973) are required.

We had carried with us to India the education and professional training of two distinctive traditions, Klaus Bruhn Jensen representing the humanities and Nick Jankowski the social sciences. Moreover, while Klaus has at different times studied and done research in the USA, he remains rooted in the cultural and research traditions of Europe. Conversely, Nick, having been trained in the USA, has migrated permanently to Europe. Thus, the editing of the Handbook has been an experience in convergence in practice with the constant but constructive discussions that this involves; we hope to convey both the potentials and pitfalls of convergence to readers in the pages to follow.

Convergence implies cooperation, but not necessarily equal contributions. Klaus has been the prime mover in developing the ideas and principles on which the Handbook is premised, establishing the contacts with a series of distinguished scholars in the field, and working with these contributors to shape an integrated handbook which would be representative of, and relevant for, current research. In matters of coordination and detailed editing, Nick has been an equal partner in the enterprise.

Acknowledgements are due to a number of people for their commentaries on draft chapters and other assistance in the process of putting together the volume. Nick is grateful to Marjan de Bruin, John Hochheimer, Ed Hollander, and Fred Wester; Klaus wishes to thank Hans Arndt, Peter Dahlgren, Torben Kragh Grodal, Erik Arne Hansen, Søren Kjørup, and, last but foremost, Grethe Skylv. Finally, we acknowledge the contributions of the other authors and their readiness to participate in the exploration of a relatively new territory in the field. The responsibility for any limitations and shortcomings in this articulation of the qualitative turn, of course, is ours.

Klaus Bruhn Jensen   Nicholas W. Jankowski
Copenhagen, Denmark   Nijmegen, The Netherlands

Introduction: the qualitative turn

Klaus Bruhn Jensen

Recent years have witnessed a significantly increased interest internationally in applying qualitative research methods to the study of social and cultural processes. The turn to qualitative approaches has perhaps been especially prominent in mass communication research. Particularly during the last decade, there have appeared a number of major qualitative studies of the institutions, contents, and audiences of mass media. In the words of James Carey, the field thus has entered into "a process of making large claims from small matters: studying particular rituals, poems, plays, conversations, songs, dances, theories, and myths and gingerly reaching out to the full relations within a culture or a total way of life" (Carey, 1989: 64). The present volume, through surveying the state of the art of qualitative science as well as examining its theoretical and political implications, aims to take stock of the qualitative turn in mass communication research. Further, the Handbook is offered as a resource for the further development and application of qualitative research in the field.

Two different sets of historical circumstances have interacted to produce the qualitative turn. First, the growth in qualitative approaches is a product of factors internally in the *scientific* community. Many scholars and institutions have come to question the explanatory power of conventional empirical approaches within the social sciences. There appears to be an emerging consensus that a great many central research issues cannot be adequately examined through the kinds of questions that are posed by hypothetico-deductive methods and addressed with quantifiable answers. At the same time, research traditions within the humanities, anthropology, and cultural studies have been seen to offer alternative or supplementary modes of analysis. Currently, as a result, the social and human sciences may be converging in an interdisciplinary re-articulation of mass communication research. One textbook which surveys key studies of media from the social sciences notes the rise of a "meaning paradigm" (Lowery and DeFleur, 1988: 455–9), even though the authors do not venture outside social science in a narrow sense to consider some milestone works which might serve to specify and explain the meaning paradigm. In retrospect, it is hardly surprising that mass communication, being at once a social and a discursive phenomenon, has challenged various social-scientific and textual disciplines in the field to rethink their theoretical and methodological categories.

Second, the qualitative turn is the product of factors of *social* history that are external to science. If one accepts the lesson of history that scientific developments are, to a degree, interdependent with changes in the broader socioeconomic context, then qualitative approaches may be seen as a scientific means of coping with a new form of social reality, what has variously been called the postindustrial society, the postmodern age, and the information society. The erosion of traditional social patterns and the rise of mass communication as a primary source of social cohesion in many regions of the world are twentieth-century trends which have accelerated over the last few decades, prompting a search for new theories and methods to comprehend social and cultural complexity and change (Jensen, forthcoming). Fragmentation of the social setting is being met with integrative, contextual modes of understanding in theory and methodology.

Whereas a detailed analysis of the interdependencies between contemporary society and qualitative science remains to be written by the history of science, the first two chapters below begin to document the varied backgrounds of current qualitative media studies. The purpose is to place mass communication research in the wider framework of research focusing on the role of human language, consciousness, and cultural practice in everyday and social life. The emphasis that is given to language and experience as constitutive elements of social practices and institutions is, indeed, a common denominator for different traditions of qualitative analysis. A related focus is found in the so-called linguistic turn of twentieth-century philosophy (Rorty, 1967), which has taken everyday language as its point of access to inquiries into the structure of reality and the conditions of knowledge. Symbolic interactionism and ethnomethodology, further, have noted the importance of everyday conceptual categories for social analysis, and semiotics, as developed in linguistics, literary theory, and other fields, has proposed to study manifold social phenomena as signs with reference to their uses in cultural, political, and religious practices. Each tradition of inquiry, in different ways, can be said to explore the stuff that social reality is made of.

DEFINING "QUALITATIVE"

Even while humanistic and social-scientific approaches to mass communication may be converging around the qualitative turn, it is still too early in the process to suggest a characterization of what a genuinely interdisciplinary field might look like. The present handbook argues for the need, as a first step, to develop common terminologies and to rearticulate research issues across what remain great divides of discipline and methodology.

The qualitative tradition in mass communication research may have been relatively slow in developing its contributions to the field in the form of journals, conferences, textbooks, and handbooks, at least compared to mainstream quantitative work. This has been due, in part, to factors of social history, as already noted: the dominant social construction of reality for a long time has remained quantitative, not least among the sociopolitical agents and institutions that confer legitimacy and funding on science, thus creating a structural bias against qualitative studies. The culture of science and politics in the twentieth century, for most practical purposes, has been quantitative (see the argument in Snow, 1964). However, as institutional and social structures become more amenable to qualitative perspectives, it is crucial to specify what different qualitative methodologies can offer and claim.

This volume, accordingly, in Chapters 1 and 2 presents both some points of contact and some fundamental theoretical and empirical differences between the two main contributors to qualitative media studies – the humanities and the social sciences. By way of introduction, it is useful to establish a few preliminary signposts locating the qualitative enterprise in relation to the field as a whole. In addition to anticipating the emphases and arguments of later chapters, a brief account of the issues and premises at stake may also help to prepare a dialogue across the field of mass communication research about the explanatory value of qualitative methodologies.

Modes of inquiry

One may begin to explore the respective contributions of qualitative and quantitative methodology by looking at the forms of knowledge that are normally associated with each. The background to the two modes of inquiry lies respectively in the humanities and the natural sciences, or, in the classic German terms, *Geisteswissenschaften* and *Naturwissenschaften*. Culture and communication, accordingly, may be conceived of as a source of either *meaning*, in phenomenological and contextual terms, or *information*, in the sense of discrete items transporting significance through mass media. As a result, qualitative analysis focuses on the *occurrence* of its analytical objects in a particular context, as opposed to the *recurrence* of formally similar elements in different contexts. (However, as Chapter 1 notes, structural forms of analysis such as semiotics may combine the two perspectives by establishing recurring deep structures beneath the heterogeneous elements which occur at the surface level.) This implies either an *internal* approach to understanding culture, interpreting and perhaps immersing oneself in its concrete expressions, or an *external* approach that seeks to establish a detached stance outside of culture. Similarly, media contents and other cultural forms may be seen to give rise to a relatively unique, indivisible *experience* through *exegesis* or, alternatively, to a set of stimuli which can be manipulated through *experiment*, thus producing variable effects that can be *measured*. Finally, where quantitative analysis would focus on the concrete, delimited *products* of the media's meaning production, qualitative approaches examine meaning production as a *process* which is contextualized and inextricably integrated with wider social and cultural practices. The following columns sum up the two perspectives normally associated with qualitative and quantitative methodology.

QUALITATIVE	QUANTITATIVE
Geisteswissenschaften	*Naturwissenschaften*
meaning	information
internal	external
occurrence	recurrence
experience	experiment
exegesis	measurement
process	product

It should be added that the dichotomies of the columns refer, above all, to the self-conception of the analytical traditions. As Chapter 2 explains in more detail, the social sciences, after an early qualitative phase, increasingly came to see the natural sciences as offering a standard of social inquiry. This is in spite of the fact that natural scientists may not see the social-scientific appropriation as very much akin to *their* standard, and indeed may perceive their work as more comparable, in several respects, to qualitative modes of inquiry. Partly in response to this development, the humanities have come to emphasize their unique, aesthetic, and historical perspectives on reality, thus also contributing to dichotomization. Today, the two elements of the dichotomies coexist uneasily in a number of scientific disciplines and fields within both the social sciences and humanities. Whereas a unified science of communication may be neither possible nor desirable, certainly in the short term, it appears worthwhile to explore the complementarity of the different analytical traditions. The purposes, ends, means, and objects of analysis are hardly incompatible in an absolute sense; the question is to what extent and in what terms qualitative and quantitative modes of inquiry are compatible.

Levels of analysis

At present, then, there seems to be no way around the quantitative–qualitative distinction. Although it sometimes serves to confuse rather than clarify research issues, the distinction is a fact of research practice which has major epistemological and political implications that no scholar can afford to ignore. It is necessary, first of all, to specify the analytical levels at which the distinction may apply. One may distinguish four such levels:

the object of analysis (as identified and characterized through reference to the purpose and context of the inquiry);
the analytical apparatus or methods (the concrete operations of inquiry, including the collecting, registering and categorizing of data);
the methodology (the overall design of the inquiry which serves to relate the constituent methods of data gathering and data analysis, further justifying their selection and the interpretation of the data with reference to the theoretical frameworks employed);

theoretical framework(s) (the configuration of concepts which specifies the epistemological status of the other levels, and which hence assigns explanatory value to the specific rendition of the object of analysis that the methodology produces).

As summed up by Anderson and Meyer (1988: 292), "it is method that generates the facts that become evidence within theory."

Even though these four levels are in practice interdependent, it will be suggested here that, in principle, the labels of "quantitative" and "qualitative" apply to methodologies and, by implication, to the methods which constitute specific methodologies. Being the juncture between the concrete acts and tools of analysis (methods) and the overarching frames of interpretation (theory), a methodology represents a heuristics, or a mode of inquiry.

The relevance of a specific methodology depends, above all, on the particular purpose and area of inquiry (for arguments to that effect, see Lang and Lang, 1985, and Jensen and Rosengren, 1990). Too often in communication studies it appears that the methodological choices have been made long before the issues and ends of inquiry have been posed, so that the methodologies become solutions in search of problems. One of the reasons why the use of qualitative methodologies in empirical studies is still relatively limited may be in fact that these methodologies are not considered as a concrete option, in part because students (and their professors) are still taught to regard survey and experimental designs as the standards of systematic science. Yet, the last few decades have produced systematic and professional conceptions of qualitative research, of which the present handbook presents a "representative" sample. Indeed, for purposes of theory development as well as applications of media studies, it is crucial that researchers assess the relevance of different methodologies with reference to the purposes and objects of analysis, asking *what* and *why* before asking *how*.

Two further specifications of the levels of analysis are called for. First, no object of analysis is by nature quantitative or qualitative, but is framed thus by the medium or analytical apparatus employed. For the sake of this opening argument, one could say that while the medium of quantitative analysis is numbers and their (numerical) correlations, the medium of qualitative analysis is human language expressing the concepts of everyday experience as they pertain to a specific context. The relevance of each medium, to repeat, depends on the purpose and area of inquiry.

Second, the qualitative–quantitative distinction in a narrow sense loses its relevance at the level of theoretical frameworks, even if qualitative and quantitative traditions tend to emphasize different types of theory. It is in the nature of the matter that theory is qualitative, insofar as it represents a configuration of interrelated concepts. At the theoretical level, geology and statistics are as qualitative enterprises as art criticism. This is in spite of the fact that much theory lends itself to formalization and numerical or graphic representation. Indeed, many, perhaps most, new insights rely on qualitative procedures, serving to relate the different levels of analysis, as witnessed also by examples from natural science. In the postscript to the second edition of *The Structure of Scientific Revolutions* (1962), Kuhn (1970: 182–4) thus refers to what he calls "symbolic generalizations" – the (qualitative) rearticulations of key terms in a field which may open the field to new forms of empirical and mathematical analysis. More generally, various forms of qualitative analysis acquire general explanatory value, despite their "non-representative" empirical samples, because, as part of the analytical procedures, continuous cross-reference is made between the theoretical and other levels of analysis.

This last point is sometimes missed in accounts of the foundations of communication theory, which tend to mistake analytical efficiency at the methodological level for explanatory value at the theoretical level, hence discounting qualitative analysis. One example is the handbook of Berger and Chaffee (1987), which aims to set standards for a comprehensive "communication science." While recognizing that "neither quantitative nor qualitative data have much meaning . . . in the absence of well-articulated theory," the authors nevertheless repeatedly imply, in their introductory sections and own chapters, that general or predictive theory is premised on the quantitative measurement of the covariation of variables or operationally defined constructs, rather than what they continue to call "unspecified qualitative techniques" (Berger and Chaffee, 1987: 18). The one chapter in their handbook that draws on the humanities, in an almost deferential discourse, presents these contributions to the study of communication as "nonscientific" (Farrell, 1987: 123).

Furthermore, Berger and Chaffee (1987: 144–5) pass over the fundamental theoretical problems that arise when "communication science" seeks to transform the level of (verbal, visual, and other) *discourse* to the level of empirical, *numerical* analysis, asserting that this "is not inherently problematic." What qualitative and humanistic researchers have been demonstrating for some time now, is that such a decontextualization of discursive meanings is precisely a key problem for the study of human communication. One may recall here the well-documented argument of Beniger (1988: 199) that, ironically, mainstream communication research, at least in the USA, may be the one field currently paying little attention to "theories of information, knowledge structures, communication, and the encoding and decoding of meaning." This situation calls for more genuinely exploratory, theoretical as well as empirical work which would acknowledge the relevance and contributions of both qualitative and quantitative traditions.

In sum, the qualitative–quantitative distinction will be taken here to apply to methodologies – the structured sets of procedures and instruments by which empirical phenomena of mass communication are registered, documented, and interpreted. The different methodologies give rise to distinctive modes of understanding media and to specific applications of the findings in contexts of media production, education, and policy. The applications and implications of qualitative media studies are taken up in Part III, while Part II surveys qualitative approaches to different stages and aspects of mass communication processes. Before turning in Part I to the legacies that have shaped current qualitative research, a brief outline of the whole Handbook is in order.

OUTLINE

Part I is devoted to *history*: the roots of qualitative mass communication studies in previous research within a number of scientific fields. Chapter 1 presents the legacy of the arts and humanities, which traditionally have centered on the interpretation and appreciation of texts, particularly literary and other aesthetic production. More recent work has examined texts in the perspective of their social uses, defining culture in anthropological terms as a set of communicative practices constituting a whole way of life. The chapter examines the special contributions of semiotics and cultural studies to current qualitative media research, and it points to a number of challenges to the further advancement of the field, among them poststructuralist theory and research on visual communication. One important methodological contribution of the humanities has been the development of discourse analysis, which offers a systematic, qualitative alternative to formal content analysis. Discourse analysis also suggests ways of integrating the social and discursive aspects of meaning production within a theoretical framework of social semiotics.

Chapter 2 surveys the qualitative tradition in the social sciences, from its prominent status in early sociology and anthropology through the predominance of quantitative methodology in the first few decades following World War II, to the return of qualitative studies since the 1960s. The survey identifies the heterogeneous origins of qualitative analysis in the social sciences, and considers, among other things, the contributions of community studies and action research to the area. During the last decade in particular, methodological advances in the form of new, systematic research techniques have contributed to the standing and usefulness of qualitative social science. Several of these developments have occurred within communications, and they have entailed theory development as well as important empirical findings regarding the role of media in the lives of individuals, communities, and whole cultures.

The eight chapters of Part II make up a *systematics* of mass communication research, examining in turn studies of the different stages of the communication process. Though some qualitative work has questioned the Lasswellian (1948) model of communication, most of the chapters do focus on either the institutions, the content genres, or the audiences of mass communication. This is, in part, because most previous research tends to assume this model, but also because the field has not so far produced a comprehensive alternative, which would take its point of departure outside the communication process itself, for example, in the media's context of social institutions and cultural practices. However, two of the chapters on systematics review studies which have served to place the media in the context of the community and of modern history. Also other chapters note that the area of inquiry includes not just the mass media as such, but, crucially, mass communication and popular culture as social practices. While there are some references to "media" research, the perspective which emerges also from Part II, emphasizes a holistic approach to "mass communication" as a social practice and cultural process in specific contexts.

Part III concludes the Handbook by addressing the *pragmatics* of qualitative research: its implications for theory development, for the politics of communication, and for further work in the field. Chapter 11 lays out what may be considered a logic of qualitative analysis with reference to the authors' own classic contributions to mass communication research, discussing the specifically qualitative research process and its relevance for theory development. Chapter 12 turns to the conclusions that may be drawn from qualitative research in the context of education and politics, outlining the possible uses of research in developing media literacy curricula and in evaluating the media's service to the audience–public. The indexes and the brief sections introducing each of the three parts, finally, have been designed to increase the accessibility and applicability of the volume for different groups of readers.

The Handbook is offered as a resource to several groups of readers. First of all, it can work as a textbook for students in undergraduate and graduate courses in mass communication, particularly on theory and methodology. It may also, it is anticipated, encourage more departments and teachers to include the qualitative dimension in the curriculum. Moreover, the Handbook represents a new reference work for researchers, practitioners, and educators in media. Increasingly, as mass communication research turns qualitative in order to comprehend new media environments (Jensen, forthcoming), scholars need to master the theory and tools of qualitative work. By the same token, practicing professionals and planners in media need qualitative evidence in order to understand how the media operate and to improve research and development. Media educators also will be able to draw on the qualitative research summed up here to develop curricula on media literacy, which are currently being included at various educational levels in many countries.

Qualitative methodology may be an especially important ingredient of education and research which addresses mass communication in different cultural contexts (Lull, 1988a). Complementing traditional research designs, which normally articulate a characteristically Western rationality, qualitative studies can contribute to the development of international research on mass media in their cultural, contextual specificity. The Handbook itself includes some perspectives, if admittedly a limited selection, outside of Anglo-American research. As mass communication increasingly becomes an agent of social cohesion and cultural interchange in a transnational perspective, qualitative methodologies may be developed further to make sense of the international media environment.

The title of the Handbook has been chosen to suggest the preliminary nature of qualitative methodology and, indeed, of the whole field of mass communication research: it is *a* handbook of qualitative methodolog*ies*. Like their objects of analysis, qualitative methodologies are in the process of being made. Qualitative studies, in conclusion, represent one contribution to the theoretical, methodological, and empirical development of an interdisciplinary field of mass communication research. Most of the studies and debates which may construct the field are still ahead of us.

Part I

History

The first part of the Handbook lays out some main lines of the "history" of qualitative approaches – their origins in various scientific disciplines and analytical traditions. Whereas qualitative methodologies are sometimes perceived as recent innovations and additions to the toolbox of mass communication research, Chapters 1 and 2 document the long history of qualitative modes of inquiry in both of the main traditions which inform contemporary communication studies.

The humanities, as examined in Chapter 1, represent centuries of textual and interpretive scholarship. While a mainstream of this research originally tended to emphasize the contemplative understanding and appreciation of particularly literary masterpieces and other high-cultural forms, recent work has included popular culture and everyday practices in the area of inquiry, studying the social and cultural uses of texts, images, and other signs. Culture, following Raymond Williams, increasingly has come to be defined as a whole way of life. One important contribution of the humanities to the study of mass communication has been the development of *theory* and of a theoretical reflexivity which may enable the field to conceive of forms of communication and culture that go beyond the familiar institutions and practices of industrial capitalism and modernity as focused on by the social sciences. A further, methodological contribution of the humanities tradition comes from its development of systematic approaches to the study of *language* and *discourse*, which constitute the primary categories and media of qualitative research.

Chapter 2 shows that qualitative modes of inquiry also had a prominent status in early social-scientific research. During the first decades following World War II, when the mainstream of the social sciences turned quantitative, qualitative research remained an undercurrent, which re-emerged and gained new momentum from the 1960s. This development had several heterogeneous origins across the social sciences. Theoretical frameworks and methods were derived from symbolic interactionism, ethnomethodology, and ethnography as practiced in anthropology and sociology. Like the humanities, these approaches emphasized the importance of everyday language and consciousness in orienting social action. Further, some studies were informed by a critical knowledge-interest as in, for instance, action research giving priority to the social applications of new knowledge. One key contribution of qualitative social science to mass communication research has been its explicit and detailed articulation of methodology, specifying *the research process* as a sequence of procedural steps which makes possible intersubjective agreement – and disagreement – on findings.

The two chapters on history suggest at least two areas of convergence – one theoretical, the other methodological. Theoretical convergence is manifest around a notion of *language as action*. Both the humanistic and social-scientific traditions of qualitative research emphasize that the conceptual categories of everyday language lend orientation to most forms of social action and interaction – what represents, in the aggregate, the social construction of reality. Language is a means of meaningful action, as suggested by speech-act theory (Chapter 1), as well as a mediator of various types of interaction from daily conversation to political and cultural activity. The *social semiotics* outlined in Chapter 1 offers a theoretical framework for further specifying the relationship between mass media, everyday language, and social action.

Methodological convergence, further, is occurring in the development of systematic approaches to the analysis of qualitative data. Whereas Chapter 2 situates the analysis of data within the research process as a whole, Chapter 1 presents *discourse analysis* as a specific method for strengthening what remain weak links of the qualitative research process: analysis, interpretation, and documentation. Later chapters also contain analysis and discussion of mass communication as a discursive practice (see especially Chapters 5, 6, 7, 8, 10, and 12).

All chapters include a large number of references to previous research, including basic textbooks that may complement this Handbook. Further, the Handbook may work well in combination with collections of materials which address particular media in their cultural context. As general reference works which cover aspects of the history of qualitative research on mass media, we add here *Keywords* (Williams, 1983b), the *Handbook of Communication Science* (Berger and Chaffee, 1987) which is also discussed in "Introduction: the qualitative turn," and the *International Encyclopedia of Communications* (Barnouw *et al.*, 1989).

Chapter 1

Humanistic scholarship as qualitative science: contributions to mass communication research

Klaus Bruhn Jensen

INTRODUCTION

For more than 2,500 years, the humanities have been studying, in the contemporary terminology, the texts of interpersonal and mass communication. Traditionally, however, humanistic studies of literary works and other major cultural forms have not emphasized the analysis of culture as communicative practices. Studies, instead, have been said to perform an exegesis, or reading, of cultural tradition, poetic genius, the *Zeitgeist*, or an ideology which found its expression in texts. The changes in concepts and terminology are significant, because, as Raymond Williams has shown, the "keywords" of a culture at different historical times imply particular conceptions both of social reality and of the purpose of scholarship about this reality (Williams, 1983b). Whereas scholars differ on the precise origins of the humanities, it may be argued that a distinctively humanistic tradition, drawing on centuries of historical and textual scholarship, began to emerge in the early nineteenth century, and that, further, the humanities assumed their current shape when "social science" was spawned as a separate area of inquiry around the beginning of this century. If the origin of the concept of communication is associated with modernity and the rise of Lockean individualism (Peters, 1989), it is only within the last century that communication and information have become keywords across the humanities and social sciences. In the humanities in particular, the qualitative turn has been a communicative turn. This past century, then, may be thought of as the century of the sign, spanning the rise of mass communication on an unprecedented scale as well as, partly as a response to this (for want of a better term) megatrend (Naisbitt, 1982), the rise of semiotics and other communication theory to explicate an opaque social reality requiring interpretation.

The present chapter traces some main lines of this complex social and scientific development from the perspective of humanistic scholarship. After introducing a common definition of communication as the social production of meaning, I present a survey of major analytical traditions, with special reference to historical studies of literacy, semiotics, and contemporary cultural studies. The chapter further considers a number of current challenges from postmodernist and feminist theories of language. A section on methodology notes a gradual shift from textual, aesthetic appreciation to the systematic analysis of specific cultural forms, particularly with the development of discourse analysis. Perhaps the key contribution of the humanities to qualitative research is an emphatic commitment to studying the *language* of particular texts and genres in their historical setting. The dark side of this literate bias is a certain blindness to non-alphabetic modes of communication, not least today's visual forms of communication, which are addressed in a separate section. In conclusion, I discuss the outline of a social semiotics which, while drawing on the categories of humanistic theory and discourse analysis, would approach mass communication as a cultural *practice*, in which issues of power, identity, and social structure are negotiated.

Communication as meaning production

To say that the mass media produce and circulate meanings in society is a more controversial statement than it may seem. Different disciplines and theoretical schools tend to define and apply the concept of meaning – its origination, interpretation, and impact – in distinctive ways. Not only must one distinguish, from a social-scientific perspective, between the definition of meaning production as a social *ritual* and as a *transmission* of contents from producers to audiences (Carey, 1989: 15). From a humanistic perspective, the contents must be conceptualized as the *expression* of a particular subjectivity and aesthetics, and as the *representation* of a particular context. These several aspects of meaning production may be specified with reference to three basic constituents of the communicative process which are shared by most contemporary humanistic as well as social-scientific models of communication: the message of communication, the communicators, and the embedding social structure; or – in a humanistic terminology – discourse, subjectivity, and context.

The concept of *discourse*, first, is a legacy of the textual scholarship that has been characteristic of most Western philosophy, theology, and other humanistic research. The underlying assumption is that language is the primary medium of interchange between humans and reality (in processes of perception, cognition, and action), and that, accordingly, verbal texts may become vehicles of knowledge and truth. Whereas traditionally this assumption applied to religious, scholarly, and literary texts, today much qualitative work employs the concept of discourse to refer to any use of language, or other semiotic systems, in social context. Crucially, discourse now is said to include everyday interaction and its categories of consciousness, thus constituting the medium of the social construction of reality (Berger and Luckmann, 1966). Through language, reality becomes social. Equally, it is through language that reality becomes intersubjective and accessible for analysis. Hence, for the purpose of qualitative research language and other semiotic systems represent both an analytical object and a central tool of analysis.

Subjectivity, similarly, has come to be defined in terms of language. In contrast to a philosophy of consciousness conceiving of subjects as relatively autonomous agents that exercise moral and aesthetic judgment, recent theories of language and subjectivity have described the subject as a position *in* language (for a survey, see Coward and Ellis, 1977). Such a position, while negotiable, tends to imply a particular perspective on the world and on one's own identity and place in the world. In Althusser's (1971) terms, the subject is interpellated or hailed to occupy particular positions. The mass media, of course, are among the main sources of interpellation in the modern period. Moreover, the positioning of subjects in language implies their excommunication from certain other positions – the unconscious. According to Lacan's (1977) reformulation of Freud, it is this process of positioning which serves to structure also the unconscious as a language. In terms of the present argument, mass communication can be said to give voice to some discursive positions while silencing others.

Finally, humanistic communication theory has approached the social structure in which mass communication is embedded as literally a *con-text* – a configuration of texts that must be "read" or interpreted, and which is the outcome of a process of historical change. This approach is in keeping with the traditional understanding of history as being, at one level, a set of stories about the past. Changing the analytical focus from specific stories as told by particular bards, to the deep structure or system of stories which dominates a given society or culture (Foucault, 1972), contemporary studies have suggested how media and other agents of socialization serve to inscribe individuals in the culture. Such stories lend a sense of purpose to the social practices in which individuals and institutions engage, pervading everyday consciousness and action.

Discourse, in sum, is the common object of humanistic inquiry. Yet, the conception of discourse has varied both in different historical periods and between humanistic disciplines. Furthermore, one conspicuous absence in much work has been the lack of an explicit examination of the *impact* of discourse with reference to particular subjects in their specific social context. The following section offers a survey of some main tenets of previous humanistic research; the survey further considers the extent to which each research tradition has examined culture as a set of communicative practices. Whereas a chapter of this nature cannot give more than a reductive sketch of what is an ancient and heterogeneous field, special attention is given to contributions from literary criticism and cultural studies, with some reference to history and psychology. The humanities, from the beginning, have been an interdisciplinary field.

HUMANISTIC TRADITIONS

From literacy to literary criticism

Whereas, in oral cultures, bardic poetry traditionally serves as the memory of the culture and its vehicle of education, Greek culture particularly from the fifth century BC came to depend, in part, on alphabetic writing for these purposes (see the survey in Thomas, 1989). Plato's attack on the poets may be taken as indicative of a gradual transition to literate culture (Havelock, 1963): poets should no longer be trusted in social matters such as politics or the writing of history, even if their poetry could still be appreciated as personal opinion or myth. In sciences, alphabetic writing may ensure a systematic and cumulative analysis. In politics, the manageable set of distinct letters makes possible a social and governmental system of significant complexity by offering a resource for organization and debate across time and space.

It is likely that the alphabet contributed to a reconception of knowledge not as memory, but as a record of verifiable statements. Reality, in the form of the alphabet, was now manifestly there as an exteriorized representation which could be studied, worked upon, and transformed. A system of writing thus represents a cultural resource with important social consequences, facilitating the distinction between past and present and, importantly, a perception of inconsistencies within received history, which may prepare conditions of conflict and change (Goody and Watt, 1963; Goody, 1987). Though much recent media theory has overstated the determination of culture by new technologies of communication (McLuhan, 1962; 1964; Postman, 1985), literacy did imply new practices of constructing social reality (Berger and Luckmann, 1966; see also Innis, 1972; Ong, 1982).

The uses of literacy in the West have been studied with reference to changing historical and social circumstances. Being a relatively affluent society with a substantial number of literate people, classical Greece enjoyed the material conditions for developing the technology of writing into forms which may, in part, account for the breakthrough of arts and sciences in that period. Building on their own experience, practitioner–theoreticians of rhetoric and poetics in the Graeco-Roman tradition accumulated a fund of systematic knowledge about the characteristics and effects of verbal messages (oral and written, fictional and factual), which was codified in classic writings by, for example, Aristotle, Cicero, and Quintilian. This knowledge, as taught in schools and academies, lived on through the Middle Ages, being revitalized and reformulated in the Renaissance and afterwards (Arnold and Frandsen, 1984).

It is important to note at this point that the social consequences of communication technologies always depend on their embedding in shifting historical *institutions*. As shown by Eisenstein (1979), it was the scribal culture of elites in medieval monasteries, as captured by Eco (1981), rather than an oral and popular culture, which was transformed by the printing press beginning in the fifteenth century. By ending the monopoly of Church institutions on the definition of knowledge, print technology became a major factor contributing to the cultural shifts of Renaissance and Reformation.

It may be added that, throughout "Western civilization," the question of how words are used to act in, and enact, a particular reality has been premised on a religious notion of the Word, which is integral to the Christian metaphysics that continues to suffuse the humanities. Words are the source of religious revelation, aesthetic experience, and scientific truth. Furthermore, the centrality ascribed to words in both religious and profane matters is rooted in the Greek logos tradition which assumes "the transcendental intimacy of thought, words, and reality" (Heim, 1987: 42). Rules of interpretation, accordingly, have been subject to continuous controversy, shaping social life and cultural practices generally. The interpretation of the Bible and other canonical texts, of course, has resulted in conflicts that could make or break individuals as well as whole societies. The sense of being present in the world through the word is, indeed, a notion which can be seen to underlie much humanistic theory. Recent work (Derrida, 1967) has challenged such a "logocentric" notion of discourse, which implies that the mental content represents an autonomous, metaphysical level of reality. What the critique still does not specify, however, is how the content of signs relates to the material and social aspects of discourse; this question will be addressed below in the outline of social semiotics.

Literacy has been a precondition for the development of modern forms of social organization and consciousness, in private as well as public life, during industrial capitalism (Lowe, 1982). Historical and literary research has noted that *genres*, in particular, bear witness to the changing social uses of communication. Thus, for example, the novel form, the news genre, and the encyclopedia, in different ways, contributed to constructing the modern social order. The novel, for one, while depending on the rise of the middle class as literary entrepreneurs, also owed its success to the development of a new realm of privacy and leisure in which that same social group became readers in search of narratives that could suggest appropriate standards of private conduct, as well as filling a new social space and time with entertainment (Watt, 1957). Equally, the discourses of news in the early press implied a redefinition of individuals, their economic rights, and their participation in political life, hence suggesting standards of public conduct with other citizens (Habermas, 1989; Schudson, 1978). The encyclopedia, finally, served to publish the contemporary range of certified knowledge in a comprehensive, but accessible form, which gave it practical, economic, and political relevance for entrepreneurs and citizens alike (Eriksen, 1987: 118–29).

With the redefinition of literature in the modern period came also a reassessment of the purpose of literary studies. While the details of this development cannot be included here (see Abrams, 1953; Eagleton, 1983; Wimsatt and Brooks, 1957), one general outcome was an emphasis on demonstrating that, and explaining how, literature as mastered by specific historical authors, may give rise to aesthetic experiences which transcend historical time and place. Literary scholarship further implied a normative approach to the education of readers, at least to the extent that readers were to learn adequate responses to the literary tradition, thus, in a sense, learning the effects of literary communication. The empirical study of such effects, however, with a few exceptions (Richards, 1929; see also Jensen and Rosengren, 1990) has not until quite recently been seen as a main purpose of literary studies. Another gradual reorientation of research entailed a move toward specialized studies of literature in its own right, away from an inclusion of literary works in primarily historical or philological studies. The process of focusing on the literary text itself, as an autonomous structure yielding various forms of aesthetic experience, reached its preliminary conclusion in the close readings of the New Criticism.

The New Criticism set out to study what was perceived as an objective, self-contained structure of textual paradoxes and ambivalences (Eagleton, 1983: Ch. 1). Any interest in the authorial intention behind, or the affective impact of, this structure was denounced as intentional and affective fallacies (Wimsatt and Beardsley, 1954). On the one hand, this approach tended to isolate literature from its broader social and historical context; on the other, the attention given to the text itself helped to improve analytical techniques, being a form of professionalization and academic legitimation which was an ambition of literary criticism in the 1930s and 1940s. It should also be kept in mind that the social context of the American universities, where the New Criticism especially was articulated, influenced its development and uses. First, close reading presented a convenient pedagogical method in a time of growing student numbers, and second, it offered a disinterested approach to the science of art for professors who were "sceptical liberal intellectuals disoriented by the clashing dogmas of the Cold War" (Eagleton, 1983: 50).

Beyond its specific historical origins, the New Criticism left its imprint on much later literary analysis. Indeed, its text-centrism was re-emphasized with the rise of structuralism and semiology, which in many literary departments now have taken the place of New Critical theory and analytical principles. While having distinctive origins, structuralism served to accelerate the shifting of emphases in the humanities from the metaphysical Word to the structured Text.

Structuralism and semiology

Rooted in early linguistics and the Russian Formalist school of aesthetics, structuralism and semiology represent a general theoretical reorientation which came to affect much work in humanistic and social-scientific disciplines in the twentieth century. Structuralism could be perceived, in certain periods, as offering the constituents of a unified science of the sign. Whereas structuralism may be said to characterize a number of human, social, and natural sciences, assigning, according to Jean Piaget, attributes of wholeness, transformation, and self-regulation to the structures being studied (Hawkes, 1977: 16), semiology is engaged more specifically in the analysis of signs and their functions, thus influencing both the humanities and the social sciences.

Semiology represents a break with humanistic tradition in several respects. First of all, the form of linguistics which Saussure outlined early in the century, and which became the foundation of a more general science of communication and culture – what he himself termed semiology, "a science that studies the life of signs within society" (Saussure, 1959: 16) – moved toward a formal and systemic approach to language and away from inclusive and historical conceptions of philology and aesthetics. Russian Formalism, similarly, emphasized the structural analysis of literature and implied a final break with the Romantic understanding of literature as, in Wordsworth's words, "the spontaneous overflow of powerful feelings" (in Abrams *et al.*, 1962: 103). Semiology went beyond the New Criticism in its insistence on examining not just the literary work itself in order to account for aesthetic pleasure, but its underlying formal structure.

It can also be argued that the rise of a pervasive formalism was related to the crisis of representation in the arts which had been signaled by the rise of Impressionism in the 1870s, partly as a response to the spread of photography, and which continued in the formal experiments of the various twentieth-century -isms (see Hughes, 1981; also Pelfrey, 1985). Realizing that the status of art as the expression of an artistic sensitivity and as the representation of a commonly shared reality was called into question, scholarship may therefore have retreated to a similar position inside language, studying art for form's sake. The crisis of representation was further accentuated by the growth of factual, "objective" genres in the press from the middle of the nineteenth century, which served to thematize the definition of social reality. The representation of social conflict and change in the press, in particular, had to be negotiated by journalists and their readers. These new forms of verbal and visual representation came to pose important objects of analysis for twentieth-century textual research efforts.

If Saussure had laid the groundwork for these efforts in linguistics and semiology, it remained for two later developments to refine and apply his insights. First, in linguistics, formalization reached a climax in the models of language production advanced by transformational-generative grammar (Chomsky, 1965). A key assumption of this school has been that the human capacity for language can be attributed to an innate deep structure which, by complex transformations, produces the surface structures that we speak and write. While this research has tended to stay at the level of grammatical form in individual sentences, later linguistics has developed a contextual approach to language use – a pragmatics which examines the variations of form and content with reference both to the social context of language and to the context made up of connected discourse, whether everyday conversation or other textual genres (Coulthard, 1977; Halliday, 1978). Such discourse analysis represents an important methodological contribution of the humanities to mass communication research, whose relevance is discussed further below.

It may be added that some linguistics relies on computers, increasingly so, for the analysis of language structures (Garside *et al.*, 1987; Grishman, 1986). In some cases the purpose is the study of large quantities of linguistic data, for example a corpus of grammatical forms; in other cases the aim is to simulate general processes of language use and structuration, as in the growing field of artificial intelligence (for discussion of its potential and pitfalls, see Hofstadter and Dennett, 1982). The computer as a heuristic model may also be seen to underlie the influential transformational-generative grammar above. Mostly, however, the computer has not been central to the development of humanistic methodologies proper. This is, of course, in contrast to the social sciences, where also qualitative studies have recently begun to employ computer software for the organization and categorization of data (see Chapter 2).

The second development of the Saussurean framework has elaborated his vision of a science of signs. Including complex modes of communication and culture among the objects of analysis, semiology of the 1960s and later has produced a rearticulation of disciplines such as anthropology and literary criticism (for a survey, see Culler, 1975). Much work over the last three decades has been devoted to interpreting societies and cultures as discourses, both in industrial (Barthes, 1973) and non-industrialized regions (Lévi-Strauss, 1963). The ambition of some studies has been to discover deep structures not just of language, but of social mythologies and, indeed, of human culture. This, further, led to the construction of models of the matrices which could be seen to underlie narratives – models which, while often based on standardized genres, appeared to be applicable to a range of textual forms (Greimas, 1966; Jakobson, 1960; Todorov, 1968). Studies in this tradition were also among the first to include popular culture in the area of inquiry, not least advertising and television (Barthes, 1973; Leymore, 1975; Silverstone, 1981; see also Chapter 6 in this volume).

A final extrapolation of structuralist principles has been made in studies of social institutions. Beyond noting the discursive structure of social life and historical change, these studies have explained capitalist social structures – their wholeness, transformation, and self-regulation – with reference to the constituent types of institutions and practices (Althusser, 1965). This approach is comparable, in some respects, to functionalism as developed in the social sciences. The conceptual points of contact between structuralism and traditional sociology have been noted, critiqued, and elaborated in recent work on the relationship between social structure and agency (Giddens, 1984).

The status and legacy of semiology are still uncertain. On the one hand, some textbooks, while recognizing certain distinctive features, tend to include semiology as one of the procedures in the toolbox of mass communication research (McQuail, 1987: 185–90). On the other hand, it can be argued that the constructivist epistemology of semiology, along with an implicit hermeneutics of interpretation, is incompatible with the analytical framework of social-scientific communication research (Carey, 1989: Ch. 3).

For the further development of mass communication research, which requires a theory of signs and discourse, it is important to distinguish semiology from semiotics. *Semiology* grows out of the logos tradition in the West. While purporting to study formal, "objective" aspects of signs, semiological analyses frequently slide into an empathetic, introspective kind of understanding, which is similar to other hermeneutics. Indeed, the elementary sign, as defined by Saussure, consisting of signifier (sound–image) and signified (concept), recalls the classic dualisms from Greek philosophy through Christian metaphysics to the Cartesian worldview – the mind–matter, spirit–body, subject–object dyads. Truth and beauty, it is implied, may reside in the signified (the Word) as interpreted by a mind (the Spirit). By contrast, the material aspect of signs may be seen as a barrier or, at best, an indirect medium for the experience of "transcendental intimacy" (Heim, 1987: 42) with reality, as noted also by the poststructuralist critique of the semiological and logos tradition. In the conclusion, I want to suggest that *semiotics*, as first articulated by Charles Sanders Peirce, represents an alternative to Saussurean semiology which avoids some of the latter's epistemological pitfalls by categorizing signs as neither representation nor expression, but primarily as action, thus hinting at a social semiotics of the uses of signs in society.

Cultural studies

The borderland between textual and social research has been given an innovative, if somewhat eclectic, articulation in cultural studies. Research in this tradition has contributed particularly to extending the concept of texts beyond high-cultural masterpieces by including both popular culture and everyday social practices among the objects of textual analysis. Whereas theory and methodology have been developed in a number of countries in Europe and North and Latin America, drawing on nineteenth-century classics (Durkheim, Marx, Weber) as well as modern European and American pioneers such as Adorno and Horkheimer (1977), Carey (1989), Gans (1974), Hoggart (1957), and Williams (1977), it is fair to say that British cultural studies have led the way over the last two decades. In summary, a Birmingham–Paris axis was established (and, later on, re-exported to the American market), which served to assimilate French social and psychoanalytic theory, including versions of structuralism and semiology, to the critical study of contemporary social and cultural issues (Hall *et al.*, 1980).

Much work in this tradition revolves around the concept of practices (Williams, 1977), in the sense of meaningful social activities. This concept serves to emphasize a cultural dimension in, and a holistic perspective on, social life, further recognizing the scope for intervention by social agents and the role of meaning for orienting social action. The center of research, thus, is located outside texts and media, which are said to be embedded, along with audiences, in broad social and cultural practices. As part of this framework, studies have examined particular cultural institutions and subcultural groups, and the concept of interpretive communities (Fish, 1979) has been introduced to suggest that audiences are characterized not simply by socioeconomic background variables, but simultaneously by their discursive modes of interpreting cultural forms, which give rise to different constructions of social reality (see also Jensen, 1991; Lindlof, 1988; Radway, 1984). For the humanities and social sciences alike, this work serves as a reminder that the relationship between cultural–discursive and demographic–social formations is not well understood.

The analytical practice of cultural studies is rooted in literary analysis-cum-interpretation, but it emphasizes extratextual frameworks of explanation. Nevertheless, while the categories of analysis are thus grounded in theories of subjectivity and social context, the primary medium of the research remains the interpreting scholar. Furthermore, the focus has tended to be placed on the overarching discourses of culture, rather than their local, empirical producers and recipients. Consequently, although cultural studies refer to the genre in question, its implied reader positions, and associated social uses, the tradition is still preoccupied with the message or discourse of communication. This is in spite of habitual, sometimes ritualistic references to the concreteness, specificity, and difference of cultural practices. The social system is conceived of as a context of diverse discourses which derive from subcultures and interpretive communities based on gender, class, or ethnicity, and which mediate the flow and interpretation of mass communication. In general, though, cultural studies have thrived on the combination of a text-centered methodology with social-systemic theories of discourse.

The theoretical framework rests on two types of assumptions: structuralism and culturalism (Hall, 1980). Where the structuralist element would emphasize the relatively determined nature of social life and cultural forms under industrial capitalism, following Althusser's (1971) characterization of cultural institutions as ideological state apparatuses, the culturalist element rather emphasizes the relative autonomy of culture as a site of social struggle and as an agent of change. The lack of public control over, in classic Marxist terms, the means of production, does not in itself entail a similar lack of influence on or through the means of discursive reproduction. The decisive theoretical issue, of course, is the degree of this relative autonomy, which raises major political issues. Whereas people may draw on frames of understanding outside the dominant social order, both as producers of their own cultural practices and as recipients of mass-mediated culture, in order to assert their difference; the question is whether this discursive difference will make a social difference so as to reform macrosocial institutions or deep-seated everyday practices. Unable to answer this classic question of effects, the structuralist and culturalist trends of cultural studies tend to coexist uneasily.

The question of effects suggests other broad issues in the politics of culture. Cultural studies have served an important function within the humanities by re-evaluating popular culture as a both pleasurable and worthy discourse and as a relevant social resource, labeling, for example, television as a modern bard (Fiske and Hartley, 1978). By focusing on the social use and value of literacy and other modes of communication, the humanities have come full circle since the rise of Greek literacy. The question remains, however, in what sense discursive resistance (what Eco [1976: 150] has called "semiotic guerilla warfare") will serve social groups that, though self-reliant in their uses of popular culture, are subject to repression and injustice. The most elaborate argument for the liberating potential of popular culture has been made by John Fiske, who tends to see the audience–public's pleasure in the media as they now exist, not just as an oppositional stance, but as a first stage in a process of social transformation (Fiske, 1987, 1989; for a critique, see Jensen, 1991). Thus, cultural studies have reiterated the question of how social and discursive levels of structuration are interrelated – which is perhaps the main question for an interdisciplinary field of mass communication research.

Rewording the humanities

As a final element of this historical overview, some recent challenges to the prevailing notions of discourse in humanistic theory and methodology should be mentioned. First, it has already been noted that poststructuralist and deconstructivist theory has challenged the implied metaphysics of semiology and more generally of the logos tradition (for a survey, see Eagleton, 1983: Ch. 4). This challenge is still in effect (for representative positions, see Baudrillard, 1988, and Lyotard, 1984), although deconstructivism has not reconstructed a concrete alternative approach to the study of culture and meaning production in their social context.

A second, related challenge comes from feminist research on the relationship between gender, culture, and textual production, which has argued that masculine and patriarchal forms of understanding are enacted, for example, through the mass media (for a survey, see Moi, 1985; for key texts of this tradition, see Marks and de Courtivron, 1981). The "masculine" bias of culture may have been reinforced, in part, because it was naturalized and therefore inconspicuous, also in scientific discourse. Fueled by the social developments around the new women's movement, feminist research has also been a constitutive part of the theoretical developments of (post-)structuralism, questioning essentialism and naturalism in the study of cultural forms and compensating for the marginalization of women in previous work. One essentialism lurking as a subtext in feminism itself is biologism – the assumption, briefly, that "feminine" culture is inherently related to the female body and psyche, rather than being a social and historical construct. At its best, however, feminism helps to differentiate other social and discourse theory. Even though qualitative analysis is not, to repeat, inherently "feminine," many of the research issues and knowledge-interests articulated by feminist scholars, thematizing gender-specific languages and worldviews, lend themselves well to qualitative methodologies.

Finally, several other fields have contributed to "rewording" the humanities. One feature which tends to unite these contributions is the primary attention given to meaning and culture as orienting action in specific social contexts. Oral history, for one, is a reorientation of historical science which has given greater scope for everyday and bottom-up perspectives on history (Thompson, 1978). Some versions of psychology, further, have emphasized that this is a humanistic or "human science" (Polkinghorne, 1988) which examines narrative and other forms of consciousness. Psychology, then, shares the predicament of mass communication research, being poised between qualitative and quantitative conceptions of science. The predicament is also shared by anthropology, which may be

defined institutionally as either a social-science or humanities subject. The "thick description" advocated for anthropology by Geertz
(1973), in many ways, may serve as a bridge between the humanities
and social sciences (for discussion and application of the concept,
see Chapters 2 and 8 in this volume). At the same time, the notion of
"thick description" reactualizes the problem of how specifically to
approach description and analysis in qualitative research.

METHODOLOGIES

For a "statistics" of qualitative research

The humanities have long relied on systematic and efficient
methods of analysis, even if these are not normally referred to as
"methodologies." Logic within philosophy, grammatical analysis in
philology and more recently linguistics, textual criticism of historical sources – all these procedures are the hallmarks of science. The
humanities seek – and find – facts.

However, there are also important limitations to the scope and
explicitness of the empirical approaches to be derived from the
humanities. The strengths and weaknesses become especially clear
in literary criticism, which has been an important influence on
qualitative research about mass media.

On the one hand, the literary notion of exegesis, or "reading,"
normally implies a cognitive operation of analysis-cum-interpretation, in which no firm line can be drawn between the analysis of
"data" and the subsequent discussion of aggregated "findings."
The primary tool of research is the interpretive capacity of the
scholar. The meaning of each constitutive element of a text is
established with reference to its con-text – the rest of the text as a
whole. The wider significance of the text may then be established by
considering also the social context of historical and psychoanalytical
factors, which offer cues to understanding specific literary periods,
authors, readerships, or discursive themes. Yet, particularly in
studies that draw on phenomenological and hermeneutic traditions
(see the overview in Eagleton, 1983: Ch. 2; a major text of the
tradition is Gadamer, 1975), while the act of interpretation may be
thought of as a phenomenological reduction extracting a textual
essence, the steps of the reduction frequently are not made explicit.
As a result, the analysis normally cannot meaningfully become the
object of intersubjective (dis-)agreement in a scientific community
or public forum. Rather, the validity of an interpretation depends

on a more universal confidence in the scholar's expertise and sensitivity, his/her legitimacy and authority, or perhaps an appreciation
of the interpretation as original and stimulating.

On the other hand, literary studies start from the fundamental
insight that language, as employed also in cultural and everyday
practices, is not transparent, but requires detailed analytical attention in order to be interpreted. Reading qualitative studies through
the eyes of a humanist, one is sometimes struck by the inattention to
the actual language that informants use. The social-scientific analysis of, say, an interview respondent's conceptual structures or
worldviews, while being supported with illustrative quotations,
often is not based on any textual analysis. Consequently, it remains
unclear how the respondent's everyday discourse was transformed
into the researcher's analytical discourse. If the humanities, notably
modern linguistics, have one lesson to contribute to interdisciplinary qualitative studies, it is this: mind the language!

Because language is a constitutive element of most qualitative
studies, one may build a typology of qualitative methodologies
around their characteristic uses of language (Jensen, 1989). Table
1.1 thus notes both productive and receptive uses of language in
qualitative research. First, language is normally the main object of
analysis, whether in the form of basic linguistic analysis of interview
transcripts (and any other type of language data) or further textual
criticism of historical sources and literary works. Second, language
is a primary tool of data-gathering in interview and observational
studies.

Table 1.1 The roles of language in qualitative methodologies

Method	Language	
	Tool of data gathering	*Object of analysis*
Interviewing	+	+
Participant observation	+	−
Textual criticism	−	+

In qualitative *interviewing* (a form of interpersonal communication) language is both the tool and the object of analysis. Communicating through language, the interviewer and respondent(s)
negotiate an understanding of the subject matter in question, which
subsequently, in the form of tapes and transcripts, becomes the

object of linguistic analysis and textual interpretation. In the case of *observation* studies, where interviewing normally is an integrated element of research, this use of language is primarily a tool for gathering further information, whereas the interview discourse mostly is not documented through transcripts or analysed in its linguistic detail. (This is in spite of the fact that field notes and other accounts of observation represent a discourse which lends itself to categories of linguistic analysis; see van Maanen, 1988.) Textual *criticism*, finally, as practiced by disciplines from history to literary criticism, is applied to written source materials as objects of analysis. Whereas written accounts may not be seen as tools of data-gathering as such, any existing textual sources will be used routinely for cross-reference with other types of evidence. The language of textual sources, then, from legislation and business memoranda to newspapers, offers cues to how, for example, political and cultural rights have been conceived in different social and historical settings.

The focus on language suggests the interesting possibility of arriving at a systematic methodology or "statistics" of qualitative research with reference to the various levels of linguistic discourse. Admittedly, linguistics is itself a specialized discipline; this is one further argument for the field to undertake more genuinely inter-disciplinary group projects. Nevertheless, linguistics does offer a number of analytical procedures which can be applied by scholars across the field. The most important level of linguistic analysis in this context is *pragmatics*, which studies the uses of language in social context (Crystal and Davy, 1969; Halliday, 1978; Leech, 1983). The study of language, which traditionally, as in classical philology, had been preoccupied with form, over the last two decades has turned to the social uses of language in everyday life.

Linguistic discourse analysis

The New Critical tradition had served to highlight language as the concrete vehicle of literary communication. Semiology, similarly, had focused scholarly attention on the formal properties of discourse. Together, these two schools drove home the point that language is not a transparent means of access to reality, and that linguistic details have important implications for the communicative functions of texts. Both semiology and the New Criticism, however, tended to concentrate on monologic, aesthetically complex texts, leaving aside the uses of language in daily conversation and a multitude of other everyday practices.

Linguistic discourse analysis, in charting this extremely complex area of inquiry, has identified three main levels of analysis. First, the most fundamental elements of discourse are utterances or statements of various types, what are referred to as *speech acts* (Austin, 1962; Searle, 1969). Each statement is defined literally as an instance of linguistic action. Language does not simply, or even primarily, work as a descriptive representation; through language, people perform a variety of everyday acts. Among the obvious examples are rituals (a marriage ceremony) and other institutionalized procedures (a sentence pronounced in a court of law), where the very pronouncement accomplishes a socially binding act. In addition, by uttering promises, questions and answers, and arguments, people also perform speech acts. Even statements which may appear purely descriptive will in most cases be performative in the sense that they are designed to produce a specific effect in the recipient(s). The typologies of language as action are still being worked out, but by relating language and social action, speech-act theory has offered one of the most important reformulations of humanistic theory since Wittgenstein (1958), specifying his dictum on language that meaning is use. "Language as action" also hints at methodologies which might bridge the gap between a social-scientific and a humanistic approach to meaning production.

At a second level, language serves to establish a mode of *interaction* between communicators, most clearly in the case of interpersonal communication, such as interviewing. Both parties introduce and develop particular themes while closing off other aspects of the discursive universe. In negotiating a form of common understanding with the interviewer, respondents can be seen to build semantic networks that are indicative of their worldviews. Also observational studies establish complex forms of interaction which lend themselves to linguistic analysis. For both observational and interview studies, mass communication research may draw on linguistic research about everyday conversation and classroom interaction (see the examples in Antaki, 1988, and Sinclair and Coulthard, 1975).

It should be added here that the interactive dimension of language has several practical implications for the conduct of qualitative research. For one thing, linguistic analysis of an interview transcript, for example, can suggest how conceptual distinctions and interrelations are established during the interaction. Such an analysis may also assess the extent to which studies fulfill the promise of qualitative researchers to generally "ground" their theoretical categories in the respondents' lifeworld (Glaser and Strauss, 1967). Conducted by another researcher, this evaluation of interviewer performance can help to address the intersubjectivity of qualitative findings. Thus, discourse analysis, in complementing traditional measures of reliability and validity in the administration and coding of interviews, may reopen the field for discussion of the criteria for producing valid knowledge. For another thing, an understanding of the interactive dimension of qualitative methodologies may help in the planning of specific designs and the training of interviewers or field-workers. For better or worse, qualitative researchers emphatically interact with their object of inquiry.

Third, it is at the level of *discourse* that the various linguistic categories can be seen to come together as a coherent structure, a text with a message to be interpreted. Both respondents and historical sources tell stories and develop arguments in forms which are comparable, in many ways, to literary or rhetorical genres. Whereas some aspects of discursive coherence are attributable to formal features (Halliday and Hasan, 1976), other aspects derive from the functional interrelations between the speech acts and interactive turns of a specific discourse. Such interrelations must normally be interpreted with reference to the discursive context and the context of use (see Jensen, 1986: Ch. 10; also van Dijk, 1977, and his Ch. 5 in this volume). Other components of discursive coherence are presuppositions and implicit premises, which refer to what is taken for granted and not otherwise elaborated in a discourse (Culler, 1981; Leech, 1974).

Because humans seem to be constantly telling stories or arguing about something, whether in formal scientific discourse, daily conversation, or public debate, any typology of discourse is of necessity complex. Bruner (1986) has suggested that one may distinguish two modes of experience and discourse: the narrative mode and the paradigmatic or argumentative mode. To be sure, further differentiation of the theories and models of everyday discourses is required; narratives work as arguments and arguments develop into narratives. Still, discourse analysis does suggest that stories and arguments draw on a relatively fixed repertoire of linguistic strategies combining premises and conclusions, assertions and substantiations, scenes, actors, and themes, even if the uses of the repertoire in different social contexts may be quite diverse

(Coulthard and Montgomery, 1981). Linguistic discourse analysis on everyday and literary discourses, in sum, offers a promising avenue for developing and applying humanistic methodology to the study of mass communication (see especially its development in Potter and Wetherell, 1987).

Stories on, and in, history

A final contribution of humanistic methodology stems from its historical awareness of texts. Beyond the historical and linguistic affinity between story and hi-story, we learn about history primarily through narratives (including this chapter), just as narratives serve to articulate a current historical setting. A major contribution of the humanities to mass communication research derives from its attention to the long waves or deep structures of society and culture – the relationship between text and context. This may be so because, traditionally, the humanities have not been exclusively focused on the social institutions of modernity and industrial capitalism, which have constituted the naturalized matrix of much social-scientific theory – and sometimes the outer limits of its theoretical imagination. (See further Chapter 10 on the historical frameworks of mass communication theory.)

The concept of *genre* helps to indicate what it means to communicate in and on history. As noted by Williams (1977: 183), three features serve to characterize a genre:

formal composition;
appropriate subject matter;
mode of address.

Painstaking studies have been conducted of the form of composition and the conventional subject matter of various genres; less attention has been given to their mode of address. Addressing their readers, genres imply both a subject position from which they may be interpreted and a set of appropriate social uses of the contents. The discussion above of news, novels, and encyclopedias suggested how genres construct and are constructed by a historically specific social order. Moreover, the "effect" of genres is due not just to the social uses of the individual genre, but as importantly to their total configuration, which compartmentalizes the social structure into the private and public realms, and into political, economic, and cultural spheres, thus projecting a particular worldview. Through language, reality becomes social; through genres, social reality becomes the object of specific forms of story-telling, argument, and action.

Genre may be the analytical level where social-scientific and humanistic modes of inquiry can be said to converge, with implications for both theory and methodology. Whereas it remains difficult to specify how different modes of understanding complement each other within interdisciplinary communication research, genre might serve as a conceptual interchange between discourse studies and social-scientific research designs. On the one hand, genre has long been key to the study of communication as representation, expression, and ritual – with an emphasis on textual form; on the other hand, genres, in particular their mode of address, motivate and structure the transfer, uses, and impact of communication in contexts of social action. For the social sciences, this may imply an extended concept of genres of social action. How to approach these interrelated aspects of genre in methodological terms may be discussed in a framework of social semiotics. Before considering the origin of social semiotics and its relevance for further research, a brief look at visual communication will serve to summarize some main points of the humanistic perspective on culture as communication.

THE CASE OF VISUAL COMMUNICATION

In contradistinction to alphabetic communication which has been studied extensively by the humanities, the study of images for a long time remained the specialized domain of art history and, more recently, film theory. Moreover, social-scientific communication research may have found it difficult to characterize visual communication processes, because the categories of content analysis and survey methodology are better suited to capture the discrete, digital elements of alphabetic communication than the analog coding of images. It is, indeed, striking that research methods have not been able the match the proliferation of visual media in the contemporary media environment (see Jensen, forthcoming). Though early work on visual perception (Dember, 1964) has been carried further by psychology and some other disciplines, in communications "the systematic analysis of audiovisual languages is still at an early stage" (McQuail, 1987: 202).

Whether visual communication in fact relies on "languages" in any conventional sense is a controversial matter. Raising classic issues of epistemology, the question tends to divide studies into two camps. First, one position holds that visual communication may be easy to understand because it approximates the perceptual processes of everyday vision (Hobbs *et al.*, 1988; Messaris, 1988). Central aspects of human perception and, by analogy, much visual communication might not be dependent upon historically or socially specific codes of comprehension, which implies certain psychological universals that correspond to the structure of reality (Piaget and Inhelder, 1948). Recent film theory, equally, has suggested a turn away from the analysis of film as language, arguing instead that reality imprints itself on film and, by projection, on the viewer's consciousness (Deleuze, 1986; 1989). These arguments, then, support contemporary Western common sense.

The second group of researchers challenges common sense and argues, in different ways, that perception and representation are constructed actively. Whereas the most emphatic articulation of constructionism can be found in philosophical pragmatism (Bernstein, 1986; Goodman, 1978; Rorty, 1989), also the mainstream of disciplines from film studies (Bordwell, 1985; Metz, 1974) to art history (Arnheim, 1974; Gombrich, 1960) and semiotics (Eco, 1976), does assume that visual communication involves a complex process of encoding and decoding. This position is supported by historical studies of changes in the forms of representation and perception (Foster, 1988; Hauser, 1951; Lowe, 1982), showing that the reality effect of visual arts depends on the prevailing psychological schemata of specific periods.

The fundamental disagreements in current studies of visual communication re-emphasize the need for communication theory generally to examine its definition of the constituents and processes of mass communication. A major part of all mass-mediated messages, perhaps the majority, represents a hybrid of visuals and alphabetic text, ranging from feature films and television to comics and advertising. Also, the total media environment exposes the audience–public to a configuration of print and visual mass media, which are interrelated through institutional and financial arrangements as well as through genres. Conglomeration, among other things, breeds intertextuality. Visual communication, hence, provides a test case for the application of humanistic methodology to mass communication research and an important area for further theoretical development.

Further research may depart from the three master concepts of the humanities: discourse, subjectivity, and context. Regarding *discourse*, one question is how the specifically visual codes affect the communicative capacity and social uses of visual media, including new hybrids of video and computer media. Visuality may enhance both the audience fascination with media content and its information value or instrumental uses, potentially but not necessarily at the same time. Moreover, while Barthes (1984a) and some later authors have suggested how text and image may be interrelated when they communicate in concert, a detailed typology of the various discourses and genres of mass communication remains to be constructed, posing a natural task for humanistic scholarship. The discourses that will carry *humanitas* in the future are likely to be visual and mass-mediated more so than in the past.

Subjectivity, next, may be reconstructed in view of new forms of visual communication. Not only do the visual media provide different means of aesthetic expression than print and audio, as exemplified by some emerging forms ranging from video art to computer graphics; in the long term, visual communication, through its modes of address and the subject positions offered to audiences (Metz, 1982; Mulvey, 1989), also may entail different modes of socialization and acculturation. Part of the social impact of mass media, thus, may be attributed to certain institutionalized forms of subjectivity associated with media reception and experience, for example the focused gaze of cinema as opposed to the distracted glance of television reception (Ellis, 1982). How such forms of media reception enter into mass communication processes and effects is a question which qualitative methodologies may be particularly equipped to address.

Context, finally, is relevant for the analysis of visual communication in at least two respects. First, the institutions and technologies of visual media are especially large-scale and complex, as in the case of network television or telematics. This tends to limit the public access to and uses of such media. Simultaneously, those same video-cum-computer technologies hold the promise of decentralization and, perhaps, democratization. The question is whether the qualities of accessibility and low cost may be combined in a social form which will make the visual technologies into general cultural resources for individuals, groups, and communities (see Chapter 9 in this volume).

Second, visual mass media may be seen to redefine, in discursive terms, their context. Television, for example, has redrawn the boundary between private and public domains, and between social reality and its representation (Meyrowitz, 1985). The constant availability of particularly visual mass communication in the modern world – in the home, the street, the workplace, and in transit – has meant the saturation of much of social time and space with cultural products. This has resulted in a qualitatively novel *media environment*, where the discourses of media and everyday life may become increasingly indistinguishable. If one traditional purpose of cultural practices has been the creation of a time-out from everyday life, the modern merging of mass communication with the rest of the social context may be creating an almost ceaseless time-in.

CONCLUSION: TOWARD SOCIAL SEMIOTICS

Mass communication is simultaneously a social and a discursive phenomenon. Signs, following the humanities, are a primary human mode of interacting with reality, entering into a continuous process of meaning production which serves to construct social reality as domains of political, economic, and cultural activities. The humanistic research traditions point beyond the aesthetic pleasures derived from texts in private, and suggest a framework for studying the social uses of signs – a social semiotics which differs markedly from the semiology of Saussure and French structuralism (for the full argument and references, see Jensen, 1991).

In contrast to the Saussurean dualism of signifier and signified, Charles Sanders Peirce proposed a basic configuration of three elements: sign, object, and interpretant (for a collection of his works, see Peirce, 1958). A sign stands for an object or phenomenon in the world, but only through reference to another sign in the mind of an interpreting subject, namely, the interpretant. The interpretant is neither identical with the interpretive agent, nor is it an essence representing the content of that person's thoughts. Interpretation, then, is a continuous process, rather than one act which, once and for all, internalizes external phenomena through a medium of signs. This does not, however, imply the solipsist reality of postmodernism, in which subjects are seen to be caught in a web of signs, being forever separated from social and material reality. To Peirce, signs are not *what* we know, but *how* we come to know what we can justify saying we know. Interpretants, accordingly, are signs by which people may orient themselves toward and interact with a reality of diverse objects, events, and discourses. The three-term model of sign use within semiotics would relate "the analysis of linguistic meaning to the idea of participants in communication coming to an understanding about something in the world" (Habermas, 1984: 397).

Peirce, further, suggested a concept of *difference* which implies an analytical emphasis on the social uses of signs, not discourse in itself. Though the sign remains the central explanatory concept to Peirce, meaning comes to be defined in relational rather than essential terms. The meaning of signs is determined not by their immanent features, but by their position, their relations of difference, within the system of meaning production as a whole. Whereas Saussurean semiology had advanced a similar argument (Culler, 1975: 11; see also Saussure, 1959), the emphasis in practice has been on the relations of difference *within* the language system, leaving aside the social uses of language and other signs. In sum, Peircean semiotics offers a framework for studying meaning production in its social context. When the discursive differences of mass media content and other cultural forms are interpreted and enacted by social agents, thus serving to orient their cognition and action, media discourses can be said, in the terminology of pragmatism, to make a social difference. Meaning is a discursive difference that makes a social difference (Bateson, 1972: 242; Goodman, 1976: 227).

Certain forms of communication and interpretation make a particular social difference and hence have a strategic importance for the understanding of society and culture. While Peirce did not give special attention to cultural practices, he identified the scientific community as an institution engaging in interpretation with definite social consequences. Scientists, in a sense, are communities of knowers who arrive at a definition and legitimation of knowledge by some public, collective procedure, sometimes with major historical implications (Kuhn, 1970; Lowe, 1982). Science, in a social perspective, constitutes an institution-to-think-with, by analogy to the anthropological, Lévi-Straussian concept of objects-to-think-with (Schudson, 1987: 56).

The mass media represent another important institution-to-think-with. Science and mass communication, in different ways, serve to place reality on a public agenda; both institutions operate through social practices that presuppose a degree of consensus regarding interpretive procedures. Whereas the specific institutional hierarchies, admittedly, differ, both are important agents, increasingly so, in maintaining the political, cultural, as well as material structures of society (Galbraith, 1967). At the same time, clearly, the interpretive communities of mass communication – the demographically and culturally specific audience groups – are more diverse, complex, and, most important, inclusive. In principle, mass communication serves to establish a cultural forum (Newcomb and Hirsch, 1984) which includes everybody and which, again in principle, may address any issue of power or social structure. Because they may, but frequently do not, fulfill this function, mass media institutions and discourses have become central sites of social conflict.

The concept of interpretive repertoires, or interpretive communities, which recent work has introduced into literary, cultural, and communication studies (Fish, 1979; Jensen, 1987; 1991; Lindlof, 1988; Radway, 1984), may help to re-establish the link between social science and discourse analysis. (The concept of interpretive *repertoires* will be preferred here, because it implies that audiences are not formal groups or communities, but contextually defined agents who employ such repertoires to make preliminary sense. See the argument in Potter and Wetherell [1987: 138–57].) The assumption underlying the concept of interpretive repertoires is that media audience groups are defined not just by their formal social roles and demographic characteristics, but as importantly by the interpretive frames or repertoires by which they engage mass media content and other cultural forms. This perspective helps to refocus research interest on the relationship between macro-social structures, such as social classes and cultural institutions, and micro-social processes (see also the argument of Giddens, 1984, and the discussions hereof in Held and Thompson, 1989). In mass communication, micro-social or discursive acts of interpretation serve to enact what represents, at the macro-social level, cultural practices. These practices can be seen to shape, as well as be shaped by, the various genres of mass communication. Genres, to reiterate, are modes of address that imply specific social uses of communication in relation to particular political and cultural practices. Being methodological interfaces between social-scientific and humanistic forms of inquiry, genres and interpretive repertoires may prove central to the study of mass media as institutions-to-think-with.

In summary, social semiotics implies a reconceptualization of the central terms of humanistic scholarship. Discourse is conceived of as genres with specific uses in social practice; subjectivity is defined in collective rather than individual terms, as the expression of socially situated interpretive repertoires; and context is related to the specific historical setting in which institutions-to-think-with serve their various purposes. Beyond a contemplative understanding of texts, the humanities can provide a concrete, language-based understanding of communication and culture. If twentieth-century scholarship has witnessed a series of interrelated linguistic or qualitative turns, the humanities have performed a communicative turn in approaching culture as a historical configuration of communicative practices. This development has helped to establish a dialogue with social science about the complementary contribution of each field to mass communication research.

Chapter 2

The qualitative tradition in social science inquiry: contributions to mass communication research

Nicholas W. Jankowski and Fred Wester

INTRODUCTION

It would be an exaggeration to claim that quantitatively oriented mass communication research is no longer predominant in the field, but methodological re-examination and renewal are clearly taking place. The content of this volume and the studies on which it draws are testimony to the transformation under way. While the previous chapter concentrates on influences from the humanities in that transformation, this chapter charts the evolution and diversity of qualitative methods in the social sciences and examines their contribution to qualitative media research. Interpretive forms of inquiry have been central to the development of qualitative social science, although the tradition also includes critical and positivist studies.

Whereas there is no unanimity regarding the core principles of qualitative methodology in the social sciences (for diversity in principles, see Bruyn, 1966; Burgess, 1982; 1984; Denzin, 1970a; Filstead, 1970; Lofland, 1971; McCall and Simmons, 1969; Smith and Manning, 1982), the following aspects may constitute a working definition. Qualitative research is a form of long-term first-hand observation conducted in close proximity to the phenomena under study (van Maanen *et al.*, 1982: 16). The research is, ideally, performed in a naturalistic setting with emphasis on everyday behavior and is often descriptive in nature. Participant observation and case studies are primary methods of qualitative empirical studies.

Three elements of this definition call for specification (Wester, 1987: 19–20). First, the concept of *verstehen*, discussed in more detail later in this chapter, is fundamental to qualitative research. Briefly, the term refers to an understanding of the meaning that people ascribe to their social situation and activities. Because people act on the basis of the meanings they attribute to themselves and others, the focus of qualitative social science is on everyday life and its significance as perceived by participants.

Second, the notion of role taking, originally formulated by Mead (1934), suggests that in order to study human behavior the perspective of the actor must be established. The researcher's task, then, becomes one of reconstructing and understanding this perspective.

These two points imply a third principle stressing the importance of identifying topics relevant to the world under study before concepts are constructed, operationalized, and measured. Problem statements in qualitative research are characterized by an initial formulation in general terms, allowing for later modification and refinement. Terms and concepts are meant to serve as guideposts for investigation and not, as in traditional social science, expressions based on theoretical constructions designed to be tested. Theoretical statements are to emerge – at least partially – from the area or object of inquiry itself.

The historical origins of these principles are outlined in the first section of this chapter. While the development of qualitative research has spanned the entire history of the social sciences, three periods can be distinguished regarding the type and intensity of qualitative research practice. Throughout the history of social science, and especially since the 1960s, the interpretive approach to social inquiry has been central to qualitative research. In the second section of the chapter, this approach is traced primarily in various currents of sociology, though other social sciences have also made contributions (Ashworth *et al.*, 1986; Bogdan, 1972; Bogdan and Biklan, 1982). In each case examples from communication studies are included. The third section considers the diversity of methods employed in qualitative research. Special attention is given here to the problems and procedures associated with analysis of qualitative data. Finally, in the fourth section we consider the accumulating evidence for a methodological reorientation among communication scholars. While expressing reservation about the current fashion of advocating qualitative research without a clear awareness of the interpretive heritage, we suggest that the qualitative tradition in social science inquiry offers the constituents of a systematic qualitative research process to be developed further in conjunction and dialogue with other traditions of mass communication research.

HISTORICAL ORIGINS

Early period: 1890–1930

During the last years of the nineteenth century and the first decades of this century, as social issues became topics of academic study, virtually all research was qualitative in nature. This is evident in early classic works by Weber, Durkheim, Simmel, and others (for references to key texts, see Berger and Berger, 1976: 26–55). As academic specializations were defined and university departments created, qualitative methods gained a solid foothold. Several factors may explain this emphasis. First, there was still a strong affiliation of social science with the mode of investigation utilized in philosophy and the humanities. Second, the social sciences were young and searching for global, overall perspectives; the essay format was more suitable to this task than that of the contemporary research article. Finally, what eventually became known as "the scientific method" had yet to be fully developed and applied to the social sciences.

The emphasis on qualitative research was especially evident in anthropology. Although methodological diversity in the discipline has since developed (see Sanday, 1983), the qualitative emphasis has continued to this day. The contributions of Malinowski (1922), Boas (1940), and Radcliffe-Brown (1952) were particularly influential in determining how field studies were conducted. Malinowski (1922: 25) is credited with encouraging first-hand observation in an effort "to grasp the native's point of view, his relation to life, to realize his vision of his world," even though, on later publication of Malinowski's diaries, it appeared that he himself had difficulty putting this principle into practice (Malinowski, 1967).

In this early period, qualitative field research was introduced to sociology in the USA, and pioneering work was conducted at the University of Chicago. Founded in 1892, the sociology department there – then combined with anthropology – came to be known as the "Chicago School." In the early decades of this century, it was to have major impact on the discipline. Under the influence of W.I. Thomas, Ernest Burgess, and Robert Park, a concerted academic enterprise developed around the study of urban life. Early Chicago studies concentrated on deviant groups in the city: hobos (Anderson, 1923), gangs (Thrasher, 1927), criminals (Sutherland, 1937). Other scholars at the university introduced community studies, later known as urban ethnography. Polish immigrants to the city were the subject of a momumental study (Thomas and Znaniecki, 1918–20), and the structure of small-town community life was also explored (Lynd and Lynd, 1929). A third, later cluster of studies examined professional life – the police (Westley, 1951), business-men (Dalton, 1959), teachers (Becker, 1951), and doctors (Hall, 1944).

The Chicago School was the home of a long list of prolific sociol-ogists, but the contributions of one stand out: Robert E. Park. Having worked for some time as a journalist, he retained interest in the media as institutions within society. In a collection of essays on the city (Park *et al.*, 1925), Park contributed a piece entitled "The natural history of the newspaper" (reprinted in Schramm, 1960). Although without empirical data supporting his interpretation of the place of print media in a historical process, the piece does exemplify Park's concern for newspapers in the context of city and community. This concern was also evident in his study of the im-migrant press (Park, 1922) in which he examined the function of newspapers among European immigrants.

Frequent reference has been made to Park's recommendation that social scientists imitate the work routine of newspaper re-porters. His instruction to a student about to begin a research project was, "Write down what you see and hear; you know, like a newspaper reporter" (quoted in Kirk and Miller, 1986: 40). Implicit in this recommendation is the assumption that the discernment of "facts" is unproblematic, and that facts can be gathered and ana-lysed straightforwardly. This position, not surprisingly, has since been challenged and modified, emphasis now being placed on the social construction of "facts" (see van Maanen, 1988: 18).

Another bit of advice Park is said to have stressed was to leave the protected confines of the university and to explore the city:

> Go and sit in the lounges of the luxury hotels and on the doorsteps of the flophouses; sit on the Gold Coast settees and on the slum shakedowns; sit in the Orchestra Hall and in the Star and Garter Burlesk. In short, gentlemen, go get the seats of your pants dirty in real research.
>
> (quoted in McKinney, 1966: 71)

Park's emphasis here on first-hand observation is often taken as evidence that the Chicago School practiced what is currently known as participant observation. Even though many Chicago sociologists became intimately familiar with the cultures studied, they seldom participated in those cultures as researchers. Most early Chicago studies relied on document analysis. In only two studies – Cressy's (1932) on dance halls and Anderson's (1923) on hobos – is there explicit reference to participant observation as a method of data collection, and even then there is limited explication of how the method was employed (Hammersley, 1989: 1–84). Harvey (1987: 50) suggests that it is misleading to consider these studies forms of participant observation as the term is now employed. (For another perspective on the place of participant observation in Chicago School research, see Chapter 3, note 2, by Tuchman in this book.)

Members of the Chicago School also conducted communication research on the effects of films on children. In the late 1920s, Herbert Blumer and Philip Hauser were commissioned by the Motion Picture Research Council to investigate the relationship between film and delinquency. As part of the so-called Payne Fund Studies (the agency which financed the research for the Council), two monographs were produced (Blumer, 1933; Blumer and Hauser, 1933; see also Blumer, 1935, reprinted in Short, 1971). This work exemplifies several aspects of the Chicago heritage. Both research projects were intended to "capture the attitudes or perspectives which mediate the effects of objective factors, in this case of films" (Hammersley, 1989: 89). The studies were exploratory in nature, with minimal methodological explication. There was heavy use of interviews and life histories, and little attention was given to data collection through participant observation.

The debate on social-scientific methodologies in the USA in the 1930s and 1940s also came to include a number of immigrants from Europe, representing different theoretical and political orientations. One group included refugees from the Frankfurt School (see Jay, 1973); their approaches comprised particularly qualitative textual analysis and historical studies (see Chapter 6 by Larsen in this volume). Another orientation was later to be developed into a mainstream of American communication research methodology by Paul F. Lazarsfeld and his collaborators, thus superseding the positions both of the Chicago School and of critical theory.

Indeed, during the period of these debates and studies, the application of quantitative methods increased. As others have noted (Bulmer, 1984; Harvey, 1987), there was never antipathy toward statistics at Chicago; quantitative methods were often employed alongside qualitative ones. But, by the 1930s a separate division with a quantitative orientation had developed at Chicago, and the methodological debate then emerging across the nation began to take explicit and emotional form.

Middle period: 1930–60

The methodological debate had its roots in the rise of positivism. Since the late 1920s and early 1930s, sociologists had begun to turn to methods of research as practiced in the natural sciences, or, to be precise, as natural science was perceived from the perspective of social science at this historical moment. It is perhaps an irony of history that social scientists were seeking to construct an objectivist notion of social reality at a time when most other arts and sciences, including physics, were arriving at a multiperspectival conception of the reality under inquiry (Lowe, 1982: 109–17). Researchers both in and outside Chicago were developing quantitative measuring devices and conceptual schemes that were intended to elevate the status of sociology to a science. The model for empirical research eventually became the one perceived as the standard in physical sciences, particularly physics. Experimental designs came to dominate research thinking, along with hypothetico–deductive reasoning, and methodologies emphasized the use of "objective" data-collection techniques and the standardization of analytical procedures.

In the course of the 1930s, then, proponents of quantitative methods gained the upper hand in the methodological struggle. The Chicago-style case study had all but disappeared as a mode of social science by the 1950s. Survey research had become *the* method in the social sciences; as Benney and Hughes (1956: 137) remarked, modern sociology had become "the science of the interview" (article reprinted in Denzin, 1970b). As the influence of positivist theory and quantitative methodology reached its peak in the 1950s, qualitative research came to be seen as a preliminary activity which could, at best, lay the groundwork for "real" science.

One of the Chicago studies of this period, expressing the tension between the qualitative and quantitative traditions, focused on the community press (Janowitz, 1952). Although clearly rooted in the early Chicago interest in urbanism and qualitative approaches, the study also systematically employed quantitative research methods. An appendix to the study elaborates on coding procedures for a content analysis, and the material presented about a survey (sampling information and instrument design) is similar to that found in most contemporary survey research monographs.

Several factors contributed to the demise of qualitative methodologies such as the Chicago case-study approach. First, there was a desire to create a genuine "science" of social investigation, modeled on positivism and the successes of the physical sciences. Second, fueled by World War II, calls were made for research to measure the impact of communication, in particular propaganda. These concerns were accompanied by a surge of funding for scientific findings. It was during this period that the Bureau of Applied Social Research at Columbia University established itself as one of the main centers of mass communication research in the USA. Last but not least, after the war there appeared to develop a structural need for social-scientific knowledge which could be applied to the development of industry and to the planning of social and educational institutions (Galbraith, 1967). Such social engineering, as witnessed by policies in many Western countries, found a theoretical ally in the functionalist perspective then taking hold. Both social policy practice and functionalist theory were well served by the survey research methodology then coming of age.

Late period: 1960–present

After functionalism and quantitative methodologies had held sway through the 1950s and into the 1960s, the theoretical and political critique of these positions intensified in the 1960s. Gouldner (1970), for example, identified the "coming crisis" of sociology as a disenchantment with functionalism and "grand theory." Where, a decade earlier, the discipline had still been preoccupied with building and securing its institutions, the movement now was toward an application of the discipline to the deep social conflicts outside academia. Rooted in political, economic, and racial inequalities, these conflicts mobilized students, blacks, other minorities, and, sometimes, social scientists (Colfax and Roach, 1971), not just to study events, but to become actively involved in organizations and demonstrations. For economic and social-structural reasons, of course, such involvement had become more feasible by the 1960s.

This societal context provided the backdrop for disillusionment with positivist versions of social science also in the academic institutions. One point of frequent criticism referred to the limitation of these approaches when studying human behavior and especially its origins in a social reality as experienced and lived. Another criticism singled out some sociologists' apparent obsession with scientific method. Herbert Blumer, former staff member of the Chicago School, became one of the most vocal critics of the increasing emphasis on quantitative methods in sociological research, an effort characterized in one piece (Blumer, 1954) as a tendency to reduce social existence to variables.

Outside Chicago, C. Wright Mills, then at Columbia University, was also a vehement opponent of mainstream sociology. His *Sociological Imagination* (1959) was a landmark critique of Parson's efforts to construct "grand theory" and the empiricism then dominant in sociology. In apparent prescience of Feyerabend's (1975) attack on traditional models of science, Mills urged all researchers to become their own methodologist (Mills, 1959: 121). Many other scholars (see Phillips, 1971; 1973) systematically listed the shortcomings of survey research and argued for a modification of standardized research procedures.

In the field of communication research, equally, criticism of predominant research methodologies was expressed. Gitlin (1978) summarized much of the reservation felt for the dominant method of mass communication research, the survey. Though Gitlin did not explicitly call for a qualitative approach to media research, he did argue that the minimal effect of communications found through surveys was largely a product of the methodology.

In a recent historical sketch of communication research, Dennis (1988) observed that media studies were conforming to a methodological metamorphosis of the social sciences generally. By the late 1970s, the supremacy of quantitative research had been "challenged by qualitative researchers – many with an ideological bent – who decried quantification and questioned the utility and value of the prevailing research tradition" (Dennis, 1988: 4). Interpretive forms of social inquiry have played a central role in this transformation.

INTERPRETIVE SOCIAL INQUIRY

Interpretive inquiry has been practiced in a number of social science disciplines, but is especially prominent in sociology. The approach has many names: interactionist (Fisher and Strauss, 1978; Silverman, 1985: 95), humanistic, phenomenological, naturalistic, or simply qualitative sociology (Wester, 1987: 14). The common heritage is Weber's (1964: 88) classic formulation of sociology: "a science which attempts the interpretive understanding of social action in order thereby to arrive at causal explanation of its course and effects." The long debate on which elements of this definition deserve emphasis falls outside the scope of this chapter (see Benton, 1977; Winch, 1958). The essence of interpretive sociology – and of interpretive inquiry generally as found in other disciplines – is the analysis and interpretation, through *verstehen* or empathetic understanding, of the meaning that people give to their actions.

Whereas there are several varieties of interpretive inquiry (Tesch, 1990), their theoretical and methodological perspectives overlap. A satisfactory typology has not yet been constructed, and in the present context we suggest that the interpretive varieties are complementary sources of methodological insight. Three methodological sources merit further discussion: symbolic interactionism, ethnomethodology, and ethnography.

Symbolic interactionism

Symbolic interactionism was the form of interpretive inquiry at the center of the theoretical and methodological reorientation of the 1960s and 1970s. It is grounded primarily in Mead's (1934) *Mind, Self, and Society*, described as the "single most influential book, to date, on symbolic interactionism" (Manis and Meltzer, 1967: 140). Others – Cooley (1930), Thomas (1928), and Dewey (1925) – also contributed to its development, but there is general agreement that the refinement of the theoretical position came from Blumer (1969). He posited, first of all, that people act on the basis of the meaning they themselves ascribe to objects and situations. Second, Blumer held that meaning is derived from interaction with others, and that this meaning is transformed further through a process of interpretation during interaction (Meltzer *et al.*, 1975: 2). Coupled to these notions was a methodology stressing respect for the world and actions of individuals as well as non-intervention by the researcher in that world, what is often referred to as a naturalistic perspective (Lincoln and Guba, 1985). Specifically, participant observation is normally associated with the naturalistic perspective and generally with the work of symbolic interactionists (Ackroyd and Hughes, 1981: 102–3; Rock, 1979: 178).

Other sociologists also contributed to the development of the naturalistic perspective. Goffman (1959), for example, is credited with creation of a distinct "dialect" of symbolic interactionism, the dramaturgical approach (see Meltzer *et al.*, 1975). Some communication scholars (Tuchman, 1978) have been influenced by one of Goffman's (1974) concepts, framing, which he himself applied to the media in his book *Gender Advertisements* (1976).

Even while symbolic interactionism is correctly considered the motor behind recent developments in qualitative methodology, it would be a mistake to assume that the two terms are synonymous. In the first place, there is a group of symbolic interactionists who conduct research from a positivist perspective. The Iowa School of symbolic interactionism has employed survey research and standardized observation techniques in an effort to operationalize the concept of self (Meltzer *et al.*, 1975: 55–9). In the second place, other varieties of interpretive inquiry have made significant contributions to qualitative methodology.

Ethnomethodology

This second form of interpretive inquiry seeks to identify the rules people apply in order to make sense of their world. Whereas ethnomethodology originates from the work of European phenomenologists, in particular Schutz (1967), the central figure in its later development has been Harold Garfinkel, who conceived the term, formulated the core ideas, and has served as a source of inspiration for other ethnomethodological researchers. For Garfinkel, ethnomethodology is a form of "practical sociological analysis" (1967: 1). This sociological analysis, however, is not merely an undertaking of professional sociologists: ethnomethodology is an everyday activity in which social agents constantly engage as they arrive at an interpretive understanding of other agents and actions through interaction, thus making sense of social reality. Media studies that draw, in part, on this approach include Molotch and Lester's (1974) examination of news as purposive behavior and Tuchman's (1978) investigation of news organizations.

There is no one research method associated with ethnomethodology. Nevertheless, participant observation and in-depth interviewing are frequently employed as elements of an open research strategy. A prominent place is almost always given to everyday conversation, this being the primary medium of everyday interaction. A special approach, refined to perfection by Garfinkel and his colleagues, is that of experiments which are designed to disrupt taken-for-granted rules of conversation. As Garfinkel (1967: 37) himself described the technique, "Procedurally it is my preference to start with familiar scenes and ask what can be done to make trouble." Douglas (1976) in particular has contributed to the development of this approach, and has in the process ignited a continuing debate on the ethical legitimacy of such research strategies (Cavan, 1978). The justification given for using a disruptive means of research is its end result: the underlying rules governing behavior in everyday situations.

A landmark study of interpretive social inquiry into media, drawing according to its references on both symbolic interactionism, ethnomethodology, and ethnography, was Lull's (1980) examination of the social uses of television. He asked how media, particularly television, "play a central role in the methods which families and other social units employ to interact normatively" (Lull, 1980: 198). Using a combination of participant observation and interview research methods, Lull and his associates examined interaction and communication patterns in their natural setting – the home. This work prepared the way for the many recent studies in the ethnography of mass communication.

Ethnography

Ethnography stems from anthropology; indeed, there was a time when the two concepts were considered identical (Kuper, 1973: 14). Today, ethnography is practiced in other disciplines, and also within anthropology several versions of ethnography now exist (Sanday, 1983; see also Clifford and Marcus, 1986; Ellen, 1984). Despite such diversity, most anthropologists seem to agree on three core principles. First, ethnographic research is concerned with cultural forms in the widest sense of the term, including the everyday as well as religion and arts (see Fetterman, 1989; Hammersley and Atkinson, 1983). Second, studies generally acknowledge the need for long-term participant observation, with the researcher serving as the primary instrument of inquiry. Finally, multiple data-collection methods are generally employed, according to Sanday (1983: 21), as a check on observational findings. (For criticism of this technique, see the discussion of "triangulation" later in this chapter.)

Sanday (1983) identifies three types of anthropological ethnography: holistic, semiotic, and behavioristic. Of these, the holistic variety has the longest tradition and is dominant within the discipline. "Holistic" refers to the scope of inquiry and specifically to the purpose of investigating many aspects of the particular group or society being studied. For this reason, anthropological ethnographies have commonly been situated in clearly defined settings such as a village or other small geographical community. Finally, the establishment of rapport between the researcher and the group studied is considered a critical element of ethnography (Seiter *et al.*, 1989b). This is one of the reasons why some researchers (Wolcott, 1975) suggest a minimum of one year for the fieldwork phase of an ethnographic project.

An increasing number of communication studies claim to be conducted in the ethnographic tradition. Lull (1988a) has edited a volume of such work which concentrates on family television viewing in different cultures. However, one problem with some of the research which is labeled as ethnographic is that it is unclear what the studies have in common with either the research tradition or its methodology. Lull himself has complained, in a critique of the cultural studies approach to media audiences, that "ethnography has become an abused buzzword in our field" (Lull, 1988b: 242).

Another critic (Braber, 1989) examined three ethnographic studies of women and popular culture, and came to essentially the same conclusion – that much of what passes as ethnography deviates considerably from what at least anthropologists mean by the term. Braber examined Hobson's (1982) analysis of the British soap opera *Crossroads*, Radway's (1984) study of female readers of popular romance fiction, and Seiter and colleagues' (1989b) research on soap-opera viewers. All three studies were limited, to varying degrees, in regard to the aspects of anthropological ethnography that Braber considered: centrality of the concept of culture, employment of participant observation, and smallness of the research setting.

Seiter's research team, aware of these difficulties, were frank in discussing the methodological shortcomings of their work: ethnographic research of television audiences, they conceded, "have not satisfied the requirements of ethnography proper, and our study is no exception" (Seiter *et al.*, 1989b: 227). Among the problems they noted in ethnographic media studies were limitations on the frequency and duration of the contact with informants and the resulting difficulty of establishing rapport. Some of these studies (Katz and Liebes, 1984; Lull, 1980) also tend to consider only a single aspect of a culture – television programming – and hence cannot claim a holistic approach.

In spite of these problems, the call for more ethnographies of media audiences is frequent and forceful. Ien Ang, in her book *Desperately Seeking the Audience* (1991), disparages the emphasis on decontextualized quantitative data, largely promoted by the television industry, and recommends "ethnographic understanding" of audiences as an alternative (Ang, 1991). Still, although she argues at length for the value of ethnography in audience research, she devotes no more than a footnote to the characteristics of ethnography as a concrete, empirical approach to conducting research.

The challenge remains, then, to explicate adequately the principles and procedures of ethnography in order to avoid its identification with any and all qualitative methods. This task is particularly urgent because of the potential of ethnography as a form of interpretive inquiry for mass communication research. For all the discussion and disagreement among anthropologists about the nature of ethnography, the anthropological consensus, as noted above, may provide the best starting point for designing ethnographic media research. At the same time, there are a number of general issues outstanding in the scientific debate on how to develop systematic and applicable qualitative research projects.

Issues of interpretive inquiry: theory and politics

Interpretive sociology generally has been the focus of much criticism, directed in particular at the non-political stance of the work. Its advocates have been accused of failing to take into account institutional power and structural determinants as limitations on the individual's freedom of action (McNall and Johnson, 1975). This critique, especially with respect to the apolitical and relativistic stance, applies to much of the work of ethnomethodologists, but less so to that of symbolic interactionists. One of the major proponents of symbolic interactionism, Howard Becker, has argued that it is not possible "to do research uncontaminated by personal and political sympathies . . . and that the question is not whether we should take sides, since we inevitably will, but rather whose side we are on" (Becker, 1967: 239). The general issue of political commitments and knowledge-interests of research has remained on the agenda of interpretive inquiry, and feminist researchers have made significant contributions to the debate.

Also within feminist scholarship there is considerable disagreement regarding appropriate methodological approaches to social science. Steeves (1987) suggests that feminists with a critical studies orientation tend to employ qualitative research methods, while those with a traditional social science background often use quantitative ones. Radical feminists generally tend to dismiss quantitative methods as "masculine" strategies of knowledge and to prefer qualitative strategies such as in-depth interviewing and participant observation. Interestingly, feminist researchers, wishing to document and highlight the everyday life of women, find methodological support in interpretive forms of inquiry from open interviews to life histories (see Roberts, 1981).

Some of the crucial issues addressed in feminist research concern the relationship between the researcher and the subject of study. One question is whether and to what degree the researcher should maintain a distance from the researched, who are frequently other women with whom the (female) researcher may empathize (Oakley, 1981). Another issue is the legitimacy of an emancipatory or action component in the research strategy, the purpose being to change an inequitable state of affairs (Mies, 1979).

Both of these issues – the politics and the epistemology of research – are interrelated and raise a fundamental question: what is the relationship between the objective of a study, on the one hand, and the objectivity of the research procedures and findings, on the other? This question, to be sure, is not unique to feminist research. In particular, the action research tradition, relying in part on qualitative methodology, also has its roots in an emancipatory objective of social science. The work of Negt (1968) and Freire (1974), stressing the involvement and mobilization of the researched, has informed participatory research, a variant of action research. Participatory research specifically has been applied to mass communication, both in communication development projects (Camilo *et al.*, 1990; Coesmans and van den Goor, 1990) and in studies of local radio stations in Latin America.

To sum up, there are affinities between the qualitative tradition and research with an emancipatory objective. However, it is incorrect to assume that most early or current qualitative research is inspired primarily by such motives. While it is true that some figures associated with the Chicago School were guided by progressive ideals (see, for example, Dewey, 1927), its research program was not designed to solve social problems. Only the Chicago sociologist

Burgess engaged in research projects that grew out of his own social and political involvement, and even then he was mainly interested in basic research, and only in the second instance in policy-oriented studies (Harvey, 1987: 36–7).

Before and after the Chicago School, of course, the personal responsibility of researchers for the political implications of their work has been a contested issue in different scientific fields, and is likely to remain so in the future. We submit that Becker's position, that we ultimately "choose sides," simplifies the matter. Few social and political issues can be reduced to categories of "underdogs" and "suppressors," allowing the social scientist an indignant rejection of the latter. Gouldner (1968), in debate with Becker, argued for choosing sociology. We would endorse that position, further recommending, as an aspect of sociology or of media research, explicit analysis of the researcher's own social and political stance, both publicly and in the academic forum. (For a discussion of such public debate on mass communication research as a form of meta-communication, see Chapter 12 in this volume.) In the process, qualitative research may gain in its relevance and legitimacy.

THE QUALITATIVE RESEARCH PROCESS

A frequent criticism of qualitative research in the past has been the lack of explicit research procedures. Explication and clarity are important in all phases of a study, both for the investigators and for other scholars assessing their findings. Whereas it may be granted that the attention given by qualitative researchers to procedures of data collection and analysis has been uneven and insufficient in the past, recent studies have begun to outline a systematic qualitative research process. This section presents the various steps of the process, and discusses the potentials and problems of work about each step, with reference also to examples from media research.

One may start by noting a development of qualitative research procedures through roughly three different phases. All three phases fall within the "late period" of the historical survey earlier in this chapter. The first period of methodological reflection began in the mid-1960s and lasted for about a decade. Analyses focused on comparisons with quantitative methodology around such issues as validity, reliability, and sampling procedures (see Bruyn, 1966; Cicourel, 1964; Filstead, 1970; and McCall and Simmons, 1969).

During the second period, spanning the 1970s, greater emphasis was placed on the mechanics of fieldwork, from gaining access to performing participant observation and conducting open interviews – the "nuts and bolts" of qualitative research. The practically oriented volume by Wax (1971), *Doing Fieldwork: Warnings and Advice*, is exemplary of the literature produced in this period as are the primers by Schatzman and Strauss (1971) and Johnson (1975).

In the third period, which is ongoing since the late 1970s, the focus has been on problems of analysing data. This phase of research has long been considered the Achilles heel of the qualitative enterprise. Conferences and theme issues of journals (*Administrative Science Quarterly*, 24, December, 1979; *Sociological Review*, 27, 4, 1979) have been devoted to the topic, and several major publications focusing on analysis have appeared (Hycner, 1985; Lofland, 1971; Miles and Huberman, 1984; Strauss, 1987). Before examining data analysis more closely, however, we consider the primary data-collection methods employed in qualitative research. Finally, we note some of the problems encountered in reporting qualitative research.

Data collection

Data collection in qualitative research involves a variety of techniques: in-depth interviewing, document analysis, and unstructured observations. Though these techniques are often referred to by a single term – participant observation – this is in fact misleading. Furthermore, in a number of cases it is incorrect to associate qualitative social science with participant observation. Many qualitative studies, for example the early Chicago studies, rely on a single data-collection method, either document analysis or interviewing.

Researchers have frequently asserted that a particular method was superior to all others. Thomas and Znaniecki made such a claim regarding life histories: "We are safe in saying that personal life-records, as complete as possible, constitute the *perfect* type of sociological material" (quoted in Madge, 1962: 61; emphasis in original). Similar assertions were made in a debate between Becker and Geer (1957; 1958), on the one hand, and Trow (1957) on the other (exchange reprinted in Filstead, 1970), the former arguing for the virtues of participant observation and the latter for interviewing.

Such declarations, we suggest, are presumptuous; Bulmer (1984: xv) has rightly pointed to the unproductiveness of engaging in a "best method" debate in an absolute sense. In fact, in Becker and Geer's rejoinder to Trow they agree with him on the point that the problem under investigation dictates the method to use. This point is illustrated further in a typology constructed by Zelditch (1970) and refined by Denzin (1970a: 30–1), in which techniques of data collection are correlated with types of information (Table 2.1).

Table 2.1 Data collection and information types: methods of obtaining information

Information types	Enumerations	Participant observation	Interviewing
Frequency distribution	prototype and best form	inadequate and inefficient	often inadequate
Incidents, histories	not adequate, not efficient	prototype and best form	adequate and efficient
Institutionalized norms and statuses	adequate, not efficient	adequate, not efficient	efficient and best form

The typology suggests that participant observation is best suited for case studies and life histories ("incidents and histories" in Table 2.1), and least suited for overviews of entire populations ("frequency distribution"). For the study of organizations ("institutionalized norms and statuses") participant observation is deemed an adequate, but inefficient data-collection method. Interviewing, according to Zelditch, seems a viable data-collection device for all three types of studies, but less appropriate for surveys of large groups or populations ("frequency distributions") than for the study of cases ("incidents") and organizations ("institutionalized norms and statuses"). What Zelditch calls enumerations refers to survey research methodology and is considered most appropriate for the study of the distribution of characteristics in a population.

There are, of course, limitations to such a typology, and they become clear when one attempts to place specific qualitative communication studies in the cells of the table. Participant observation, for example, was the primary data-collection method employed by Gans (1979) in his study of news organizations; his results were more than "adequate." Interviewing, on the other hand, has been employed in a wide variety of studies of media organizations and institutional procedures, but, we suggest, it is far from always "efficient" or the "best form." As Deutscher (1973) demonstrated, there is often a discrepancy between reports of attitudes gained through interviews and observations of the behavior related to those attitudes. Once again, the "how" of research (methodology) should be deliberated carefully in each particular case with reference to "what" and "why" (the subject matter and purpose of inquiry).

In order to examine the explanatory value of specific methods, we next consider more closely participant observation, which is frequently identified as the ideal method for qualitative research. Second, we discuss the relevance of employing multiple methods, what is commonly known as "triangulation."

An often quoted definition of *participant-observation* has been offered by Becker and Geer (1957: 28):

> By participation observation we mean that method in which the observer participates in the daily life of the people under study, either openly in the role of researcher or covertly in some disguised role, observing things that happen, listening to what is said, and questioning people, over some length of time.

The primary purpose of participant-observation research, accordingly, is to describe in fundamental terms various events, situations, and actions that occur in a particular social setting. This is done through the development of case studies of social phenomena, normally employing a combination of data-collection techniques. Other definitions further stress the multiple methods of participant observation:

> it is probably misleading to regard participant observation as a single method ... it refers to a characteristic blend or combination of methods and techniques that is employed in studying certain types of subject matter: primitive societies, deviant subcultures, complex organizations ... social movements and informal groups ... [it] involves some amount of genuinely social interaction in the field with the subject of study, some direct observation of relevant events, some formal and a great deal of informal interviewing, some systematic counting, some collection of documents and artifacts, and openendness in the direction the study takes.
>
> (McCall and Simmons, 1969: 1)

One problem with this latter definition is that it includes nearly every form of data-collection and interpretation under the heading of participant observation. Hence it becomes difficult to discriminate and, most important, to compare and assess the findings that different data-collection methods generate. Participant observation is best suited, in comparison with survey or experimental designs, for interpretive inquiry into social interaction from the perspective of the people involved.

In previous research, the multiple method approach is best known under the term *triangulation*, and has been advocated most vocally by Webb and colleagues and, later, by Denzin:

> If no single measurement class is perfect, neither is any scientifically useless . . . for the most fertile research for validity comes from a combined series of different measures, each with its idiosyncratic weakness, each pointed to a single hypothesis.
>
> (Webb *et al.*, 1966: 174)

> Triangulation, or the use of multiple methods, is a plan of action that will raise sociologists above the personalistic biases that stem from single methodologies.
>
> (Denzin, 1970b: 27)

One of the assumptions of a multiple method strategy is that such an approach provides for more valid results than a single research strategy. Or, as Jick (1979: 604) puts it, the basic assumption of all triangulation is "that the weaknesses in each single method will be compensated by the counter-balancing strengths of another."

Various forms of triangulation have been proposed (for example, Brewer and Hunter, 1989). One of the most elaborate developments of the technique includes four types: triangulation of the data, the investigator, the theory, and the method (Denzin, 1970b). Data triangulation refers to the dimensions of time, space, and analytical level in which information is obtained. Investigator triangulation involves the more standard approach of using several analysts or coders, often as part of a multidisciplinary team of scientists. Theoretical triangulation suggests application of concepts and perspectives from diverse theories and disciplines. Finally, methodological triangulation constitutes a research strategy in which different methods are employed for data gathering and analysis around a single object of study.

Some calls for triangulation may be rooted in a scientifically naive notion that multiple methods can reveal a single, "true" reality beyond frameworks of theory and interpretation. Phillips (1973: 91), for one, has raised the question of whether triangulation actually increases rather than reduces biases inherent in particular data-collection methods. In spite of such reservations, triangulation may become a constructive force in the development of methodology as well as theory. For one thing, it can stimulate inventive uses of familiar research methods, and thus may help to uncover unexpected dimensions of the area of inquiry. For another, given appropriate theoretical and meta-theoretical reflection on the status of each set of data and findings, it may at times allow for more confidence in the conclusions of qualitative studies. Perhaps most important, triangulation can assist in constructing a more encompassing perspective on specific analyses, what anthropologists call "holistic work" or "thick description" (Jick, 1979: 608–9; also Geertz, 1973).

What should be noted, finally, is that triangulation does not absolve qualitative researchers of interpretive work. Indeed, when findings derived from different methods conflict or fail to corroborate each other (as well as when they support each other), this signals not the end of the study, but the beginning of a phase of theoretical analysis examining the nature of agreements and disagreements. To repeat, further empirical but also theoretical work is needed to specify the explanatory value of different methods of data collection. This may become a priority of qualitative research, along with the development of systematic analytical procedures.

Participant observation, often including triangulation, has been applied also to processes of mass communication. In particular, studies of media organizations have been a proving ground for this data-collection method. Exemplary works include Gans' (1979) study, *Deciding What's News* and Tuchman's (1978) *Making News*. At the audience end of the process, Lull (1980), as already noted, has conducted pioneering work on television audiences based on participant observation, which has inspired a new generation of audience researchers committed to ethnographies of media use in the natural setting of the home (see Lull, 1988b). However, it is striking that in these media studies, as in much research from other disciplines, there is little or no indication of how the collected data were analysed.

Analysing qualitative data

Early writers in social science who attempted to convey the craft of qualitative analysis to other scholars, seldom went beyond recommending filing systems for documents, wide margins on field notes to pen in codes, and carbon copies of all documents to allow later cutting and pasting of the material. The lack of sophistication of these aids and procedures has not passed unnoticed by critics of the qualitative approach. Also researchers who recognize the relevance and legitimacy of qualitative research have reservations about the systematicity of current approaches, as summed up in the following question: "How can we be sure that an 'earthy,' 'undeniable,' 'serendipitous' finding is not, in fact, wrong?" (from Miles, 1979; quoted in Miles and Huberman, 1984: 16). Above all, there is a call for explicit and systematic procedures of analysing qualitative data sets. In the words of one sympathetic critic over a decade ago, there was, at that time, a strong need for "systematic methods for drawing conclusions and for testing them carefully – methods that can be used for replication by other researchers, just as correlations and significance tests can by quantitative researchers" (Miles and Huberman, 1984: 16). It would be an exaggeration to suggest that fully developed and systematic methods of analysis are now available, but developments have since occurred both in aids to organizing and conducting analyses, and in analytical procedures.

Aids to analysis

Among the basic aids to analysis are the various primers on the mechanics and procedures of fieldwork already noted (Johnson, 1975; Schatzman and Strauss, 1971; Wax, 1971), suggesting practical approaches and rules of thumb for various purposes of qualitative analysis. An important recent contribution to the literature is Miles and Huberman's (1984) volume *Qualitative Data Analysis: a Sourcebook of New Methods*, which provides suggestions and examples of how to systematize three aspects of analysis: data reduction, data display, and the drawing of conclusions. Data reduction refers to the processes of selecting, distilling, and otherwise transforming the information – data – found in field notes or interview protocols. Data display refers to various methods for visually rearranging data in the form of matrices, graphs, and charts. The suggestions of Miles and Huberman represent additions and, in some cases, advances in relation to the aids already available for performing qualitative analysis. It should be noted, however, that "the drawing of conclusions" cannot be reduced to such aids, but centrally involves the researcher as an agent of analysis and interpretation.

One noteworthy aid of recent vintage is the computer. The application of computers to qualitative data analysis has lagged considerably behind their uses in quantitative research, in part because of prejudice among qualitative scholars. According to Denzin (1970a: xi), computer analysis and other high-speed data-processing techniques "too often become substitutes for the sociological imagination." Such reservations have diminished with time, and many efforts have gone toward using computers for performing aspects of qualitative analysis, in particular various time-consuming administrative chores. A special issue of the journal *Qualitative Sociology* on computers in qualitative research was published in 1984. Since then, several other authors (de Graauw *et al.*, 1986; Peters and Wester, 1988; Pfaffenberger, 1988; Tesch, 1990) have devoted attention to this topic.

A review of the various tasks which can be performed by computer is offered by Peters and Wester (1988). First, the machines can store and retrieve material better than any mechanical system. Through elementary editing or word-processing programs it becomes possible to type interview or observation protocols into computer files that can be printed on demand. Second, such files can be segmented, organized, and reorganized once codes have been assigned to their elements, thus dispensing with laborious and personalized cut-and-paste schemes. Various computer programs – "The ethnograph" (Seidel and Clark, 1984), "Qualog" (Hiemstra *et al.*, 1987), and "Kwalitan" (Peters and Wester, 1990) – provide the possibility of coding data and then sorting the material through combinations of codes. Finally, computer files of qualitative data sets allow other researchers to gain access to the materials and hence to conduct further analysis. This development is likely to contribute to the perceived applicability and legitimacy of qualitative analysis among the community of media researchers.

One major use of the computer in qualitative research is for analyses of data sets through repeated iterative or cyclic procedures. Analysis of the "raw" data takes place continuously throughout the qualitative research process, even while the nature and intensity of the analysis may change depending on the specific stage of the study (Lofland, 1971: 117–18). The relevance of cyclic analysis stems from a central characteristic of much qualitative research whose purpose is theory construction – the exploration and refinement of concepts during the course of the study itself. The computer facilitates repeated coding and recoding of the basic data as theoretical notions and concepts are reformulated and developed.

For all of the potential of a computer, it is important to stress that the machine is doing no more than facilitating or aiding the process of analysis. The core value of the computer in qualitative research is accuracy and speed in the organization and administration of data. For example, in the selection of materials to illustrate a particular point or to develop a typology, there is much less opportunity to miss relevant material, which may frequently happen when the sorting of data is done by hand. Ultimately, however, the agent of analysis at each step of the qualitative research process is the researcher, not the machine (Peters and Wester, 1988: 337).

Analytical procedures

These aids to analysis, then, should be seen in relation to systematic procedures for performing qualitative analysis. Two analytical procedures – analytic induction and grounded theory – are of special interest here because of their historical origins and substantive contributions within social science. (See also the account in Chapter 1 of discourse analysis as a possible "statistics" or systematics of qualitative analysis.) Other procedures, such as ethnographic (Spradley, 1979; 1980) and phenomenological analysis (Hycner, 1985), represent refinements specifying the steps to follow in concrete analysis, but they are essentially varieties of the other, established procedures, and are not considered further in this context.

Analytic induction. Perhaps the earliest explication of a procedure for qualitative analysis was analytic induction, which involves "an exhaustive examination of cases in order to prove universal, causal generalizations" (Manning, 1982: 280). The procedure has been most elaborately worked out in a twelve-step sequence by Denzin (1970a; 1978). Basically, the procedure calls for, first, constructing a general description of the phenomenon under study. Next, the characteristics which the researcher initially assumes are the most important are elaborated and specified. Then, a specific case is examined to establish whether the assumed characteristics apply. If the case does not fit the characteristics, then either the description is modified so as to manifestly exclude the case, or the originally hypothesized characteristics are changed so that the case may become part of the phenomenon under study. This procedure is repeated until there are no more cases left to categorize, or until no cases arise which do not fit within the parameters of the phenomenon.

As a practical form of analysis, analytic induction is time-consuming and has found limited application outside exploratory sociological studies (see Lindesmith, 1947). It is, moreover, doubtful whether it lives up to the claim of being able to predict events, establish causality, or produce universal statements (Manning, 1982: 294). The technique does, however, offer a procedure for thoroughly examining cases that might be related to a concept in development. One example of work in communication research that relies on analytic induction can be found in the Lang and Lang (1953) investigation of the differences between the television coverage of the MacArthur Day Parade in Chicago and the perceptions of the event among the spectators along the parade route (see Chapter 11 of this volume).

Grounded theory. The procedure of analytic induction provided part of the inspiration for other researchers who were concerned with theory development while, at the same time, wanting analyses to remain "close to the data." Glaser and Strauss (1967), two of these researchers, proposed that new theoretical formulations were needed which would be based or "grounded" in empirical data. They recommended relying on "sensitizing concepts" to guide such theory development, a phrase originally coined by Blumer:

> Hundreds of our concepts – like culture, institution, social structure, mores, and personality – are not definitive concepts but are sensitizing in nature. They lack precise bench marks which allow clear-cut identification of a specific instance, and of its content. Instead they rest on a general sense of what is relevant.
>
> (Blumer, quoted in Rock, 1979: 9)

One of the difficulties with this proposal stems from the principle of staying close to the data. The question is how close to the data one can be and still undertake theoretical work, which of necessity requires a certain level of abstraction and hence distance from empirical data. Addressing this question, Glaser and Strauss (1967: 3) speak in terms of "criteria of fit" and "criteria of relevance." Relevance, for them, not only has an analytical dimension, as in traditional deductive use of theory, but also a substantive dimension. Theories thus should "fit" the specific field under observation; the theoretical concepts are in this way "sensitized" to the subject of research.

While the analytical procedure proposed by Glaser and Strauss received widespread attention, it was also strongly criticized for being a polemic rather than a constructive intervention into scientific debate. As it turned out, researchers who set out to practice the precepts of grounded theory frequently went aground in uncharted analytical terrain. Glaser (1978), Strauss (1987), and Strauss and Corbin (1990) have made attempts to solve such difficulties in subsequent volumes, and other researchers, such as Turner (1981), have contributed to a further codification of analysis within grounded theory.

One of the most comprehensive efforts so far in this area is Wester's (1984; 1987) procedural approach to grounded theory. This approach is comparable, in certain respects, to analytic induction, consisting of four phases which each in turn contain some fifteen procedural steps. The initial, or exploratory, phase is intended to extract preliminary concepts from the collected material. In the second or defining phase, the researcher tries to construct variables based on the concepts. In the third or reduction phase, the aim is to formulate the core of a theory. In the fourth and final phase, termed integration, the concepts are related to one another and the relations tested on the data. The cycle of reflection, observation, and analysis is repeated throughout the research process in each of the four phases until the theoretical formulations have exhausted the available data (Peters and Wester, 1990).

As was the case for analytic induction, communication research seldom makes explicit use of grounded theory. Lull (1988a: 16) does refer, albeit briefly, to the "compelling argument of Glaser and Strauss," and he further explains his own preference for the grounded theory approach thus:

> the theoretical essence of our work emerges quite spontaneously within each research project. I believe that we should not simply conduct research that is programmatically influenced by any fixed theoretical perspective if we are to really "let the data speak to us."
>
> (Lull, 1988a: 17)

Data of and by themselves, however, cannot generate theory. It is only through intervention by a researcher, operating within a theoretical perspective, that data can be examined and used to develop theory. For this reason, many researchers employ "sensitizing concepts" or ideal types in the preliminary phases of their empirical investigations. Such concepts may help to orient the researcher theoretically, while at the same time allowing the kind of flexibility which Lull was referring to. Most of the chapters in this book provide examples of the specific relevance of qualitative methodologies for theory development (see especially Chapter 11).

Reporting qualitative research

The final step of the qualitative research process – reporting the work – is sometimes overlooked, but deserves mention in this context since it is the point of contact with other researchers as well as with the interested lay public. Some authors, in fact, suggest that it is during the writing up of qualitative research that the final analysis of the data takes place (Maso, 1987: 118; Miles and Huberman, 1984: 213).

According to Burgess (1984: 182) there are three forms of qualitative research reports: (1) descriptions which make little or no reference to theoretical perspectives; (2) analytical discussions based on concepts emerging from the study; and (3) substantive accounts intended to contribute to general theory. Other scholars have attempted to discern the essential nature of the qualitative research report. Lofland (1971: 5) proposed that, (a) the report should get "close to the data" and should be based on a relation to the subject of inquiry for a substantial period of time; (b) it should be "truthful" and written in "good faith"; (c) it should contain much descriptive material and liberal quotations from those studied; and (d) the procedures for data analysis should be explicit. In addition, Agar (1980: 61) has argued that reports should be written in a style which makes sense to members of the group studied, so that the research may attain later relevance in the context of their own everyday lives.

With more specific reference to the style or rhetoric of scientific accounts, van Maanen (1988), discussing ethnography, identifies two primary types of tales: realist and confessional. The realist tale is the most common and is generally told from the point of view of the subjects of study, with much use of quotations and a focus on everyday life. Confessional tales, instead, stress the field-worker's point of view and often are intended to explain (and justify) the activities of the researcher. Both realist and confessional tales, however, imply that writing style may be important for the findings that are communicated. This aspect of qualitative research, and more particularly of ethnography, then, "raises the question . . . whether ethnography (of any sort) is more a science, modeled on standardized techniques and reporting formats, or an art modeled on craftlike standards and style" (van Maanen, 1988: 34). Rock (1979: 21), like van Maanen, has recommended use of literary techniques such as integration of metaphors and analogies in the discourse of research.

In several of these prescriptions, more attention is given to writing style than to the development of theoretical concepts. We submit that both aspects are important for the further development of qualitative research. As a first step, most traditional criteria for research reports also apply to the presentation of qualitative studies, calling for a clearly formulated research problem based on an explicitly stated theoretical perspective; thorough presentation and discussion of relevant literature; adequate elaboration of the chosen methodology; and logical presentation of findings and conclusions. However, because an understanding of the lived experience and everyday reality of research subjects is key not just to the conduct, but also to the appreciation and assessment of qualitative findings, readers should be given an opportunity to relive this experience. Qualitative research findings are constituted through the subjects' categories of meaning and experience. It is the integration of discursive criteria of scientific reporting with more traditional, substantive criteria which van Maanen characterizes as artistic craftsmanship. One challenge for qualitative social science is to contribute to the current development and clarification of the rhetoric of science (Nash, 1990; Simons, 1989).

There are abundant examples of qualitative sociology which demonstrate artistic craftsmanship. To name a few: Goffman's (1959; 1963) work on communicative interaction processes; Becker and colleagues' (1961) examination of medical training and socialization; and the study by Glaser and Strauss (1965) on "leave taking" by patients during the process of terminal illness. All of these studies demonstrate the potential of qualitative methodologies for representing specific social realities. Similar examples from qualitative communication research, while remaining fewer in number, include Epstein's (1973) *News from Nowhere*, Tuchman's (1978) *Making News*, and Gans' (1979) *Deciding What's News*. It is the task of further studies to integrate such qualities of scientific reporting with an explication of the methodologies employed, the specific approaches to data collection, and, not least, the analytical procedures of the qualitative research process.

CONCLUSIONS

Mass communication research has followed the cycles of method-ological development prevalent in the social sciences. In the early decades of the century, communication studies were primarily qualitative in nature, concerning themselves mainly with historical, ethical, and legal questions. Readership surveys began to make their way into print by the 1930s, and, as noted in the historical survey, during the 1940s and 1950s quantitative research generally increased. In 1957, Wilbur Schramm published a review of the research methods of studies published in *Journalism Quarterly* be-tween the mid-1930s and mid-1950s. He found that only 10 per cent of the articles between 1937 and 1942 were based on quantitative data, whereas, a decade later, in the period 1952–6, almost half of the published articles could be classified as quantitative.

Whereas no explicit replication of Schramm's (1957) study is available, Faulkner and Spector did conduct a comparable study (discussed in Faulkner, 1982) of the publication policy of five major sociology journals between 1973 and 1978. In two of the most traditional titles, *American Sociological Review* and *American Journal of Sociology*, less than 10 per cent of the articles published were categorized as qualitative research. This is indicative of a quantitative trend which, as mentioned at the outset of this chapter, has remained predominant to this day, but which at present may be under transformation. Among the indicators of change, beyond the growing body of theoretical and empirical qualitative studies reviewed above, is the introduction of new journals to the field which stress interpretive sociology, such as *Urban Life*, *Symbolic Interactionism*, and *Qualitative Sociology*.

In the field of mass communication, while there is no similar collection of new qualitative journals, it is interesting to note that established journals such as the *Journal of Communication*, *Media, Culture and Society*, and *Critical Studies in Mass Communication* provide considerable space for qualitative studies. Other signs of methodological re-examination and renewal are also evident in the attention paid to qualitative research in textbooks of both media studies and communication research. Generally speaking, in the past there has been either no mention of qualitative research (for example, Wimmer and Dommick, 1987) or it has been characterized from a positivist perspective. In one introductory textbook, for example, the authors matter-of-factly stated: "Being scientific, it [communication research] is, of course, also *quantitative* research" (Agee *et al.*, 1985: 364; emphasis in the original). Recent exceptions include the research methodology textbook edited by Stempel and Westley (1981), which contains three chapters devoted specifically to qualitative research methods. Also McQuail (1987) notes the explanatory value of qualitative methodologies, for example semiotics, in the study of media contents and audiences. Moreover, Anderson (1987b), in a new methodology text, goes even further in this direction and devotes half of the volume to qualitative methodology. A final substantial indicator of the qualitative turn in mass communication research is the documentation provided by the contributors to this volume. A great many of these studies are at the "cutting edge" of research and have found expression in monographs and central journals in the field.

Most of this work originates from academic researchers who have been influenced by the methodological upheavals in the humanities and social sciences. However, practitioners coming from another institutional context have also contributed to qualitative methodology: marketing researchers make extensive use of open and group interviews, and other exploratory techniques. Indeed, one of the major marketing-research organizations in the field – the European Society for Opinion and Marketing Research (ESOMAR) – has for many years organized seminars on qualitative methods and published materials on their applications (see, for example, Sampson, 1987). This is a trend which is also noticeable in the growing number of qualitative sessions at conferences of the International Association for Mass Communication Research (IAMCR) and the International Communication Association (ICA). Although being constrained by their commercial framework and focusing primarily on technical questions, the contributions from marketing research still may provide productive insights to qualitative researchers working in an academic environment (see further references and discussion of commercial qualitative research in Chapter 12).

To summarize, the application and social uses of qualitative methodologies is expanding in a number of contexts, if not always with a recognition of the interpretive heritage from which the qualitative turn emerged. There seems to be a move toward synthesis of quantitative and qualitative practices in communication research (Anderson, 1987b: 366–70). There is also increasing methodological openness and a growing willingness to apply qualitative approaches.

At this point of the qualitative turn, we suggest, there is reason for expectation, indeed excitement, but some constructive reservations are also warranted. First, there is currently a tendency for practically everyone to claim that they conduct some form of qualitative research. Whereas Lull (1988b) took researchers from the cultural studies tradition to task for performing "ethnography" without a recognition of what ethnography entails, his charge can be generalized: qualitative communication research too often falls short in demonstrating its methodological basis and in explicating its procedures of data collection and analysis. It is not surprising, further, that the call for more methodological rigor in qualitative research is being voiced by self-defined positivists within social science; it is more interesting to note their openness in principle to the qualitative turn. Miles and Huberman, in their important contribution to qualitative methodology, state that, "we think of ourselves as logical positivists who recognize and try to atone for the limitations of that approach. Soft-nosed logical positivism, maybe" (Miles and Huberman, 1984: 19). On the one hand, they require valid and verifiable research methods; on the other, they see the value of "a more inductive methodology for illuminating social processes" (Miles and Huberman, 1984: 20). Qualitatively oriented communication scholars, taking up this challenge, may reap the benefits of the enterprise – the illumination of social processes – only if they pay the scientific price – the development of systematic methodologies.

A second reservation springs from a tendency that the methodology becomes everything to everybody, and that, as a result, the relationship between the techniques applied in qualitative research, on the one hand, and the interpretive frameworks in which the methodologies are grounded, on the other, are confused. While we would also welcome plurality in the interpretation of what qualitative methodology stands for and how it may be applied, our pluralism does not extend to Feyerabend's (1975: 28) principle of "anything goes."

In conclusion, our argument has been that the elements of interpretive inquiry outlined in this chapter point to the key sources of qualitative social science research. The value of this tradition for mass communication research derives both from its specification of the steps of the qualitative research process and from the associated interpretive frameworks for understanding and defining the meanings which people give to their actions and to social events. The meanings ascribed to various media and genres by both producers and audiences of mass communication are areas of inquiry that are currently being reformulated with the aid of qualitative methodologies.

These are among the areas of qualitative mass communication research which are surveyed in Part II – Systematics. The term implies, following the present Part I on History, a systematic investigation of the communication process, examining in turn different stages and aspects of mass communication. Systematics also implies a focus on the development of qualitative methodologies for purposes of systematic inquiry.

Part II

Systematics

This part of the Handbook, "systematics," examines the process of mass communication from a number of vantage points. Its structure conforms to the typology of Lasswell's (1948) and similar communication models, characterizing the institutions, contents, and audiences of mass communication from qualitative perspectives. However, two chapters examine the broader context of social and historical institutions and practices embedding media; the remaining chapters each relate their focal element to other aspects of the communicative process. Indeed, a main feature of qualitative media studies is the attention given to the context from which particular empirical data derive, and which constitutes a frame of their interpretation. Contexts include different historical and cultural settings, but also the characteristic genres through which culture is communicated and the sum total of available media – the media environment – to which the audience–public has been socialized.

The chapters and their authors speak for themselves, articulating a variety of positions on the systematics of doing qualitative work. We only refer here to a few general issues and implications which emerge from the chapters of Part II as a whole.

The two chapters on media institutions serve to highlight the importance of various links between the *micro-social* and *macro-social* levels of analysis. The procedures and routines of both news production and TV drama production within specific mass media organizations simultaneously shape and are shaped by the wider political and cultural practices associated with mass communication. The news genre, as examined in Chapter 3, is perhaps the archetypal case of texts with specific social uses and functions in relation to specific political institutions. Chapter 4, further, explores the scope for creativity at the micro-level of TV program production while also recognizing the importance of various macro-forces influencing production, and the chapter presents suggestions for further research which detail the several relevant levels of analysis.

Qualitative content analyses draw on at least two different traditions which are represented in Chapter 5 on (linguistic) discourse analysis and Chapter 6 on (literary) semiological analysis. Despite these differences, both chapters emphasize the importance of examining the *language* or *signs* generally of media texts. Chapter 5 presents a concrete illustration of how discourse analysis may be applied to news texts; Chapter 6 further discusses the relevance of textual analysis for the study of visual communication. In addition to the study of media contents, discourse analysis and semiotics have also proven relevant for analysing other forms of data such as interviews or observation protocols. Discourse analysis, then, may become a *general method* for several forms of qualitative research.

The chapters on audience studies together point to what may be the clearest example of convergence between the humanities and social sciences in qualitative research, identifying mass commmunication and its reception as simultaneously *social* and *discursive* phenomena. Whereas Chapter 7 focuses on studies of the decoding of particular media texts and Chapter 8 concentrates on broadly ethnographic studies of media audiences, they concur in their emphasis on the *contexts* of media use, whether the domestic or the broad cultural setting. Audience research needs to examine the interaction between media and audiences, rather than the two agents in isolation. And, the findings must always be interpreted with reference to the negotiation of social and cultural identity that media users engage in. This also suggests the limits of empirical data about the experience and impact of media and the importance of theory for the study of mass communication processes.

The role of *theory* is re-emphasized in the two chapters on media contexts, which thus represent a transition to the wider, social and scientific implications of qualitative research that are taken up in Part III. Chapter 10 particularly argues that the current limitations of our broad historical understanding of mass communication stem less from problems of research techniques than from a narrow theoretical vision of what communication is. History is constructed, in part, as stories; Chapter 9 similarly suggests the importance of the conceptual relation between communication and community.

Qualitative research, currently and in the past, has made important contributions to theory development. Moreover, qualitative studies, which frequently rely on multiple methods, may help to develop *meta-theory* that enables researchers to weigh different kinds of evidence, either specifically in combining qualitative and quantitative methodologies or generally in a triangulation of different sources and forms of data – a point raised in Chapter 9 and several other contributions.

It should be added that the part on Systematics does *not* include chapters on the "nuts and bolts" of qualitative research. This is, in part, because a number of volumes on this aspect are already available (see especially the references to the research process in Chapter 2; also the subject index under entries about specific methods – interviewing, participant observation, discourse analysis, and so forth). Furthermore, as argued in the general introduction to this volume, this Handbook wishes to raise questions of *what* and *why* before addressing *how*.

Chapter 3

Media institutions
Qualitative methods in the study of news

Gaye Tuchman

INTRODUCTION

As do many academics who live in small apartments and have smaller offices, periodically I winnow my books to separate what I must own from what I have enjoyed. This year I once again performed that task, carefully saving all books pertaining to news and placing them in some logical order. Marching down rows of still crammed shelves, my books on news insistently remind me that from the earliest to the most recent American and European studies, the most valuable research has been qualitative.

There is no innate reason that these good books are based on historical inquiry, interviews, or participant observation. The old rule remains valid: the method one should choose when approaching any topic, including news, depends upon the question one wants to answer. But it is not so surprising that the most significant work on news is qualitative. Theoretically the most interesting questions about news and news organizations concern either process, such as the general relationship between news and ideology, or the specific processes by which news reproduces or alters ideology.[1] And when one considers the impact of news on either individuals or institutions, the best answers are also process-oriented and require examination of either micro-interactions, such as how people read the newspaper or watch television news, or the course of unfolding events, such as how what was first viewed as a minor burglary resulted in the resignation of President Richard Nixon.

Ultimately, one sees the importance of qualitative methods by considering such a seemingly straightforward question as "what is news?" Early twentieth-century sociologists turned to *verstehen* –

phenomenological understanding – to answer this question, not to content analysis.

NEWS AS PHENOMENON

Just as a reductionist might say that art is anything displayed as art by a museum or gallery (institutions with the power to define art), so too someone might respond that news is any item that is not advertising and is presented by a news medium. Using quantitative logic, the next step for this reductionist would be content analysis, a systematic determination of what is disseminated as news.

Such reductionism seems as absurd in the case of news as it does in the case of art. The early sociologists clearly recognized that news was more than the items found in the newspapers of their day. One early social-scientific statement about news is Max Weber's comparative discussion of news in Germany versus news in the Allied nations during World War I. The terms of the comparison are not particularly relevant today. What matters more is the context: Weber commented about journalists and journalism in "Politics as a vocation" (1918/58), the companion to his classic "Science as a vocation." Situating his argument in a discussion of politics, Weber makes clear that news is not mere information. He explicitly adds that journalists are not best viewed as purveyors of either information or scandals (although they may do both), but are rather "professional politicians." Furthermore, newspapers are not simply profit-making capitalist enterprises, as was the case in England during the Great War, but political organizations which "function" as political clubs. To talk about news, Weber claims, is to talk about politics in society.

The ex-journalist Robert Park wrote the earliest extensive treatment of news by an American social scientist. He asked different questions than Weber. Rather than considering politics in the context of war and the aftermath of Versailles, situations clearly important to Germany, Park addressed an American social problem: growing urbanization produced by European immigration and internal migration (the movement from farms to growing urban centers). Park (1922) wanted to know not simply what news was, but rather how it functioned in cities composed of very different groups living largely in segregated enclaves. His answer seems simple: news is the functional equivalent of the town crier who once made his rounds announcing "Ten o'clock and all is well," or, perhaps, "Eleven o'clock and Mrs Smith just birthed a healthy boy." But, Park knew well, city life is inextricably different from life in a village. In a city there are so many births and deaths each day that each one is irrelevant to those not personally touched, church bells compete for attention, and groups adhere to conflicting norms. Furthermore, news in an American city of that time might serve different functions than news in a European setting. Park's Chicago was a tumultuous city; like other major American urban centers, it faced the problem of integrating vastly different groups into a sociopolitical entity. For Park, news entailed the task of building social cohesion. The purpose of news was to locate what everyone had to know to act in their environment and through their actions to build a common identity.

Perhaps because he had studied in Germany, Park reflected on the nature of news, including the nature of culture in the modern era. Systematic reflection on his previous occupational experience as a journalist (retrospective participant observation, if you will) had led Park to place news in a literary context and so to raise issues of culture as well as of form. Park mistakenly believed that news would replace the short story as a literary form. The short story is still alive and well in North America, but Park's mistake is less important than his comparison. For Park's error led him to identify a characteristic of news so basic as to be sometimes invisible: news is a story. Stories follow their own intrinsic and coherent logic. News stories may be responses to the general American query, "what's new?" As stories, they may also make one stand up and take note. Park (1940) wrote that news is a story that may make the reader say "Gee Whiz!"

For the most part, the reflective and systematic examination of imaginable alternatives (qualitative reasoning) later diminished in social scientists' study of news – although at least one of Park's students, Helen MacGill Hughes, continued creative musing about the nature of news (see Hughes, 1940). However, by the 1950s, how Americans studied news had shifted significantly, as seen in the work of another Chicago sociologist, Morris Janowitz (1952/67). I discuss a Chicago work because through the late 1950s many University of Chicago graduate students were still being trained as participant observers.[2]

Janowitz' work represents a change in two ways, one in methods and the other in theoretical focus. To study the community press, Janowitz used both qualitative and quantitative methods. Unlike

some earlier Chicago sociologists, Janowitz did not identify participant observation as either a systematic or a rigorous method. In the
preface to the second edition of his book, he explained, "*The
Community Press in an Urban Setting* was an exercise in the Chicago
school of sociology with an attempt to incorporate more systematic
research procedures" than participant observation, such as survey
research (Janowitz, 1967: viii). In 1967 Janowitz also criticized
some of the interview techniques he and his assistants had used as
"too primitive" (p. xviii). Thus, by 1967, the year the second edition
was published, Janowitz seems to have accepted more of quantitative researchers' criticisms of participant observation than he had in
1952.

Additionally, reflecting on his work in the preface to the second
edition, Janowitz noted the theoretical breach between his work
and earlier studies of news. Unlike Weber, Park, and Hughes, who
had addressed themselves to cultural and political issues, Janowitz
asked questions relevant to what by the 1950s had become identified
as communications research. As he put it,

> No doubt we were able to identify the social role of [the com-
> munity press] as one aspect of the normative system of the urban
> community. In another sense our definitions and our assumptions
> in retrospect were too limited. There was an *excessive concern
> with the strategy of communication research* which focuses on
> specific responses, and not enough on the natural history of a
> social institution [a particular concern of Park's] and the collec-
> tive representations it created.
>
> (p. xvii; emphasis added)

In *The Community Press*, the term "politics" refers to the activity of
politicians who, Janowitz explained, keep close ties with the community press. The term was bereft of its earlier association with
ideology, demagoguery, and the newspaper as a political club. In
this retrospective self-criticism Janowitz seems to foreshadow what
would become the theoretical approach to news in the 1970s and
1980s.

Through the 1950s and 1960s, especially in the USA, the empirical study of news concentrated on aspects of communications research – "who said what to whom in which channel with what
effect." Most research entailed either content analysis or, during
and after the 1950s, quantitative examination of the decisions of
individuals termed "gatekeepers." One of the best known of these

is based on actions and justifications for action given by the pseudonymous "Mr Gates" (White, 1950). The few studies depending on participant observation were sometimes dismissed by quantitative researchers (as was Lang and Lang's "Unique perspective of television," originally published in 1953) or placed in a functionalist context.[3] Warren Breed's "Social control in the newsroom" (1955) is a good example of this latter tendency.

Studies of news have always been responsive to political conditions. In the late 1960s, a period of dissent in many Western capitalist nations, researchers again turned to qualitative methods to raise critical issues about news, culture, and society. In the 1970s, analyses of news began to contain semiotic analyses. For instance, in his doctoral dissertation Peter Dahlgren (1977) used semiotics to parse the meanings implicit in the opening of the CBS evening news, including the sense of urgency created by the sound of a wire service machine clicking in the background.

By the 1980s, qualitative methods included additional systematic means of reflection, such as discourse analysis (see van Dijk, 1988a and in this volume, and German studies discussed below). As does much of the research on news organizations undertaken during and after the 1960s, discourse analysis emphasizes how the ideological significance of news is part and parcel of the methods used to process news. Thus, ultimately linguistic and discourse analysis of news content raises the same epistemological questions addressed by the participant-observation studies of news organizations of the 1960s and 1970s.

STUDIES OF NEWS ORGANIZATIONS

In the 1960s the Cuban Missile Crisis (Gans, 1979), the civil rights movement (Epstein, 1973), and the Vietnam War (Gitlin, 1980; Halloran *et al.*, 1970; Tuchman, 1978) provoked a series of participant-observation studies of news organizations. Many of these emphasized how the processes of making news resulted in embedded ideological meanings. Within the decade, racism (Hall *et al.*, 1978), the war in Northern Ireland (Schlesinger, 1978), anti-unionism (Glasgow Group, 1976), and conservative views of deviance (Chibnall, 1977; Cohen and Young, 1973; Fishman, 1980) prompted more participant-observation studies with similar conclusions. Although these studies were done in both Britain and the USA, at local media organizations and at national media, their conclusions were so similar that they seemed to replicate and so to validate one another.

These studies were a significant departure from earlier work in three ways. First, their unit of analysis was not the individual reporter or editor, such as the pseudonymous Mr Gates; rather, they examined news organizations as complex institutions. Second, although framed in "neutral" academic language, these studies were implicitly political. Their authors sought to understand how news came to support official interpretations of controversial events. Third, sometimes implicitly but often explicitly, these studies raised a key epistemological issue: how do news organizations come to "know" what they "know." At least three participant observers (Fishman, 1980; Gans, 1979; Tuchman, 1972; 1978) compared the validity of news reports with the methods of social science. Doing so, they explicitly worked at the juncture of the sociologies of organizations and of occupations and professions. Additionally, by examining how organizations define "facts," they challenged ideologies of facticity common to both news and American sociology (see Tuchman, 1980).

Although key studies in the USA and Britain used participant observation, researchers employed that technique in several different ways. I will concentrate on the American studies. I employed classic old-style Chicago sociological observation (see Junker, 1960, including the introduction by Everett Hughes). That is, I observed the activities of news staff both inside and outside of the newsroom, following stories from their assignment through their editing and dissemination. (In the case of television, they were aired at 6:30 p.m. and 11:00 p.m. At the newspaper studied, I attended morning editorial meetings and sat in on the copy desk through the revision of the second edition at 11:30 p.m.) I attended events with general reporters, made the rounds with beat reporters (some identified by editors as their "best" and others as their "weakest"), and put in time at news bureaus. I did general open-ended interviewing as well. All observations and interviews were recorded in field notes the day they were made.

Herbert Gans (1979) followed similar procedures at the organizations he observed. However, he complemented his observations and interviews with quantitative content analyses that revealed some general characteristics of news reports (they are more likely to tell about people who are "knowns" than those who are "unknowns") and American news values (such as pastoralism and ethnocentrism). He analysed reporters' professional and political attitudes (what he termed their "para-ideology") as well.

Mark Fishman (1980) and Marilyn Lester (1975) were less observers and more participants than either Gans or I. My "participation" was frequently reduced to the role of "go-for" (the person who returned film to the studio or fetched coffee) and personal confidant. Both Fishman and Lester spent time as novice reporters. Fishman worked as a reporter for seven months at a local newspaper; Lester, as a summer intern at a national daily. However, Fishman and Lester approached their participation differently. Lester favored participant observation guided by what Glaser and Strauss (1967) have termed "grounded theory." That is, as the fieldwork proceeded, she developed hypotheses and systematically gathered data to test and refine them. This type of participant observation claims to link theory and data more closely than the other variants I have described. But other ways of being a participant–observer include ways to link theory and data. Gans' content analysis helped him to develop the hypotheses he would test in the field. Fishman was able to look more intensively at some news practices than had other researchers because D. L. Wieder provided him with the field notes of Wieder's own "extensive participant observation" (Fishman, 1980: 24) gathered roughly ten years earlier at one of the newspapers where Fishman worked.

Finally, Todd Gitlin's (1980) work was guided by past participation in the phenomenon he studied, the impact of reporting on the anti-war movement. A founder and past president of Students for a Democratic Society, Gitlin had saved many documents from the late 1960s and early 1970s, and had access to other key activists and to news workers, as well. When interviewed, they described their memories of specific events, including encounters between activists and reporters and between reporters and editors. Gitlin also used archival materials, such as telecasts and news reports.

Each type of participant observation had advantages and drawbacks (reviewed in the essays in Filstead, 1970). Accounts that reporters and sources give about stories covered years before may have been altered by informants' retrospective construction of events. Participation may facilitate an insider's view, but may hamper one's ability to understand other aspects of the editorial process. Lengthy periods of daily observation are tiring. Some days I observed from 8:00 a.m. until midnight so that I might follow a story from assignment to either the revision of the first edition or the end of the 11:00 p.m. news. Exhausted when I got home and enervated at the thought of returning to observe in the morning, I sometimes took such shortcuts as tape-recording what I thought were the days' highlights instead of writing field notes before I slept. I necessarily lost information. As young graduate students, Fishman, Lester, and I may have received confidences that would have been withheld from older researchers; we could have been seen as young people to take in hand. However, we might not have had access to some sorts of information gathered by Gans, who was the peer of his most senior informants.

Despite such variations, one might argue that these five research-ers had enough in common essentially to reproduce one another's key findings. All five American researchers have vaguely similar political ideals, varying from what Americans would term left–liberal to what Americans would call social democratic. Some had similar theoretical grounding. But I do not believe that either similar theoretical perspectives or political leanings account for the resemblance among their studies. Many of the same themes about how the constraints and resources of news organizations influence the news process occur in British studies (see especially Schlesinger, 1978). I find it especially significant that all of these studies linked the news process to ideology (or in Gans' case "para-ideology") and argued that news organizations necessarily developed special ties to legitimated and centralized sources of information. Indeed, these same themes occur in more recent qualitative research that concen-trates on the interactions between reporters and sources.

REPORTERS AND SOURCES

Two recent studies are particularly significant, because they affirm the participant–observers' findings that news organizations are heavily dependent on legitimated sources, even while using differ-ent sources of data than the earlier studies of news organizations. One book is *Negotiating Control: a Study of News Sources* (1989) by Richard V. Ericson, Patricia M. Baranek, and Janet B. L. Chan; the other, *The "Uncensored War": the Media and Vietnam* (1986) by Daniel C. Hallin. Both are qualitative. Ericson, Baranek, and Chan based their book on fieldwork, interviews, and a supple-mentary content analysis of letters to the editors. To reconstruct the processes influencing news reports about both the war and dissent from government policies, Hallin used historical documents, news

reports, and "deep background" interviews with reporters, corre-
spondence with officials, and content analysis – though he did not
present his content analyses in tabular form.

Ericson *et al.* (1989) confirm both Herbert Gans' insistence that
most news is about "knowns" (roughly fifty people, Gans [1979]
suggests) and my argument (Tuchman, 1972; 1978) that the statement of an official source is an "event." In their conclusion they
stress,

> News is a product of transactions between journalists and their
> sources. The primary source of reality for news is not what is
> displayed or what happens in the real world. The reality of news is
> embedded in the nature and type of social and cultural relations
> that develop between journalists and their sources, and in the
> politics of knowledge that emerges on each specific newsbeat.
>   (Ericson *et al.*, 1989: 377; see also Shibutani, 1966)

Because Ericson *et al.* (1989) used participant observation, they
could learn what those "politics of knowledge" were. Most important, by being with reporters they could analyse what reporters chose
not to report and demonstrate how the proverbial exception proves
the rule. Such information could never be gleaned from a content
analysis of published material (see Tuchman, 1977; also Molotch
and Lester, 1975). For instance, Ericson *et al.* (1989) explain that
the politics of knowledge gained on the court beat led a reporter to
go against what he knew to be his editor's preferences. A court
reporter did not file a newsworthy story about a very reputable man
who had shoplifted a toothbrush even though he felt the story would
have received page-one coverage. Such coverage would contravene
the sense of fairness that the reporter had developed interacting
with routine sources on his beat. But, Ericson *et al.* note, such
decisions are still framed within the pragmatics of newswork. This
reporter could choose not to file his story, because he found another
story to file that day and so could satisfy the primary requirement of
his job – producing copy.

Furthermore, because they had used participant observation,
Ericson *et al.* (1989) could glean richer data in their interviews with
sources. Frequently, having observed occurrences in which sources
interacted with reporters, they were able to hold concrete discussions about published stories and the sources' interactions with
reporters. Such data transform the "non-observable" into the "ob-
servable." They are far preferable to inferences, even when the

inferences seem statistically irrefutable (see Molotch and Lester, 1975). They enabled statements about how sources tried to influence reporters and the conditions under which they succeeded. They also facilitated generalizations about how sources could react when they felt that reporters had been inaccurate or unfair. In this specific sense, these researchers' data are superior to responses elicited by scenarios constructed to serve as the basis of interviews. (However, "constructed scenarios" may facilitate statements about representativeness, such as "Given a set of variables we can predict how a source will react to this scenario 95 per cent of the time.")[4]

Qualitative historical research also emphasizes the importance of negotiations with sources. Studying American coverage of the Vietnam War, Hallin notes that reporters ignored issues about the war that their sources would have found beyond the pale. This tendency was probably exacerbated by the seeming confluence of sources' views. Particularly in the early years of American military involvement, reporters never even conceived of such issues as "Should the United States have wanted to persist in Indochina, or to intervene there to begin with? . . . What outcome was best for the people of Indochina?" (Hallin, 1986: 214).

American journalists only began to question the war when elite sources were willing to disclose their disagreements with one another. As Schudson (1989: 268) summarizes Hallin's generalizations,

> The behavior of the American press in questioning the Vietnam war . . . can be understood as happening only because the political elite was divided much more profoundly than it ordinarily is. Even then, the press seems largely to have gone about its *normal business of citing official leaders* – it just so happened that the officials were at odds with one another.
>
> (emphasis added)

So long as Presidents John F. Kennedy and Lyndon B. Johnson were able to control leaks within their administration, reporters had no one to whom to turn for an "official" dissident view.

Discourse analysis of content, participant observation within news organizations, and interviews with sources thus all confirm that official views are embedded in news accounts. In this specific sense, news is ideological. However, although the news media may unconsciously embed a "preferred reading" in their stories, even that "preferred reading" may constitute a "contested terrain"

(Hall, 1979). That is, groups of readers or viewers (or individuals) may reject the preferred reading or argue about its validity.

IMPLICATIONS: EFFECT AS PROCESS

Since individuals and groups may reject the preferred reading embedded in a news story, why is it important to understand the process of making news? The "constructionist" approach to news offered by Gamson and his associates (Gamson and Lasch, 1983; Gamson and Modigliani, 1987; 1989) suggests the reason is grounded in the symbolic condensation of frames inherent in media discourse.[5] As Gamson and Modigliani (1989: 3) explain,

> media discourse can be conceived of as a set of interpretive packages that give meaning to an issue. A package has an internal structure. At its core is a central organizing idea, or *frame*, for making sense of relevant events, suggesting what is at issue. . . . This frame typically implies a range of positions, rather than any single one, allowing for a degree of controversy among those who share a common frame.

The frames or "condensing symbols" of news packages are a form of "shorthand, making it possible to display the package as a whole with a deft metaphor, catchphrase, or other symbolic device" (Gamson and Modigliani, 1989: 3). They may resound with cultural themes, as does the frame that nuclear energy involves a "bargain with the devil." People who have read an editorial identifying nuclear energy as a devil's bargain may debate the terms under which such a bargain should be made. But whether they agree with the editorial or contest it, they are reacting to the embedded meaning of the news story (the frame of "devil's bargain").

As do other discourses, indeed as does culture itself, frames mutate as structural conditions change. ("Devil's bargain" is a relatively recent frame.) Thus the frames themselves constitute "contested terrain" (Hall, 1979); proponents of each frame try to establish their way of organizing information about nuclear power as the way to debate issues. As news sources, these proponents deliver their frames as organizing ideas for stories about nuclear power.

Journalists need not passively accept these frames. Reporters and editors engage in an active process. They both make and consume their society's culture. I construe culture "as a 'tool kit' of symbols, stories, rituals, and world-views, which people may use in varying configurations to solve different kinds of problems" (Swidler, 1986: 273; also van Dijk, this volume). Reporters and editors necessarily use some of the same tools as their readers and viewers. The idea of nuclear power as a bargain with the devil draws upon Christian cosmology and is meaningful to residents of even the most secularized Western nations. Similarly, the frame of nuclear power as progress encodes twentieth-century adaptations of the nineteenth-century faith that humanity marches toward a better world. By (re)producing symbols familiar to their audience, reporters and editors proclaim the "preferred reading" of a text.

Members of the audience for news may reject that preferred reading. It may not resonate with the conditions of their own lives, including personal concerns set by the structural conditions influencing their mundane affairs. Nonetheless, even the rejection of a preferred reading is a response to the frame promulgated by the media, as seen in the following examples about illegal drugs.

Stories about the horrors of illegal drug-use frequently employ the frame that drugs destroy lives (see Reinarman and Levine, 1989, and literature reviewed therein). This frame may prompt some to use drugs even as it inhibits others. Consider two possibilities. First, the preferred reading may be antithetical to the "cognitive schema" of a news consumer (Graber, 1984). The frame may contradict the news consumer's experience; she or he may know individuals whose lives have not been destroyed by illegal drugs or, with eternal optimism, may view herself or himself as the exception to the rule. Second, the preferred reading may produce a response antithetical to that intended by "news promoters" (Molotch and Lester, 1974) and media workers. Media stories – even televised anti-drug public service announcements – often note that some illegal drugs provide a powerful high. Recent research indicates that some news consumers yearn to experience that "orgasmic high" and therefore seek out the condemned drugs (Reinarman and Levine, 1989).

Finally, the process of making news embeds the effect of news in yet another way. Even stories as dramatic as coverage of Watergate, including the Senate hearings about impeaching President Nixon, had their greatest impact on politicians, many of whom used these accounts as indicators of public opinion (Lang and Lang, 1983). Ultimately, then, the process of transforming occurrences into news stories feeds on itself; it resembles the hermeneutic circle.

Official interpretations set the news frames inherent in packaged stories; these packages are in turn interpreted by officials, who use them as guides to action. Interpretation spawns interpretation; news makes news.

As Raymond Williams explained in *Marxism and Literature* (1977), a cultural hegemony spawns the terms of its own rejection. Williams was discussing early Marxist reactions to capitalists' criticism of their theory and politics, but his insight also applies to news. Qualitative researchers have demonstrated that the process of making news encodes both cultural understandings and official sources' frames in news packages. Thus, news consumers are pulled into the frames vital to the news process. Even when news consumers use interpretive strategies that reject specific news frames, they react to the discourse of their culture. Like reporters and editors, they participate in the creation of news as a cultural response to structural conditions.

NOTES

1 Joanne Miller (personal communication) reminds me that some quantitative techniques, such as latent structure analysis, can examine process. However, unless the quantitative researcher has a firm understanding of the hypotheses to be tested and so clear knowledge of the data to be gathered, such analyses are prohibitively laborious "fishing expeditions." The articles in Wellman and Berkowitz (1988) explicate the ideas associated with this form of analysis.

2 According to the late Everett Hughes (personal communication, circa 1965), in the 1920s Robert Park instructed graduate students to use their jobs and their communities as sources of data for term papers and theses. Hughes continued this practice during his tenure at Chicago. Some student papers, such as Howard S. Becker's work on dance musicians and Fred Davis' on taxi-cab drivers, were eventually published as articles; most were not. Hughes also taught a graduate course in participant observation. According to Herbert Gans (personal communication), in the 1950s Hughes assigned students to gather data about specific census tracks and then to institutions within the region under study. (For instance, Gans was assigned an area in Chicago's Hyde Park.) Hughes continued this method of teaching participant observation when he moved to Brandeis University in the early 1960s. At that time most graduate students at Brandeis University, including me, saw themselves as having inherited the mantle of "old Chicago sociology."

However, it is unclear precisely what this "mantle" was. In the 1950s when Herbert Blumer moved from Chicago to the University of California, some Berkeley students also claimed the "Chicago mantle" (Arlene K. Daniels, personal communication) because Blumer was an important proponent of symbolic interactionism. However, Blumer did not engage in participant observation. (For further discussion of the place of participant observation in Chicago sociology, see Chapter 2 in this volume.)

It is clear that at the University of Chicago in the 1950s, Everett Hughes was the primary faculty proponent of participant observation, and graduate students were the main practitioners of this method. Both Herbert Gans (personal communication) and I agree that extended participant observation is a method for the young: when one is in one's twenties or thirties, it may be possible to observe for ten to sixteen hours and then type notes before sleeping. Later in life such long hours pose problems.

3 This article was not even cited by Bernard Berelson (1959) in his classic discussion of the state of communications research.

4 Joanne Miller (personal communication) points out that because latent structural analysis charts networks, it may discover relationships hidden from a participant observer who cannot know indirect ties of which informants themselves are unaware.

5 The idea of frame originated with Bateson (1955/72), was introduced to cultural sociology by Goffman (1974), and then became a key idea in participant observation studies of news (Fishman, 1980; Gamson, 1984; Gamson and Modigliani, 1989; Gitlin, 1980; Tuchman, 1978). The sociologists have used the term "frame" in slightly different ways. But they all stress how frames render socially intelligible what Goffman termed "strips" of behavior.

Chapter 4

Media institutions
The creation of television drama

Horace M. Newcomb

INTRODUCTION

While television is used in many ways, for many purposes, in different contexts, there is no question but that one of the most pervasive uses is the dissemination of dramatic entertainment. For this reason, if for no other, we might be interested in the central question of this chapter – how does that "moment" of dramatic entertainment come to be? In spite of our general familiarity and ease with the medium, this aspect of television remains mysterious, for viewers and scholars alike. My own interest in this general area focuses on a specific question: what is the role of individual creativity in the context of mass art? One result of that interest was a collaborative effort with Robert S. Alley, a book-length study of prominent television producers (Newcomb and Alley, 1983). Our thesis, auteurist in tone, was that "strong" producers could manipulate this mass industrial system as much as they were manipulated by it. The thesis was substantiated with interviews and critical analysis.

In the study of television production, any such specific interest must be considered in light of other concerns, which can be reduced to broad conceptual terms. Most often, in a suspicious construction, the questions are summarized in this way: what options are made available to creators by an industrial system working in its own interests and the interests of dominant groups, and how do those options systematically constrain the production process? A more optimistic formulation can also be presented: given the recognition of these limitations by creators, how are they accepted, rejected, appropriated, or otherwise used in diverse ways?

To examine these broad topics, the generalized questions must be seen to contain others. What is the specific industrial process by which television drama production is currently organized? What are the roles of specific points of influence such as writers, supervising producers, executive producers, directors, and actors? What influence is exerted by "external" forces such as networks, advertisers, special-interest groups, and regulatory agencies? What is the power of the "star" in shaping such a process? What is the role of "forms," historically developed by interested parties, or "culturally given," in shaping and maintaining content? What is the organization of labor within collaborative media industries, and how do professional guilds monitor, participate in, and manipulate that organization? What is the role of technological development in maintaining or changing that organization and in shaping content? Still other questions arise if we apply historical perspectives. How does current practice differ from that in earlier periods, especially in the transition from radio and film to television? Similarly, how has the process of making television been affected by competition from newer forms of media distribution such as video cassette and cable television? The purpose of this chapter is to explore ways of understanding these processes, asking these questions, and providing overviews related to other aspects of media study.

We can proceed by citing significant examples of prior work. That survey completed, I will attempt a synthesis of questions and approaches into principles (not theories with predictive value) that might guide similar research, and I close by outlining some specific, much-needed projects within this area of media studies.

PREVIOUS RESEARCH

Three models

Three significant studies demonstrate, in my view, differing approaches to some of these questions and can serve as models for further research. The first of these, an obligatory beginning point for any production research, is Philip Elliott's *The Making of a Television Series* (1972). Even though Elliott deals with the making of a specific form of documentary (a series of programs designed for an adult-education project), many of the issues he deals with are central to our concerns. Indeed, in his conclusions, he attempts to generalize from his findings, and specifically assesses the utility of his work for examining the production processes of dramatic television. Elliott's approach is also valid in studying broadcasting systems of very different sorts than his own focus, Britain's Independent Television Authority (ITA). His work can certainly be used as a basis for comparison, if not as a model, in studies that cross modes of organization, regulation, financing, and distribution.

One great strength of Elliott's work lies in its detail. Perhaps because it was an early example of its kind, drawing as much from analysis of other social phenomena and from the sociology of art as from media theory or film analysis, the book walks us through each step in the production process. By tracing the series from its original conception, through a research and development phase, into production, postproduction, and broadcast, Elliott is able to examine the points of decision making. This enables him to identify critical conjunctures involving personnel, conceptual, technical, and aesthetic choice, division and organization of labor, and levels of authority. The chronology of the production process becomes the organizing principle of the book, a strategy common to much production research that follows.

The book is also highly self-conscious regarding its methods. Elliott places his approach in the context of prior versions of media study, pointing out strengths and weaknesses of his choices in relation to survey research and traditional sociology. The conclusion carefully draws lines of connection from the single case study to other possible versions of similar research, and the author considers the limitations and possibilities of participant observation in a special appendix to his work. I also discuss these and other methodological issues below with reference to a case study.

Moreover, Elliott is vitally concerned with linking his work to larger theoretical considerations within media studies. As in most such studies, it is clear that the theory does not grow inductively from the case study. Rather, the study is suffused with assumptions which are brought fully to the surface only in the conclusion.

The second book I see as a model for production research actually appeared before Elliott's work. Muriel Cantor's *The Hollywood Television Producer: his Work and his Audience* was first published in 1971, and reprinted, with a significant new introduction, in 1988. Cantor's book, grounded in traditional occupational sociology, is based on tape-recorded interviews with fifty-nine television producers. These interviews are supplemented with public and private documents and with field observation of studios.

The values of this book are, for our purposes, many. First, it gives a precise picture of television work, through the perspective of a significant group, at a particular historical juncture. Second, directly related to this is a sense that this perspective is fully contextualized by a thorough knowledge of the television industry as a whole.

Third, the book's focus on a particular occupational group serves as a model for much-needed work with other groups. No other study has provided comparable depth and breadth in discussing writers, directors, actors, or executives in the television industry.

Finally, Cantor's work draws on a particular perspective of mass communication and individual creativity. Thus, the book reaches the general conclusion that creativity and autonomy are highly controlled, if not stifled. Television drama is seen as mainstream, maintaining the status quo despite potentially more progressive values among producers. This is attributed to the general profit motive of the American television industry, an industry central to capitalist ideology. Theories of culture in this work are not nearly so well developed as theories of society. The core of Cantor's argument lies in what is, in my view, a limiting notion of "creativity" or "autonomy." Still, it is the view held by many in the industry as well as by the scholars who study them.

Both these strengths and weaknesses inform the third major work in this group, Todd Gitlin's *Inside Prime Time* (1983), which combines several aspects of the two previous models and adds significantly to both. Gitlin draws his conclusions from several hundred interviews and some observations of television production. His topics range from explanatory overviews of network research and industry ratings systems, to case studies of the production of particular television dramas. The book offers the multiple perspectives of professional participants rather than the sorted and reasoned descriptions of a participant–observer.

The descriptive portions take us through an apparent chaos, presenting the perspectives of writers, producers, actors, and production company and network executives. Conflict and contradiction are apparent throughout. The result is a more dynamic and fluctuating picture than that offered by either Elliott or Cantor. In comparison with Elliott, this difference may be seen to emerge from systemic (Hollywood vs ITA) and generic (dramatic entertainment vs instructional documentary) distinctions. Differences with Cantor emerge from distinctions in method. Gitlin includes detailed case studies, examines and evaluates fictional content from a text-analytical perspective, and speaks with a wider range of individuals. Cantor's emphasis on occupational sociology is replaced by an emphasis on the sociology of art, communication, and culture.

Ultimately, this complexity in the struggle over meaning and expression is seen as thoroughly meretricious. For Gitlin, television entertainment is a debased form of expression growing from, and contributing to, a social and political world already debased by consumer capitalism. The result in the television industry is a non-critical, indeed celebratory acceptance of "recombinative" art suggesting "cultural exhaustion" (Gitlin, 1983: 325–35). This dark view leaves little hope for creators, who are described with obvious interest on Gitlin's part, but with great irony. Nor does it hold out much value for audiences, who are described, despite a few disclaimers, disdainfully.

Comparisons of these three models in terms of focus and organization show us at least three ways of doing production research. The organizing principle of Elliott's work, and of much research in this area, is the case study through time. It can be seen as a micro-level analysis, tracing the choices made, the points of power and influence, the negotiations, and the final product. Generalizations from such analyses are usually tentative and theory-driven, rather than clear empirical findings. Given the variety of productions and production techniques in television, many comparisons must be made before reaching actual conclusions.

The principle informing Cantor's work is the role of the occupation in context. This study can be termed "mid-level." Individual productions are cited; "stories" are told about negotiations. But because we see those cases from individual perspectives, it is only as they accumulate that an analytical perspective can be gained. Still, because most of these producers have worked on multiple projects, their experience is more wide-ranging than the history of single productions.

Gitlin operates primarily at the macro-level. His work opens with an overview of the television industry and closes with a generalized argument regarding contemporary American culture. He traces individual productions through time, as does Elliott, and he offers testimony of many individual perspectives from television professionals, thus amplifying Cantor. The evidence, however, is offered to support larger claims. Media study becomes a crucial example of a much broader analysis of culture, society, and politics, so that much of what Gitlin suggests could be claimed in other contexts of education, religion, or social policy.

Other helpful studies

Hazell: the Making of a TV Series (1978), by Manuel Alvarado and Edward Buscombe, offers a rich parallel to Elliott's work. The focus here is on a dramatic, limited-run series (miniseries) adapted from a detective novel. Alvarado and Buscombe were able to secure the cooperation of Thames Television and follow the entire development, production, and broadcasting history of the series.

Doctor Who: the Unfolding Text (1983), by John Tulloch and Manuel Alvarado, takes a different direction. Following the history of this long-running series, the authors discuss production decisions and philosophies within the context of a comprehensive cultural analysis of the program. The work is described as "an investigation in terms of the industrial, institutional, narrative, generic, professional and other practices which, originally existing outside the programme, have operated in different ways to shape it" (Tulloch and Alvarado, 1983: 2). In many ways this book is a model for the sort of analysis called for in this chapter. Researchers seeking a model for a cultural studies approach rather than a more specific focus on production research will find this a powerful exemplar.

While these two books focus on television series, following Elliott's lead and one direction of Gitlin's analysis, Newcomb and Alley parallel Cantor in *The Producer's Medium: Conversations with Creators of American TV* (1983). Our aim was to show that the television industry does not necessarily stifle creativity. The book presents condensed versions of interviews with eleven very successful producers, and links their own perspectives to our critical analysis of their work.

Joseph Turow's *Playing Doctor: Television, Storytelling, and Medical Power* (1989) offers a thorough version of production research on television drama. His concern is with representations of medical professionals and the institution of medicine. The focus is on the circuits of power uniting television, the institution of medicine, and the viewing public. Few studies deal with the production of specific content areas, and this is a good example.

Many studies of production processes have also been captured in careful essay-length studies. Judine Mayerle's (1989) study of *Newhart* guides the reader through the entire production process by examining the production and postproduction of a single episode. It does not, however, deal extensively with the process of constant rewriting that is necessary in television comedy. Another article does tackle this issue. Jimmie L. Reeves' (1988) study of *Newhart* is based on access to all versions of a single script from the freelance writers' first "pitch" notes through the finally edited and aired version. Taken together, these two articles provide the rich detail which is necessary to understand the production of episodic television.

In addition, scholars interested in production research will find extraordinary help in material often overlooked from an academic perspective. These sources appear as memoirs, fans' books, instructional and informational material, journalistic overviews of business and industry, and so on. For example, important "instructional" information is offered by Blum and Lindheim (1987), Chambers (1986), and Shanks (1976; 1986). Descriptions of "backstage" events and practices, sometimes accompanied by "insider accounts," are offered by Broughton (1986), Christensen and Stauth (1984), Floyd (1988), Hill and Weingrad (1986), Lynch (1973), and Ravage (1978). Useful insider accounts and memoirs are presented by Levinson and Link (1981; 1986) and Metz (1975). Overviews of various aspects of the television industry are available in Eliot (1983), Mair (1988), and Morgenstern (1979). And case studies of the making of specific programs are offered by Pekurny (1980) and Ravage (1977). Many more examples of this work are available, and are often more accessible in public libraries than in academic research collections.

METHODS AND ISSUES

Preliminaries

Qualitative research is often dependent on factors not fully controlled by the researcher. The first of these is *access*. At times, opportunity, rather than logic, guides the work. Many researchers, however, are surprised at the ease with which they can gain access to those involved in high-level media production. All the common courtesy protocols – preliminary letters and telephone calls outlining specific needs, dates, times, and references – must, of course, be observed. Once a relationship has been established with one individual or group, access develops out of recommendation, reference and trust. Media professionals are quick to realize the researcher's needs and to offer suggestions and introductions of other persons who can act as sources. Thus, access is constantly renegotiated during the course of research. Somewhat more disconcerting, at times, is a deeper form of renegotiation required when the researcher realizes that additional access and new information are redefining the entire project.

Access is also enhanced by *specific knowledge* of professional, organizational, and technical matters. Professionals do not have time or opportunity, for the most part, to teach researchers. They will be able to provide information about specific technical matters, work routines, and individual practices, but the researcher must have a high level of specific knowledge "going in."

Access is made easier, finally, by careful attention to *timing*. Most media industries have routinized work procedures that range from seasonal emphases to daily schedules. Researchers must be aware of the best time of the year, the week, and the day to reach media professionals. They must also be prepared for meeting times to be shifted at the last moment, and to see this as a necessary part of their work, not an attempt on the part of their subjects to avoid them.

Methods

The two primary methods of production research are participant observation and interviewing. Each has strengths and limitations, discussed particularly cogently by Elliott (1972). I add my own perspective here.

The strengths of *participant observation* are rooted in its actual, "on the ground" observation of *process*. Researchers are able to observe actual work routines, in the course of the observation recording decision-making processes, conflict, negotiation, and compromise, all of which are part of the production process at different levels. Key to analysing the processes of production are observations of the exercise of power. In negotiation, who and what control the driving forces that enable conflicts to be resolved? Observation can also be made of the final outcome of this process, the application of decisions. This may lead to discussions of successes and failures, as production personnel see the results of their actions and choices even while the researcher sees the results of her or his work. The greatest opportunity of participant observation, then, is the constant refinement of questions, goals, and directions as the work continues.

The degree of success in participant observation is related, in some cases, to the level of participation. In this regard, the more knowledgeable researcher has advantages. If the researcher knows little or nothing of the technical processes involved, observations will be limited, narrowly directed, or simply incorrect. Again, there is little time for learning "on the job."

The primary disadvantages of participant observation are frequently rooted in limited access. Dependence on the goodwill of host institutions or individuals may result in too easy acceptance of their point of view. Participant observation is also limited to the duration of the researcher's access, and it is difficult to generalize from "snap-shot" experiences. This is doubly the case when the observer is considered an intruder and treated with suspicion. All these matters rest, finally, in another: whether the presence of the observer alters the normal procedures one wishes to observe. Since "invisibility" is impossible, the only recourse is, again, extensive and varied background information.

The primary strength of *interviewing* as a method is its capacity to range over *multiple perspectives* on a given topic. Multiple interviews can be used to increase information and broaden a point of view. All interviews can be used as heuristic devices, as new information leads to new perspectives and questions for later subjects. Interview data further facilitate the gathering of historical perspectives. Subjects have usually been involved in many projects, often for many years. They thus are able to point to changes caused by technological, financial, or regulatory factors. In this way, they actually do some of the researcher's comparative work; one of the pleasures of interviewing is to discover how analytically aware practitioners are.

All these factors lead to what is perhaps the interview technique's greatest strength – the gathering of more comprehensive information than might be possible in participant observation. Because even the most rigid interview schedule can be altered in process, the researcher is free to follow leads and expand questions. The more extensive, or more precise, questions can lead to more detailed responses, more leads to other subjects, more opportunities for comparison, and even a thorough revision of the entire project.

Eventually, the researcher must confront the most formidable issue of interview work – the reliability of informants. While the participant observer might be faced with her or his own versions of this issue, on-the-scene activity provides some check on the explanations given. After-the-fact descriptions offered in interviews must be examined very carefully for everything from accuracy of detail to basic truthfulness. Related problems include a tendency to ask for information that will confirm the researcher's own assumptions; the realization that the informant has a "canned" response to many familiar questions; the less likely discovery of intentional deception; and the more likely recognition of self-serving answers to questions.

Using either of these primary methods for research on the production of television drama demands constant cross-checking and amplification with other methods and sources. In the ideal situation, participant observation and interview will be used together. Furthermore, interpretations must be supported with reference to several types of explanatory frameworks. I consider these below in terms of the historical, economic, technological, textual, and organizational issues involved in production research.

Issues

Any production research must consider questions in at least five major categories: cultural, institutional, organizational, group, and individual. At the risk of making a sometimes chaotic process much too rational and rigid, we can consider a checklist of sorts which may remind us of significant factors in production research.

In dealing with television drama, it is incumbent on us to have some theory of how drama, particularly popular entertainment, works in *culture*, of drama's role historically and in the new mass-mediated context, and of the ways in which audiences attend to it. Television's relation to other forms of expression, histories of genre, theories of narrative and of textual analysis, will shape both the questions and observations of researchers. Television drama may be a "product," but it is a product with special cultural uses. The "culture industries" thus are different in significant ways from other industries, no matter how similar in other ways.

As is always the case, these special features are affected by *institutional* arrangements. Production research must account for macro-level arrangements such as whether a television system is defined as public service or commercial, the policies and economic structures supporting each type, and the relevant agents of power at these various levels. A study of television drama production for the Public Broadcasting Service in the USA, for example, will focus on different issues than a study examining commercial net-work television, even while inevitably asking many of the same questions.

Within these institutions, *organizational* structures impinge directly on the production of drama. For example, I have used the term "drama" throughout to refer to fictional, dramatic program-ming for television. Within the commercial networks, however, there are formal Divisions of Drama (referring to one-hour pro-gramming in the action-adventure and melodrama forms), Comedy (referring to half-hour programming, usually, but not always comic in nature), and Long Form (referring to made-for-television movies and miniseries). Day-time and Prime-time are also separated formally, and Children's programming is yet another division. De-partments focused on Development are distinct from those dealing with Current programming. Financial, contractual, and personal matters are treated similarly in some ways, differently in others in all these areas. Moreover, organizational questions can also be specific to the level of production of individual series.

Groups within each of these organizations establish particular work routines which accomplish actual production. Often these groups are regulated contractually by unions or guilds that monitor their relations with other groups, with work demands, pay scales, and so on.

Finally, *individuals* make choices within all these contexts, modifying, accepting, rejecting, subverting, circumventing, and creating. Their work, in a highly collaborative, regulated, con-strained context, ultimately contributes the elements of television drama.

A CASE STUDY

With these issues in mind, I will present as an example the project I am now beginning, titled "Writing/television: creativity in an indus-trial setting." The project focuses on the work of writers for prime-time, series television, and while the title suggests a sociological perspective, my main concerns are aesthetic and cultural. In fact, "creativity" may be the wrong term here, for I am actually more interested in "authorship."

I am interested in this topic for several reasons. I am intrigued by the problem of how one writes for a set of characters one did not invent, within genres one did not inflect. I am even more concerned with the narrative structures of series television, in which long-term narratives are planned, for financial purposes, not to end. Put another way, since series television violates formal Aristotelian notions of beginning, middle, and end, how does one write for a "perpetual middle," or a perpetual second act, especially when episodes do often conform to traditional principles? Given the historical and narrative focus of these questions, I place them in the *cultural* arena.

I am acutely aware, however, of the *institutional* constraints on television writers, beginning with the difficulty of breaking into this position, and of the various levels of control that exceed the traditional notion of authorship as an individual autonomous voice. Certain legal rules apply at this level. The Writers Guild Minimum Basic Agreement with producers mandates, for example, that at least two episodes of every series be given to freelancers, writers not on staff. I will be particularly concerned with how writers perceive their role within these institutional contexts and with how they perceive those roles to have changed.

The same issues will be addressed at the *organizational* level in a more immediate way. Television writers are constantly rewritten by other writers who have more autonomy within the organization. I am especially interested in how writing and rewriting differ between comic and dramatic productions, within the context of specific shows (personalities and professional styles come into play here), and at different studios and production companies.

At the *group* level, I am interested in the writers' collective perceptions. The study will focus on the different perceptions of comedy and drama writers, freelancers and staff, new and old, successful and unsuccessful writers, and so on. The history of the Writers Guild, of various negotiations and strikes, will be pertinent here, as well, as is the choice of many successful writers to become "hyphenates," producer–writers who create new shows, hire writers, and supervise their work. This topic is especially important in the current state of the American television industry, where successful writers, particularly comedy writers, have become exceptionally powerful, commanding multi-year, multimillion-dollar studio contracts. Finally, of course, I am interested in how an *individual* writer accomplishes his or her daily work in this complex context.

I will use both participant observation and interviews to gather data for this study. Because I have written for series television and continue to work in that arena, I know most of the basic rules of the game. I also have extensive access to writers and writer–producers. As a member of the Writers Guild, I have access to contractual documents, Guild officials, and computer bulletin boards to communicate with other writers. Because many writers and producers go on to network positions, I also have access to network officials who deal with writers.

Once the interviews and observations have been collected, however, the work of the production researcher has just begun. Any researcher in this area is faced with more material than can be used. To sort and cull the material, the researcher must draw conclusions that are not obvious in the data, search for patterns of significance, and apply those patterns to previous research. (For details of analytical procedures, see Chapter 1 on discourse analysis, and Chapter 2 on the research process.) This is so despite the fact that production research appears to be more empirically grounded than other forms of interpretation.

It should be clear by now that the simple question posed at the beginning of this chapter – how does an episode of television drama come to be broadcast? – is woefully inadequate as a guide for this interpretive process. At best, the question is a microcosmic example of these larger issues, so that the individual episode can be seen as a point of conjunction where the issues and the forces behind them meet. But it is with the macrocosmic scale that we must end. Production research, then, is conducted not merely to describe interesting examples of one of the most prevalent forms of communication in today's world. It will also be shaped by researchers' assumptions regarding issues such as "art" and "communication," "society" and "culture," "high art," "popular culture," "mass communication," and "the audience."

We can see these issues most clearly by returning briefly to our primary examples of previous research. All three authors assume that television, as constituted in specific industrial settings, fails to reach its progressive ideological potential. (Underlying some of these assumptions is another which suggests that television is incapable of reaching that potential.) For Elliott, the problem lies in the inherently contradictory notion of "mass" communication. For Cantor, the issue rests in the appropriation of the medium by those who would use it solely for profit, must therefore depend on the mass audience, and consequently must mold content in the most acceptable fashion, stifling individual creativity in the process. For

Gitlin, the problems are the same, but even more fundamental: commercial television, creature of consumer capitalism, has become the perpetuator of it, the best conduit for monitoring and instructing a culture in the throes of exhaustion. Only with these assumptions in mind can we fully appreciate the significance of method and technique.

SUGGESTIONS FOR FURTHER RESEARCH

It should be clear, then, that there are few, if any, "theories" specifically of production processes, despite the fact that most studies have been theory-driven. This is primarily because we have an insufficient number of studies for thorough comparison. As a result, any individual study is potentially unique, potentially aberrant. To correct this situation, the following types of continuing research are needed.

High-level institutional studies. Like Gitlin (1983), these studies would provide systemic overviews into which individual studies could be placed. First, we need cross-cultural and system comparisons. There is much information on the structure of broadcasting industries throughout the world, but little information on how those structures affect the day-to-day production of drama, news, or other program types (but see Chapter 3 in this volume). The same is true for comparisons of advertiser-supported and public-service systems, broadcast and cable systems, or multinational as opposed to national production companies.

Second, we need historical studies. We have no good institutional histories of networks or public broadcasting companies as those histories might reflect on the production process. Film study has moved far ahead of television studies in this area (see, for example, Bordwell *et al.*, 1985). In some cases, this is because access to archival material, especially corporate records, is still limited for television. But we can counter this situation to some extent by attending to the personal information available from those who literally invented the television systems we live with.

Mid-level institutional studies. Here we need careful, historically oriented studies of specific studios, production companies, distribution processes, technological innovations, and so on. Again, the focus should be on the ways in which production is affected. I would include here certain types of textual studies on the rise and fall of genres, responses in the industry, and the consequent re-creation of narrative strategies. Also needed are more studies comparable to Cantor's book on producers; occupations, their professional organizations, crafts and skills groups should all be studied.

Ground-level studies of individual productions. Like Elliott's, these studies should focus on the production of specific program content, in limited or continuing runs. Television history would be immeasurably enriched by careful studies, historical and contemporary, of individual programs. Accumulating this data would allow us to discover whether generic, organizational, network, or certain historical factors were common forces shaping production practices. Until we have such material gathered, individual studies will be interesting in and of themselves, but of little use in describing and evaluating an industry central to contemporary life.

That, ultimately, should be the goal of production research. Our work should exceed fascination, our own and that of the general public, with television production. But it cannot do so until we have more – and more systematic – studies from which to proceed.

Chapter 5

Media contents
The interdisciplinary study of news as discourse

Teun A. van Dijk

INTRODUCTION

This chapter presents a discourse-analytical approach to the media. Discourse analysis emphasizes the obvious, but as yet not fully explored fact that media "messages" are specific types of text and talk. The theories and methods of the new interdisciplinary field of discourse analysis may be brought to bear in a more systematic and explicit account of the structures of media messages. Since discourse analysis is a multi-disciplinary enterprise, it is also able to relate this structural account to various properties of the cognitive and sociocultural context. Because the other chapters of this book pay detailed attention to the production, reception, uses, and sociocultural functions of media discourse, the present chapter only briefly deals with such a broader study of those aspects of mass communication.

Discourse analysis emerged as a new transdisciplinary field of study between the mid-1960s and mid-1970s in such disciplines as anthropology, ethnography, microsociology, cognitive and social psychology, poetics, rhetoric, stylistics, linguistics, semiotics, and other disciplines in the humanities and social sciences interested in the systematic study of the structures, functions, and processing of text and talk (for details, see the contributions in van Dijk, 1985b; also Chapter 1 in this volume and Chapter 6 on earlier and related forms of textual analysis of media discourses). In order to limit discussion of the vast domain of discourse-analytical media research, I shall focus on the study of news in the press. For further theoretical details, and for extensive applications in the study of various cases of press coverage, the reader is referred to van Dijk (1985b; 1988a; 1988b).

THE DISCOURSE APPROACH IN MEDIA RESEARCH:
A BRIEF REVIEW

Although the discourse approach in mass media research has now become more or less accepted as an alternative or addition to classical content analyses (Krippendorff, 1980), the number of systematic discourse studies of mass media messages is still limited. The applications of discourse analysis in media research are as varied as the very fields of discourse studies and mass communication themselves. Much work has a linguistic orientation, such as the early stylistic studies of Leech (1966) and Crystal and Davy (1969), and the later critical linguistics approach of Fowler et al. (1979), Fowler (1991), Kress (1985), and Chilton (1985; 1988), among others. Much of this work, as well as recent work on social semiotics (Hodge and Kress, 1988) has been influenced by Halliday's systemic grammar (Halliday, 1978; 1985).

Better known in mass communication research, and equally diverse in orientation, is the critical work of the Glasgow University Media Group (1976; 1980) on the media representation of industrial disputes, the contributions in Davis and Walton (1983), and the cultural studies approach of the Centre for Contemporary Cultural Studies (Hall et al., 1980). While also dealing with language, discourse, and images, these approaches are not part of linguistics proper, but pay special attention to ideological and political dimensions of media messages. Despite the theoretical and ideological diversity of these and other current approaches, we witness increasing integration of linguistic, semiotic, and discourse-analytical approaches (van Dijk, 1985a; Hartley, 1982).

It is striking that most of this work has been done in the UK (and now also in Australia). Until recently, there was little linguistic or discourse-analytical work on the media in the USA, where most media studies were either anecdotal or focused on sociopolitical issues (see, however, Geis, 1987). The same holds for France, despite its early semiotic studies of some genres of media discourse (Barthes, 1973). Research in Germany is generally inspired by various approaches in text linguistics (Luger, 1983; Strassner, 1975; 1982) and its later developments across the boundaries with other disciplines, including semiotics and psychology (Bentele, 1981; Schmitz, 1990). In Austria, critical media research from an interdisciplinary discourse-analytical perspective is carried out especially by Ruth Wodak and her associates (see her study of the anti-semitic discourse, also in the press, accompanying the election of Waldheim: Wodak *et al.*, 1990).

THE TEXTUAL ANALYSIS OF NEWS IN THE PRESS

The study of news reports in the press is one of the major tasks of discourse-analytical media research. Indeed, as the works reviewed above suggest, apart from advertising probably no media genre has received so much scholarly interest from mass communication researchers, semioticians, linguists, and discourse analysts. This attention is justified when we realize how important news is in our everyday lives. Most of our social and political knowledge and beliefs about the world derive from the dozens of news reports we read or see every day. There is probably no other discursive practice, besides everyday conversation, that is engaged in so frequently and by so many people as news in the press and on television. Let us therefore examine the structures of this genre in more detail.

To enhance the practical usefulness of this chapter, I discuss the various levels and dimensions of news discourse through a *partial and informal* analysis of a concrete example taken from a British newspaper. Further, I briefly indicate which structures of news discourse have particular social, political, or ideological implications, so that they may be focused on in a more critical analysis of news.

One of the characteristics of discourse analysis is that it describes text and talk in terms of theories developed for the several levels or dimensions of discourse. Thus, whereas classical linguistics and semiotics made an overall distinction between the form (*signifiants*) and meaning (*signifiés*) of signs, current discourse analysis recognizes that text and talk are vastly more complex, and require separate though interrelated accounts of phonetic, graphical, phonological, morphological, syntactic, micro- and macro-semantic, stylistic, superstructural, rhetorical, pragmatic, conversational, interactional, and other structures and strategies. Each of these levels has its characteristic structures, which may be interpreted or function at other levels, both within and outside the traditional linguistic boundaries of the sentence, as well as in the broader context of use and communication.

Note that such a complex analysis of discourse is not limited to "textual" analysis, but also accounts for the relations between structures of text and talk, on the one hand, and of their cognitive, social, cultural, or historical "contexts," on the other hand. Also textual production and comprehension processes, interactions among language users, and the societal or cultural functions of discourse are important objects of research in such a transdisciplinary approach. In this analysis of a news report, however, I shall focus on textual structures.

Example

As the example of analysis, I use a news report that appeared in the British *Daily Mail* of 21 January 1989 (see the appendix to this chapter). It deals with the last act of a dramatic episode that had angered Conservatives, and hence the right-wing press, for a long time: the sanctuary sought by a Sri Lankan refugee, Viraj Mendis, in a Manchester church. After having lived for more than two years in the sacristy of the church, Mendis was finally arrested during a massive police raid on the church, which led to protests not only from church officials, but also from many anti-racists and other groups defending the rights of immigrants and refugees. When a last recourse to the courts failed, Mendis was finally put on a plane to Sri Lanka, and it is this event which our news report is about.

This news item is part of a corpus of news reports, background articles, and editorials in the press about ethnic affairs which I studied as part of a project on racism in the press (van Dijk, 1991). This media project is itself part of a larger research program about the reproduction of racism in discourse, including not only media discourse, but also everyday conversations and textbooks (van Dijk, 1987a; 1987b). As will become clear from our analysis of this particular news report, the Western press, and especially the right-wing press, (re)produces and further emphasizes a negative image of minorities, immigrants, and refugees, and thereby contributes to increasing forms of intolerance, prejudice, and discrimination against Third World peoples in Europe and North America.

TEXT SEMANTICS

Local and global coherence

Both discourse analysts and ordinary language users are primarily interested in meaning: what is this text or talk about, what does it mean, and what implications does it have for language users? Part of the answer to such questions is given in text semantics, which formulates interpretation rules for words, sentences, paragraphs, or whole discourses. One important semantic notion used to describe meaning is that of proposition, which may be roughly defined as the conceptual meaning structure of a clause (van Dijk, 1977).

One of the important notions studied in text semantics is that of the *local coherence* of the text: how are the subsequent propositions of the text bound together? One of the major conditions of such local coherence of texts is that their propositions refer to facts that are related, for instance, by relations of time, condition, cause, and consequence. In the *Mail* report we see that the first sentence of the lead paragraph expresses two propositions ("Mendis is flying to Sri Lanka," and "There was a bid to release him"), which are both temporally ("after") and (indirectly) causally related (he was deported because the attempt to get him released failed). Note that two expressions in these propositions also refer to the same person, Viraj Mendis, participating in the two events that are thus related.

The propositions are also conceptually related ("flying" and "airport," "illegal" and "release"). Indeed, as we shall see below, these concepts are part of the so-called scripts of air travel and arrest. Our shared, social knowledge of such scripts provides the numerous "missing links" between the concepts and propositions of the text, which is, so to speak, a semantic iceberg of which only the tip is actually expressed, whereas the other information is presupposed to be known by the readers. This dependence on world knowledge and beliefs also may make coherence subjective and ideological: what is coherent for the journalist may not be so for all readers.

Besides this kind of *referential* local coherence, propositions may also be *functionally* coherent: for instance, when the second proposition has the function of a Specification, Paraphrase, Contrast, or Example, relative to the first proposition. Propositions in news reports are often connected by a relation of Specification: more general propositions are followed by more specific ones that give further details. We see in the next sentence what the "dramatic bid" consisted of: who did what, where, and how. Similarly, later sentences may feature paraphrases ("demand," "plea") of previous ones, and they may have ideological functions when they carry specific evaluative implications, as is clearly the case in the *Mail* report.

It is a crucial property of discourse that it is not only locally but also globally coherent. Beyond meaning relations between subsequent sentences, a text also has overall semantic unity. This *global coherence* is described by what we all intuitively know as themes or topics. Topics conceptually summarize the text, and specify its most important information. In theoretical terms such topics can be described as semantic macro-propositions, that is, as propositions that are derived from sequences of propositions in the text: for instance, by macro-rules such as selection, abstraction, and other operations which reduce complex information. The hierarchical set of topics or macro-propositions forms the thematic or topical structure of the text. Language users employ such *macro-structures* in order to understand globally and to summarize a text. In news discourse, the top of this macro-structure is conventionally expressed in the headline and the lead paragraph.

The report in the *Mail* may be represented as a list of propositions, subsequently reduced to a shorter list of macro-propositions or main topics. Through repeated applications of the macro-rules (macro-rules are recursive) we arrive at a list of main topics such as:

> Viraj Mendis was deported to Sri Lanka;
> an attempt by a priest to have him released in Zurich failed;
> at Gatwick airport many groups protested against his deportation;
> Mendis was arrested after having sought sanctuary in a Manchester church.

In order to derive such topics (macro-propositions), we again need vast amounts of world knowledge: for example, that expulsion may involve (air) transport as well as police officers, and that it may lead to protests, which involves demonstrators and, sometimes, police officers. Special emphasis on specific topics may have ideological implications. Thus, the *Mail* pays much attention to the topic of the demonstration, unlike, for instance, the report in the *Guardian* (21 January 1989) on the same event, which focuses on the expulsion and its political implications.

Implications

One of the most powerful semantic notions in a critical news analysis is that of *implication*. We saw earlier that much of the information of a text is not explicitly expressed, but left implicit. Words, clauses, and other textual expressions may imply concepts or propositions which may be inferred on the basis of background knowledge. This feature of discourse and communication has important ideological dimensions. The analysis of the "unsaid" is sometimes more revealing than the study of what is actually expressed in the text.

There are various types of implication: entailments, presuppositions, and weaker forms, such as suggestion and association. In our example as well as generally in discourse about minorities and refugees, especially in right-wing news reports about minorities, the use of the word "illegal" not only means that Mendis has broken the law, but also associates him and other immigrants or refugees with crime (van Dijk, 1991). Similarly, the use of "Marxist" has negative implications, and makes Mendis a less credible refugee. Doubts about credibility are also raised by the description of demonstrators "who arrive in luxury coaches." Thus, the whole article uses many descriptions of demonstrators and Labour which imply or suggest that they are wasting taxpayers' money and that their protests are not serious ("they make a living out of complaining").

Many ideological implications follow not only because too little is being said, but also because too many, irrelevant things are being said about news actors. The well-known example in news reports about minorities is the use of irrelevant ethnic or racial labels in crime stories. We find this strategic use of *irrelevance* here when Mendis is called a Marxist, and when the demonstrators are associated with revolutionaries, blacks, lesbians, and gays, associations that are hardly positive for most *Mail* readers. Mentioning an irrelevant detail like the cost of the coaches used by the demonstrators further suggests that they and the "loony Left" are wasting taxpayers' money, a suggestion that likely has a powerful persuasive impact on many taxpayers/readers.

SUPERSTRUCTURES: THE NEWS SCHEMA

Topics are usually organized by an abstract schema, consisting of conventional categories that specify what the overall function is of the topics of the text. Such a schema is called a superstructure (van Dijk, 1980). Just like stories or argumentations, news reports follow a hierarchical schema, consisting of such conventional categories as Headline, Lead (together forming the Summary), Main Events, Context, History (together forming the Background category),

Verbal Reactions, and Comments. Typical for news stories is that these categories, as well as their global semantic content, are expressed discontinuously, as "installments," throughout the text: of each category the most important information is expressed first, a top-down strategy which assigns a so-called relevance structure to the text.

The assignment of importance or relevance may have ideological implications. The Headline, "**Mendis flown out as police face 'rent-amob' fury**," expresses two macro-propositions (topics): namely, that Mendis is deported (by plane) and that (at the same time) the police are confronted with the angry reactions of protesters. These two propositions summarize the main information of the text and thereby signal that for the *Mail* both events are important. Other newspapers may only highlight the event of the expulsion. The Lead and the subsequent sentences provide further details of these topics, in the Main Event category (featuring information about the expulsion and demonstration) as well as in other categories such as a brief History (Mendis having been in Britain for thirteen years) and some general Context (the policies of the Church regarding sanctuary).

It is characteristic of a right-wing tabloid like the *Mail* that little attention is paid to the social or political background of the events, whereas relatively many details are given about the demonstrators and their Labour supporters. Information in the Verbal Reactions category is limited to the negative opinions of a policeman about the "great unwashed." These opinions are consistent with those of the *Mail*. This also shows that news gathering and quotation in news are often biased through the choice of sources and the uses of source texts. Demonstrators and Mendis are not allowed to speak, as I have generally found for the role of minority speakers in ethnic affairs coverage (van Dijk, 1991). Finally, the Comment category is expressed discontinuously throughout the text by the various negative descriptions of the demonstrators and their Labour supporters. In other words, also the organization of the schematic superstructure of this news report is consistent with the ideological position of the *Mail*.

STYLE AND RHETORIC

Style is the textual result of choices between alternative ways of saying more or less the same thing by using different words or a different syntactic structure. Such stylistic choices also have clear social and ideological implications, because they often signal the opinions of the reporter about news actors and news events as well as properties of the social and communicative situation (their use in a tabloid) and the group memberships of the speakers, for instance that a specific journalist is white, male, or middle-class. Thus, the use of "mob" and "rentamob," instead of "crowd" and "demonstrators," may be interpreted as signaling the ideological position of the reporter about left-wing demonstrators, while at the same time discrediting them for the readers. The same is true of the use of "howling," "screaming," and "fury," instead of "vigorously protesting." Besides expressing negative attitudes and manufacturing the consent of the readers (Herman and Chomsky, 1988), the use of such words also shows a cultural dimension of news language: the everyday, popular style of tabloids.

Another aspect of style is the syntax of sentences: for instance, when agents of negative actions, typically those of the authorities, are left out. In the headline clause, "**Mendis flown out,**" it is not said *who* flew him out, or *who* put him on the plane (for details, see Fowler *et al.*, 1979). The rhetoric of this report mainly resides in the hyperboles used to describe the demonstrators, as we have seen above, and in typical tabloid alliterations such as "howling their hatred," both emphasizing the negative properties of the demonstrators.

In sum, at various levels of analysis, those of local and global semantics, news schemata, and style, we find a consistent pattern of discursive features that imply or signal the ideological position of the *Mail* in the account of this event. In addition, the relevance structure of this report favors attention to those aspects of the situation that are important for the *Mail*, while leaving out important information and evaluations about the immigration and refugee policies of the Thatcher government, the courts, the police, and other white authorities.

SOCIAL COGNITION AND SOCIOCULTURAL CONTEXTS

Discourse analysis of news is not limited to textual structures. We have seen that these structures express or signal various "underlying" meanings, opinions, and ideologies. In order to show how these underlying meanings are related to the text, we need an analysis of the cognitive, social, political, and cultural context. The cognitive approach is premised on the fact that texts do not "have" meanings, but are assigned meanings by language users, or, to be precise, by the mental processes of language users. In other words, we need to spell out the cognitive representations and strategies of journalists in the production of the news report and those of the reader when understanding and memorizing it (van Dijk, 1988a; van Dijk and Kintsch, 1983).

A few theoretical notions are necessary to explain what mental structures and processes are involved here. First, in textual understanding, the meaning of the text itself is gradually and strategically constructed and represented in memory as a *text representation*. Second, language users, and hence journalists and readers, have a unique, personal representation of the news events referred to by the text, in our case the expulsion and demonstration. This knowledge representation in memory is called a (situation or event) *model*. A model represents what a language user has understood of the event that the text is about, and we have understood a text if we have been able to build a mental model of that event.

This model not only features the information which is expressed through the text representation; it also contains much other information about this event, such as details about flying, expulsion, demonstrations, and Labour, possibly including personal associations and evaluations of readers. This information is not expressed in the text, because it is assumed to be known by the readers, or because it is found irrelevant by the reporter. Some of this presupposed information is derived from the *scripts*, as mentioned above, about expulsions and demonstrations. Such scripts are culturally shared, conventional knowledge representations about well-known episodes of social life. Thus, whereas models may feature personal and biographically unique information, scripts are general and social.

Similarly, people also have a specific mental model of the present communicative context, a so-called *context model*, which features information about the goals of the discourse, its communicative acts, and the properties of the audience. It is this context model that controls what information from the event model will be found communicatively relevant for inclusion in the text. For instance, in discourse about minorities, both in the press and in everyday conversations, prejudiced language users usually not only express negative opinions about minorities, as represented in their models of ethnic events; in addition, they will add disclaimers such as, "I have nothing against Blacks (Turks, refugees), but . . ." These disclaimers are designed to avoid a bad impression ("He is a racist");

they "save face" for the speaker (for details about such strategic moves in racist discourse, see van Dijk, 1987a). It is the context model that manages this interactional, communicative aspect of discourse and which relates discourse with social situations and structures.

We have seen, then, that event models in memory not only feature knowledge, but also opinions or evaluative beliefs about events and their participants, as has been more than clear in the *Mail* report. The many evaluative implications of the text we have encountered above may now be explained by spelling them out in a description of the mental models of the journalist. If a news report is "biased," this is usually because the mental model of the journalist features structures and opinions which favor a specific ideological perspective on an event. Hence, critical analysis of the meaning of discourse in fact often involves the tentative reproduction of the beliefs in the underlying models of the speaker/writer.

In the same way that models feature instantiated (specified) knowledge from scripts, they embody specific opinions that are derived from general, socially shared opinion structures such as attitudes. More generally, then, we say that models are based on *social representations* or *social cognitions*, for instance about immigrants, refugees, or demonstrators (Farr and Moscovici, 1984; Fiske and Taylor, 1984). Unlike specific opinions, which may be personal, such social cognitions are characteristic of groups, such as the group of tabloid journalists, or the larger group of right-wing people in Britain (Gordon and Klug, 1986).

If social cognitions about different social groups and social events are similar, we say that they are being monitored by the same fundamental interpretation framework, that is, by the same *ideology*. Such an ideology features the basic norms, values, and other principles which are geared towards the realization of the interests and goals of the group, as well as towards the reproduction and legitimation of its power.

Thus, if we say that the news report of the *Mail* is "ideological," we thereby mean that the structures and meanings expressed in it, first, reflect the structures and contents of the specific mental model of this individual reporter about this specific event, but that this model, second, may be based on general social–cognitive schemata (prejudices) about demonstrators or refugees, and that such schemata are finally monitored by underlying group-based ideologies. Hence, an ideological analysis requires a complex description not only of the text, but also of the intricate cognitive representations and strategies used in the production and comprehension of the text.

Unfortunately, in critical semiotics, in linguistics, and discourse analysis, and in mass communication research, such a cognitive analysis is often neglected, or given only in very superficial and intuitive terms, such as "consciousness" or "meaning production." However, it is precisely through a detailed account of social cognitions that we are able to relate discourse and speakers with social structure and culture, that is, through the representations that language users have *about* social structures. These social cognitions also allow us to relate the micro-structures of discursive action and communication with the societal macro-structures of groups (journalists, demonstrators, refugees, minorities) and institutions (newspapers, governments, courts). In a theoretical framework that is vastly more complex than that of traditional "effects" research, we are thus able to describe and explain in detail how this news report in the *Mail* may contribute to the legitimation and reproduction of anti-immigration ideologies and racism in British society.

In other words, models and social cognitions are, so to speak, the interface between text and context. This is how and where white male journalists have represented their group and class membership, and it is this general representation of ingroups and outgroups that is used strategically in the formation of models about a specific news event, models which in turn govern the news-gathering routines, the interpretation of sources and source texts by the reporter, as well as the ways in which the news event is described in the news report. In our opinion, it is in this way that the analysis of discourse as presented in this chapter should be related to the work presented elsewhere in this book.

APPENDIX

CLASHES ON STREETS AND AT AIRPORTS AS REBEL IS DEPORTED

Mendis flown out as police face "rentamob" fury

By BOB GRAHAM and DANNY BUCKLAND

ILLEGAL immigrant Viraj Mendis was flying home to Sri Lanka last night after a final dramatic bid for his release at Zurich Airport.

As his plane touched down en route to Sri Lanka, a supporter accompanying him demanded that Mendis be allowed off.

The plea came from the curate of the Manchester church where Mendis claimed sanctuary. The two British policemen sitting either side of Mendis re-handcuffed him and refused to budge and Swiss police were called in. After a bitter argument on the tarmac, it appeared the Swiss were about to agree to let him go, but their senior officer intervened and the plane took off for Colombo.

Mendis, a 32-year-old Marxist and Tamil supporter, said: "I'm going home to almost certain death." It was as if Home Secretary Douglas Hurd was "holding a pistol to my head himself and pulling the trigger," he said.

He had left Gatwick amid screaming protests from the "great unwashed". Passengers were jostled as Left-wingers surged into viewing areas, howling their hatred of the Government. Four women and a man rushed barriers leading to the tarmac where his Air Lanka plane flight waited. Police, security staff and an airline crew dashed to stop them, scuffles broke out, and the five were arrested.

Dirty

As the plane left Britain the West German Embassy said the state of Bremen might accept him and discussions were taking place with the federal government.

Three luxury coaches had taken many of the demonstrators to Pentonville Prison, where Mendis had been held, then on to Gatwick. They were paid for with £1,700 of ratepayers' money, allocated by leaders of Manchester's Labour-run city council.

The council's Tory group leader, John Kershaw, protested last night that the money, meant for genuine cases of hardship, had been spent without any committee authorisation.

At Pentonville, the "rentamob" protesters who had gathered outside the walls included the Revolutionary Communist Group, the Black Women for Wages for Housework group, the North West Campaign for Lesbian and Gay Equality and the King's Cross Women's Centre. Last night, bottles were thrown at police vans after a rally in support of Mendis in Manchester, at which Labour MP Anthony Wedgwood Benn spoke. Five hundred demonstrators marched through the city vowing vengeance against Margaret Thatcher and the Home Secretary, and responding to anti-police slogans shouted through loudspeakers from a truck supplied by the council cleansing department.

The column included the Palestine Solidarity Campaign, Manchester University students and trade unions.

One senior police officer who monitors Left-wing protest groups said: "The same faces reappear all the time at demos. We know them as the great unwashed, because they all seem to wear the same dirty mode of dress. They make a living out of complaining."

Mendis, who spent 13 years illegally in Britain, was seized by police on Wednesday from the Church of Ascension in Hulme, where he had claimed sanctuary for more than two years. The Home Secretary later warned churchmen to be cautious about sheltering people defying the law and yesterday the Archbishop of Canterbury reminded clergy that sanctuary was abolished 350 years ago and told them that they must obey the law.

Daily Mail, Saturday, 21 January 1989.

Chapter 6

Media contents
Textual analysis of fictional media content

Peter Larsen

INTRODUCTION: THE CRITICAL HERITAGE

In historical accounts of mass communication research, the term *qualitative content analysis* is sometimes linked with the name of Siegfried Kracauer, the German sociologist and cultural critic who moved to the USA as a refugee in the late 1930s and later established himself as an important film theorist in the 1940s and 1950s. Kracauer may not have been the first to use the term, but he did indeed write what may be regarded as the manifesto of qualitative content analysis. In "The challenge of qualitative content analysis" (1953), Kracauer dealt a severe blow to the type of quantitative content analysis practiced by many contemporary mass communication researchers, and instead made a plea for qualitative, hermeneutic, or humanistic procedures. While the article is rooted in the author's own analytical and political experiences in the context of the Frankfurt School and in the works of fellow refugees such as Theodor Adorno and Leo Lowenthal, there is a clear continuity of Kracauer's argument with later and current debates on the relevance of qualitative approaches to media content. Thus, the article offers a useful framework for considering some general principles and issues of textual analysis of fictional media content.

Taking as his point of departure Bernard Berelson's classic *Content Analysis in Communication Research* (1952), Kracauer argued that the proposed quantitative strategies for determining the content or meaning of media messages are, if not useless, then certainly not as objective and reliable as suggested by Berelson and others. Indeed, quantitative studies may only serve as a supplement to qualitative analyses. According to Kracauer, the inadequacy of quantitative analyses stems from the methods themselves: when trying to establish the meaning of texts by breaking them down into quantifiable units (words, expressions, statements, etc.), analysts in fact destroy the very object they are supposed to be studying, since the atomistic character of the resulting data precludes a relevant examination of the relations within each text as a meaningful whole. Though, in quantitative research, the textual units are often rated with reference to various graded scales, still the initial segmentation of the text, the choice of scales, as well as the rating of textual units tend to be based on tacit categories of a fairly primitive kind, which, furthermore, originate outside the text. In Kracauer's (1953: 637) words, the categories are "opinion-laden short cuts" to analysis.

By contrast, Kracauer's central argument is that the content of a text must be conceived as *a meaningful whole*, and hence that analysis necessarily involves an act of interpretation which, like other readings, is based on specific assumptions to be made explicit in the course of analysis:

> Documents which are not simply agglomerations of facts partici-
> pate in the process of living, and every word in them vibrates with
> the intentions in which they originate and simultaneously fore-
> shadows the indefinite effects they may produce. Their content is
> no longer their content if it is detached from the texture of
> intimations and implications to which it belongs and taken liter-
> ally; it exists only with and within this texture – a still fragmentary
> manifestation of life, which depends upon response to evolve its
> properties. Most communications are not so much fixed entities
> as ambivalent challenges. They challenge the reader or the ana-
> lyst to absorb them and react to them. Only in approaching these
> wholes with his whole being will the analyst be able both to
> discover and determine their meaning – or one of their meanings
> – and thus help them to fulfill themselves.
>
> (Kracauer, 1953: 641)

The text, then, should not be regarded as a closed, segmented object with determinate, composite meanings, but rather as an indeterminate field of meaning in which intentions and possible effects intersect. The task of the analyst is to bring out the whole range of possible meanings, not least the "hidden" message of the text.

The distinction between manifest and latent, or surface and deep, meanings is well known from the humanistic tradition of textual interpretation (see Chapter 1 in this volume); for Kracauer, qualitative content analysis is synonymous with exegesis. The humanistic tradition, specifically the German *Geistesgeschichte*, receives a characteristic inflection in Kracauer and other representatives of the Frankfurt School. Even while media texts are thought of as complex and indeterminate, they are also said to be historically determined to the extent that they express the general ideological trends (*Zeitgeist*) of a given period, which minimizes the danger of "subjective" misinterpretations. Crucially, following the knowledge interests of the Frankfurt School, the deciphering of latent meanings through qualitative content analysis implies a deconstruction of ideology and a critique of its social origins with a view to political action.

Like other early qualitative content analysts, Kracauer did not offer any systematic methodology or approach. Studies of film, popular fiction, news, and some other genres relied on procedures from traditional literary analysis of canonical works, offering interpretations or "readings" of media (and not very "close" readings) (see Kracauer, 1947 and 1974 on film; Kracauer, 1963 on bestsellers; Lowenthal, 1961 on popular literature; also the overviews in Jay, 1973, and Negt, 1980). Compared to research on a small number of literary "masterpieces," modern media texts posed problems of both heterogeneity and sheer quantity. However, during the 1950s and 1960s more adequate tools of analysis were being developed, particularly within general semiology or semiotics, which promised to solve both these problems. This development calls for a brief overview of previous research in the next section. Next, some specific examples of studies of media texts are presented in order to illustrate the procedures of qualitative content analysis. In conclusion, this chapter discusses the continued relevance and possible integration of literary analysis in mass communication research.

THE SEMIOLOGICAL HERITAGE

In founding European semiology, Ferdinand de Saussure had made a key distinction between the manifest uses of language (*parole*) and its latent, underlying system (*langue*) (see the survey on structuralism and semiology in Chapter 1). Semiology was to become a science of sign systems and their social uses, focusing on the rule-governed, transindividual aspects of concrete signifying practices. In a later introduction to the first major collection of semiological analyses, the French theorist Roland Barthes put special emphasis on the mass media as modern signifying practices, and suggested that sign systems also operate behind the various "images, gestures, melodic sounds, objects, and complexes of those substances to be found in rituals, ceremonies, or public spectacles" (Barthes, 1964: 1). (The rise of mass communication itself may, in part, explain the development of a systemic, semiological mode of analysis. See the Introduction to this Handbook.) Mass-communicated messages may be experienced in immediate terms as an immensely differentiated complex of signs. But, in fact, the signs can be broken down analytically so as to capture the latent systems which generate the variety. Behind the *parole* of media texts lies a *langue* or a set of semantic elements and syntactical rules – a code which governs the production of meaning through media. For text-analytical purposes, this model suggests that the analyst will be able to reconstruct such latent codes, just like a person who has never played chess before would be able to reconstruct the rules underlying the infinite number of possible games by attentively following a finite number of concrete games.

The most rigorous formulation of guidelines for such an analysis is Roland Barthes' *Elements of Semiology* (1984c). Semiological analysis, according to Barthes, should establish the "synchronic" state of a given signifying system, thus excluding considerations of how this system has developed historically, in the "diachronic" dimension. Furthermore, the analysis should examine a corpus of signifying objects from the point of view of their immanent meaning, leaving out or only later introducing "other determining factors of these objects (whether psychological, sociological or physical)" (Barthes, 1984c: 95). With *The Fashion System* (1983), a meticulous study of texts from major French fashion magazines during one year, Barthes himself delivered an example of a synchronic analysis of this kind. However, the study also demonstrates one side-effect of working with such a fixed perspective of texts. While producing an extremely precise description of one *langue*, unless it is interpreted with reference to relevant historical, social, economic, psychological, and other contexts, the analysis remains "formal," as formal, in some respects, as the quantitative approaches being replaced.

Early semiology, as exemplified by Barthes' work, generally argues that the emphasis given to the "closure" of signifying objects around *particular* meanings was only an analytical strategy and a preliminary solution made necessary by the unfinished state of the general theory. Yet, the implicit argument frequently is that this formal, closed analysis is sufficient, so that one may proceed directly from the textual structures to consider their external, socio-historical determinations as well as their possible ideological effects. The underlying assumption is that the conceptual meanings (signifieds) of the text are relatively unified or homogeneous. In some cases, such homogeneity is ascribed to the industrial, standardized character of mass media production (see, for example, Eco, 1976: 13). More often, however, the argument is premised on a particular conception of the relationship between texts and *ideology*. Again, Roland Barthes' work provides an illuminating example.

In *Mythologies* (1973) Barthes analysed a variety of everyday phenomena (advertisements, popular films, sports events, etc.) and showed that they hold two kinds of meaning: one which is immediately understood, and another which is "carried" by the first meaning. To exemplify, the image of a black soldier saluting the French flag on the front page of *Paris Match*, on the one hand, means just that: "black," "soldier," "military salute," and so forth. On the other hand, this, as it were, "natural" meaning is reappropriated in the production of a "cultural" or, to be precise, "ideological" message. When read within its sociohistorical context of consensual concepts and values, the *Paris Match* cover becomes a sign of "French imperialism."

In later works, Barthes used the linguistic terms *denotation* and *connotation* to refer respectively to the "natural" and "ideological" meaning of a text. Emphasizing the ideological character of connotation even further, he argued, in "Rhetoric of the image" (1984a), that, even while texts may vary in terms of their signifiers, connotation

> holds all its signifieds in common: the same signifieds are to be found in the written press, the image or the actor's gestures. . . . This common domain of the signifieds of connotation is that of ideology, which cannot but be single for a given society and history, no matter what signifiers of connotation it may use.
>
> (Barthes, 1984a: 49)

In early semiology, then, this notion of a single ideology is the implicit reason for claiming that the analysis of media messages is a critical practice, in spite of the exclusion of historical and social circumstances.

In summary, there are striking parallels between the semiological heritage and the critical heritage of Kracauer and the Frankfurt School, both regarding the assumed homogeneity or closure of media content around one ideology and regarding the status of qualitative content analysis as social critique. At the same time, the parallels suggest that this may be a fairly common understanding of the relations between text, ideology, and society, rather than the consequence of the specific theoretical frameworks. Moving beyond the notion of ideological homogeneity to a differentiated conception of ideologies and social communication systems, later semiological analyses have proved their relevance as forms of social understanding and critique.

FROM SEMIOLOGY TO NARRATOLOGY

Since the mid-1960s, narratology (the study of narratives) has been one of the most fertile fields of semiological research. Reworking traditional literary theory and drawing on Russian Formalism, French scholars such as Barthes, Genette, Todorov, and others developed a set of concepts and analytical procedures which became a major source of inspiration for qualitative media studies (for an overview of narratology, see Barthes, 1984b, and Chatman, 1983).

The case of Bond

One particularly instructive example of narratology as applied to media contents is Umberto Eco's study of Ian Fleming's bestselling novels about secret agent James Bond, "Narrative structures in Fleming" (1987b). Eco's main concern, again, is with *langue*, in this case the narrative system behind the individual novels. At one point, he compares a Bond novel to "a game of football in which we know beforehand the place, the numbers and personalities of the players, the rules of the game, and the fact that everything will take place within the area of the great pitch" (p. 160), adding that in this particular case even the result of the game is known beforehand.

More generally, Eco regards the ten Bond novels as the work of "a machine that functions basically on a set of precise units governed by rigorous combinational rules" (p. 146). The narrative *units* are described as a series of oppositions. First, a limited number of central, opposed characters with fixed features and spheres of action appear in all novels, constituting a set of narrative *agents* (for example, Hero/Villain). Second, a set of basic *values* is the background on which these agents act. In establishing the *combinational rules* of the narrative units, Eco employs a procedure inspired by the Russian Formalist Vladimir Propp's (1958) influential study of the fairy-tale. Using the main actions and events of the novels and their causal connections as his elements, Eco breaks down the narrative of each novel into a string of narrative "moves," showing that not only do the same types of action appear in each novel, but they also appear in the same order, with only minor modifications. Each novel, accordingly, may be said to represent a variation of a single "archetypical" narrative, which Eco, with a touch of irony, summarizes as "Bond moves and mates in eight moves" (p. 156). Whereas the underlying narrative system is established by reducing the richness and variety found at the textual surface, the resulting deep structure or "archetype" does not imply reductionism. The novels are actualizations of this organizational framework, which, among other things, is what the reading public presumably expect from a Bond novel. Moreover, Eco later in the study examines the surface features in some detailed stylistic analyses.

Still, Eco's discussion of the (ideological) message of the Bond novels is premised on their system or deep structure. In opposition to earlier conceptions of ideology within semiology, however, his argument is that such texts do "entail ideological positions, but these do not derive so much from the structured contents as from the way of structuring them" (p. 161). The opposing values which are put into play by Fleming's narrative machine are often political or racist stereotypes, and do as such carry ideological implications. But the point is that while the specific ideological message may vary according to its historical context, the deep structure of opposing values is permanent: "If Fleming is a reactionary at all, it is not because he identifies the figure of 'evil' with a Russian or a Jew. He is a reactionary because he makes use of stock figures" (p. 162). Perhaps, then, the structure is the effect.

Media and myths

Also in terms of its methodology, Eco's study differs radically from traditional textual analysis. Exegesis has been replaced by a systematic approach identifying fundamental narrative structures. Furthermore, compared to previous semiological work, the analysis of signifying structures here serves as the point of departure for an interpretation of the connections between the texts and their social and historical context.

Later narratological studies have elaborated this relationship between textual structure and social context within the conceptual framework of Claude Lévi-Strauss, the French anthropologist. According to Lévi-Strauss (1967), the myths circulating in "primitive" societies may be regarded as conceptual tools by which people classify and interpret their everyday experiences in an attempt to solve or explain the conflicts which arise from the very same experiences. Thus, myth is not a direct statement or "expression" of the ideologies or worldviews that are dominant in a given society, but the means or medium of a specific ritual and symbolic interaction between individuals and society. A similar role is played by media in modern, industrialized societies.

A large number of media studies have relied on a narratological methodology as exemplified by Eco.and on a Lévi-Straussian framework of interpretation. One example is Will Wright's work on Western movies. In *Six Guns and Society* (1975), he not only shows that most Westerns hold a common archetypal or mythical structure, but further demonstrates that this structure articulates a particular set of norms and principles stemming from social institutions and serving to order social life in general (for a similar analysis of the Western, see Cawelti, 1970). The viewing of Westerns, then, can be understood as a ritual action serving to reinforce rather than to challenge dominant American social beliefs. Silverstone (1981) and Fiske and Hartley (1978) have carried this argument even further: in analyses of the "mythological" structures underlying major television genres, they argue that the television medium itself, being a central institution of modern society, has taken over the integrative and socializing functions performed by the storyteller in oral societies.

GENRE: A MEDIUM LEVEL OF ANALYSIS

The rejection of quantitative methods by early proponents of qualitative content analysis had left unsolved the very problem that these methods were meant to address – the quantity and heterogeneity of media texts communicating through verbal language, fixed and moving images, sound, music, and so on. One practical way of solving the problem was, and still is for some purposes, to analyse what are arguably significant examples from a larger corpus of texts. However, narratological studies, as indicated, may provide a more satisfactory solution. Large groups of texts can in fact be broken down into their basic signifying components and structures by means of qualitative procedures – without breaking up the text as a meaningful whole. Previous studies further demonstrate that such procedures can be applied to texts carried by different media.

An important product of these structural and systemic approaches has been a new understanding of textual *genres* (for an overview of recent discussions, see Feuer, 1987). According to traditional literary theory, a genre is a system of aesthetic or textual conventions. In the semiological terminology, however, a genre may be studied as a latent *langue* governing the production of individual works. Further, in a Lévi-Straussian perspective, genre may be regarded as a "mythical" structure serving to interpret social conflicts to the audience in ritual or symbolic terms. Specifically, genres may hence be said to function "ideologically" in the sense that they reproduce and reinforce beliefs of how social reality is (and should be) structured. The studies of Westerns by Wright (1975) and Cawelti (1970) are examples of genre analysis in this social perspective. Further examples are Altman (1987) on Hollywood musicals, Cawelti (1976) on crime, adventure, and melodrama in popular literature, Schatz (1981) on major Hollywood genres, and Feuer (1987) on television situation comedies. (See also Chapter 1 in this volume on genre.)

The introduction of genre as a "medium level" of analysis makes possible a reconceptualization of the relationship between text and ideology, which serves to differentiate the positions of early qualitative content analysis and early semiology. While the media in general can be said to function "ideologically" in as much as their texts carry norms and values, they neither express nor convey a single ideology. Instead, the various genres imply particular, partial versions of social reality; they also address different audiences and presumably may mean different things to different people. A conclusion emerging from recent work is that textual analysis in itself is not a sufficient basis for characterizing the interaction between texts and audiences. This has entailed a shifting of the analytical emphasis in qualitative content analysis during the last two decades.

FROM TEXT TO RECEPTION

There are at least three bodies of research indicating a general reorientation of qualitative content analysis. First, one major tendency has been a displacement of the analytical focus from *langue* to *parole*, and from the level of signifieds or conceptual content to that of the signifiers, emphasizing now the specificity, materiality, and concrete uses of signs in mass communication as a social practice. This tendency is evidenced, for instance, in a number of "close readings" of classic Hollywood films (see studies presented in the British journal *Screen* in the 1970s and 1980s; also Bellour, 1986, and Heath, 1981). These readings focus on individual films and characterize their meaning not as a fixed structure, but as a process which serves to transform the *langue* or generic codes of cinema into a specific discourse, an instance of *parole* emerging at the precise moment when the images are seen to proceed across the screen. Significantly, these studies pay special attention to any differences of how meanings are articulated through these moving images, as opposed to, for example, verbal, written language. Even though such analyses focus on a quite limited material, the ambition has been to use the analysis of sample films for the broader study and interpretation of how the cinema audience may have "read," and currently read, Hollywood films of the classic era.

A related perspective is found in a second body of works studying what is termed *enunciation* – the specific modes in which cinematic and other texts address their audience. The assumption is that such modes of address serve to "situate" the addressee in a particular position *vis-à-vis* the media message. Thus, enunciation is said to play a crucial role in the very structuring of media content and of the form in which it is understood. Drawing on so-called reception theories as developed in recent European literary studies, much of this research examines the general techniques through which texts work to direct the recipient's attention and understanding (for a general overview of reception theory, see Eco, 1987a; also Chapter 7 in this volume). The application of reception theory to media studies, further, is discussed by Allen (1987), who also includes analyses of different types of television programs from a reception perspective. Other work in this tradition examines the modes of address which are specific to particular media or genres (see Bordwell, 1985 on film, and Morse, 1985 on popular television genres). Some of the most interesting studies in this area approach the problematic of reception from a broadly feminist perspective. Arguing that the principal modes of address are biased in terms of gender – especially that the structuring of content which is characteristic of most media and genres presupposes a male audience – these studies have served to differentiate further the notion of ideology and of the nature of ideological impact in qualitative content analysis. The seminal work remains Mulvey's (1986) analysis of the implicit spectator in classic Hollywood films, but a great deal of later research has developed this perspective in concrete analyses (for an overview, see Kaplan, 1987).

The third body of research shifts also the empirical focus of the analyses from text to *audience*. In the first two groups of studies, the analysis of textual features normally is used to infer certain general conclusions of how texts and genres are read or assimilated by the audience. The "reader" is, in a sense, constructed from within a textual–theoretical perspective, being regarded as an implicit position in the text which serves to frame the reading process, and which the reader presumably occupies in order to make sense of the text. However, much recent mass communication research (see Chapters 7 and 8 in this volume) has challenged this argument, and has been devoted to the study of actual readers and reading processes in a qualitative perspective. Whereas these studies rely mainly on such methodologies as participant observation and varieties of interviewing, they frequently include qualitative content analyses as part of their design. The assumption is that textual analysis, first, can provide guidelines for interviews with empirical readers about texts, and, second, that textual analysis, as applied to both the media texts and interview texts, may serve as a general approach to interpreting and explaining empirical readings.

One interesting example of this combination of textual analysis and qualitative audience research is Janice Radway's (1984) study of the genre of "romance" in popular literature. Basing her study on a series of group interviews, Radway provides a detailed description of how a specific group of American female readers respond to and make use of the group of novels published as "Harlequin Romances." In the course of the interviews, it turned out that most of the women made a spontaneous distinction between "ideal" and "failed" romances, a fact which prompted Radway to select a group of novels in each category for closer examination. Analysing the novels from a narratological point of view, she demonstrates that what the women intuitively experienced as "ideal" romances were in fact a type of novel which had been built on a specific narrative structure consisting of thirteen major events or actions that were carried out by a limited set of agents endowed with a limited set of features. Further, this sequence of events enacts a movement from an initial situation in which the heroine suffers a social and emotional loss, to a final situation in which she is reintegrated into society and achieves emotional fulfillment. This textual analysis, in turn, led Radway to a renewed examination of how her empirical readers responded in the interviews to such "ideal" texts. Ultimately, Radway (1984) is able to establish a plausible connection between the conflicts that are solved in the novels by textual or narrative transformation, and those real social and emotional conflicts which dominate the lives of their female readers.

From one point of view, Radway's content analyses may be said to lie squarely within the tradition of semiological and other qualitative textual analysis, since she employs many of the analytical procedures developed from the 1960s. Indeed, her general conclusions regarding the social functions of texts for their audiences do not differ substantially from those of most genre studies in the Lévi-Straussian tradition. Nevertheless, Radway's account of the relationship between text and audience is more specific and differentiated because of the dual strategy of analysis. While the interviews with readers point to groups of texts and to discursive details which deserve closer examination, the textual analysis returns the analyst to a reinterpretation of the readers' interview statements and, further, to theorizing on the social functions of texts. A social theory of communication may be substantiated, above all, by further research which simultaneously considers media texts and audiences.

CONCLUSION

Qualitative content studies of the last few decades have served to change or differentiate many of the early assumptions in the area. The outcome is a growing awareness of the complexity of mass communication – a realization that media texts are not carriers of single meanings, let alone a single, dominant ideology; that their "content" is carried, in part, by the mode of address; and that audiences are active in interpreting media, genres, and texts. One of the most important consequences of this development has been the rise of reception studies, or audience-cum-content analysis.

At the same time, qualitative content analysis continues to play a major role in contemporary media studies, perhaps less as an end in itself than as a constituent of other qualitative procedures. As suggested by, for example, Radway's (1984) work, the detailed study of media messages provides the researcher with a framework for further studying their reception, and textual analysis similarly represents a key method for examining and interpreting interviews, observation protocols, and other empirical "data." The insights of textual studies may help to remind other qualitative researchers that while data sets hold information, they are, first and foremost, texts which must be analysed and interpreted to yield that information. If the media of qualitative research are language and texts, then various forms of textual and discourse analysis are necessary for several areas of mass communication and several levels of inquiry (see also Chapters 1 and 5 in this volume).

Qualitative content analysis also remains an area of inquiry in its own right which is important for the understanding of mass communication as a social and cultural phenomenon. To conclude, a few remarks, pertaining also to the relationship between theory and methodology, may suggest directions for further content studies.

The ambition of semiology, which has been the conceptual framework of this area since the 1960s, has been to develop concepts and models for the study of signs and sign systems *in general*. Mass communication researchers have been able to benefit from advances in semiology that are relevant for studies across the whole spectrum of media. Importantly, there has been a close relationship between theoretical and practical, analytical studies, so that concrete analytical insights have informed further theoretical work.

More recently, research has emphasized the *specificity* of different media, and the study of visual communication has emerged as the central and most promising aspect of content analysis. Studies have demonstrated that a better theoretical understanding of how meaning is produced by (sequences of) images, as opposed to written texts, is a necessary precondition for the detailed analysis of heterogeneous visual media messages and their reception (see, for example, Bordwell, 1985; also Chapter 1 in this volume on visual communication). In view also of the importance of visual media in contemporary society, the study of visual communication should have a central position in future qualitative content analysis. Further research on visual media contents, then, may contribute both to the development of a semiotic theory of different types of media texts and to an understanding of their significance for social contexts.

Chapter 7

Media audiences
Reception analysis: mass communication as the social production of meaning

Klaus Bruhn Jensen

INTRODUCTION

To say that reception analysis draws its theory from the humanities and its methodology from the social sciences is a helpful overstatement introducing this chapter's argument. The humanities, first, have contributed the conception of mass communication as a cultural practice producing and circulating meaning in social contexts. The social sciences, next, have informed the use of particular modes of empirical inquiry into the process of interaction between mass-mediated messages and their audiences. It is the convergence of these roots, albeit in different forms, which may explain the emergence of a new form of audience research during the 1980s that represents an emphatic articulation of the qualitative turn.

One of the main premises of reception analysis has been that audience research, in order to construct a valid account of the reception, uses, and impact of media, must become audience-cum-content analysis. Whereas Chapters 1 and 2 of this volume respectively document the attention given by the humanities to the interpretation of textual contents, and by the social sciences to the cognitive and behavioral impact of contents, traditionally the two research enterprises have in practice been segregated. By contrast, reception analysis submits that texts and their recipients are complementary elements of one area of inquiry which thus addresses both the discursive and the social aspects of communication. In two words, reception analysis assumes that there can be no "effect" without "meaning."

In elaborating these programmatic statements, this chapter briefly traces the roots of recent audience studies in fields as diverse as literary criticism, philosophy of language, and social theory. The rise of reception analysis is characterized in the context of other forms of audience research, and some preliminary findings regarding specific decodings, of particular genres of communication and by particular audience groups, are reported. (This chapter emphasizes studies of the reception of particular media discourses, which normally employ interviewing, whereas Chapter 8 addresses ethnographic approaches to the uses of media in different contexts.) The section on methodology emphasizes the development of a systematic, comparative analysis of audience discourses and media discourses. The case study examines the reception of television news; it found major differences between the journalists' news and the viewers' news, thus illustrating the interpretive scope also of a "realistic," factual genre. In conclusion, the radical implications of reception analysis, both for communication theory and for a politics of mass communication, are assessed.

THE SHORT HISTORY OF RECEPTION ANALYSIS

The history of reception analysis is, indeed, short, but turbulent because of its profound theoretical and political implications. It is commonly acknowledged that the pathbreaking work of Dave Morley (1980), while emerging from the British cultural studies tradition, summed up a long prehistory that had pitted two conceptions of communication against each other. The first broadly conceived school is associated with the logos tradition of the *humanities* (see Chapter 1), and has approached *texts* as the locus of meaning to be extracted by (more or less) competent readers through a hermeneutic act. Though similar in certain respects to the ritual view of communication (Carey, 1989: 18), work in this tradition has tended to focus its analysis around the text itself rather than its cultural uses. Most important, the tradition as applied to mass media has implied a view of media effects as acting directly and powerfully on audiences. The strong version of this position may be found in the cultural criticism of the Frankfurt School (Adorno and Horkheimer, 1977). Another influential version of text-centrism came from film theory, particularly that associated with the journal *Screen* in the 1970s, which, in assuming powerful, subconscious effects, collapsed the discursive subject anticipated by the text with the concrete social subject interpreting the text.

The second research tradition that has been rearticulated by reception analysis is the so-called dominant paradigm (Gitlin, 1978) of *social science* research. Rejecting the transmission model of some early scholarship on effects, in part because the quantitative evidence suggested rather limited effects of media despite their manifest social significance (Katz and Lazarsfeld, 1955; Klapper, 1960), much work in this tradition had turned to a *uses-and-gratifications* approach, asking now what individual users do with the media rather than vice versa (Blumler and Katz, 1974; Rosengren *et al.*, 1985). However, following this conceptual advance, most studies have remained within the dominant tradition, being functionalist in theory, quantitativist in methodology, and consensualist in politics.

The reconstructions of audience studies imply a new perspective on the social and discursive aspects of communication theory (Jensen, 1991). In response to the social-scientific tradition, reception analysis notes that any study of media experience and impact, whether quantitative or qualitative, must be based in a theory of representation, genre, and discourse that goes beyond the operationalization of semantic categories and scales. In response to humanistic textual studies, reception analysis suggests that both the audiences and contexts of mass communication need to be examined as socially specific, empirical objects of analysis. The common denominator for the dual social and discursive perspective on communication, then, becomes the social production of meaning. Much theoretical and empirical work has specified this perspective with reference to the asynchronous processes of encoding and decoding media content (Hall, 1973). At each point of the communicative process there is a scope of indetermination which allows for several potential meanings and impacts to be enacted. Also reception is a social act that serves to negotiate the definition of social reality in the context of broad cultural and communicative practices.

The empirical findings on reception so far imply an important theoretical distinction between potential and actualized meanings, concepts which have been developed in literary criticism and semiotics, not least within German reception aesthetics (for a survey, see Holub, 1984; also Suleiman and Crosman, 1980; Tompkins, 1980). The prevalence of readings that differ from the relatively few readings anticipated by media professionals or textual scholars, points both to the *polysemy* of media discourses and to the existence of quite different interpretive strategies that are applied to the same discourse by different audiences. Such interpretive communities (Fish, 1979), or, better, *interpretive repertoires* (see Chapter 1 in this volume), relying on specific contextualized frames of cognitive and affective understanding, appear to crisscross, to a degree, standard socioeconomic audience categories, hence mediating the further impact of media in ways that are only beginning to be explored in empirical research. Also in cases where socioeconomic and interpretive categories can be seen to denote similar groups, it seems clear that a discursive or interpretive conception of reception is a necessary constituent of a comprehensive theory of the audience.

While being a young area of inquiry, the new qualitative audience research produced several summary volumes in the late 1980s (Jensen, 1986; Lindlof, 1987; Lull, 1988a; Seiter *et al.*, 1989a). Early studies had focused on factual genres, particularly news (see especially Lewis, 1985; Morley, 1980), and had found a variety of alternative or oppositional decodings, depending on the audience's class and other socioeconomic background, of what appeared to be the (ideologically) "preferred" reading (Hall, 1973). Other work noted that the very mode of address of the news genre carries ideological implications about the substantive role of news and its respondents in political processes (Jensen, 1990a; see also Morley, 1981, on genre). A second body of research shifted the focus from ideology in a political sense to the question of pleasure, asking how the media appeal to recipients as gendered individuals. In particular, "feminine" genres such as the various subtypes of soap opera (Ang, 1985; Hobson, 1982) and romance novels (Radway, 1984) were seen to carry use value, indeed an emancipatory potential for audiences in their family and other social contexts. Also historical and theoretical psychoanalytic work has addressed the relationship between media use and (gendered) identities (de Lauretis, 1984; Modleski, 1984). A further, more heterogeneous group of studies have examined variations in reception with reference to the ethnic, cultural, and subcultural contexts of audiences (e.g. Liebes and Katz, 1990; Lull, 1988a), identifying mass communication as an important resource within other cultural practices. Finally, a few studies have attempted to capture the specific experiential qualities of particular media, for example the difference between film and TV reception (Ellis, 1982), as well as the interrelatedness – intertextuality – of contemporary media as whole media environments (see Bennett and Woollacott, 1987; for a survey, see Jensen, forthcoming). It may be added that similar, qualitative as well as quantitative studies that are of relevance for reception analysis have been undertaken in political science (Graber, 1984) and social psychology (Livingstone, 1990), witnessing an interdisciplinary convergence also in the methods employed.

METHODOLOGIES OF RECEPTION

Whereas other forms of communication research have proposed to integrate the study of contents and audiences, notably in work on agenda setting (McCombs and Shaw, 1972) and cultural indicators (Gerbner and Gross, 1976), reception analysis has made a new departure in studying in depth the actual processes through which media discourses are assimilated to the discourses and cultural practices of audiences. A summary definition of reception methodologies may refer to a comparative textual analysis of media discourses and audience discourses, whose results are interpreted with emphatic reference to context, both the historical as well as cultural setting and the "con-text" of other media contents. Three main elements of this definition may be explicated in terms of the collection, analysis, and interpretation of reception data.

First, the *collection* or generation of data centers on the audience side. Media discourses are more readily accessible in practice, notwithstanding the real problems of copyright and archiving in historical research (see Chapter 10 in this volume). The approaches to audience discourses coincide with the general techniques listed in Table 1.1 on page 32: interviewing (of individuals or groups); observation (with varying degrees of participation by researchers); and textual criticism (of historical sources or other texts). Further materials may include letters (Ang, 1985), classroom interaction and student productions (Masterman, 1985), and records of group encounter sessions (Jensen, 1990b). The present chapter focuses on interviewing; however, it should be stressed that textual criticism or discourse analysis remains a key constituent of reception methodologies, not just for the analysis of interviews and other current discourses, but also for the diachronic study of media-related discourses in a historical perspective (see further Chapter 8 on observation and ethnography). Each of these methods, of course, poses classic problems of validity and reliability that have begun to be addressed in the context of reception analysis (Höijer, 1990; Jensen, 1989; also Kirk and Miller, 1986).

Second, the *analysis* of interviews and other audience discourses draws on techniques and models from linguistics and literary criticism. After some early discussions in the area had questioned an implicit, sometimes impressionistic approach to extracting striking quotations from hundreds of pages of transcripts, recent work has outlined more explicit, systematic approaches to qualitative audience research as a discursive practice. This is evidenced both in attempts to establish a framework for cumulative studies (Liebes and Katz, 1990) and in analyses of the theoretical status of audience discourses (Jensen, 1989; Morley, 1981). Whereas the general principles and relevance of discourse analysis are laid out in Chapter 1 (see also Chapter 5 for an application to news discourse), here it should be emphasized that, beyond documenting a respondent's line of thought and argument, discourse analysis offers a powerful tool for evaluating the interaction between interviewer and respondent. Similarly, discourse analysis offers a set of linguistic criteria for assessing the intersubjectivity of later interpretations, which makes possible reflection and discussion of disagreements, rather than a simple measure of intercoder agreement.

Third, then, reception studies make no absolute distinction between the analysis and *interpretation* of audience experience of media. While moving beyond the vague notion of "reading" as aesthetic appreciation, reception analysis insists that, for most research purposes, an operationalization of categories that establishes aggregated, decontextualized sets of "data" which only subsequently are interpreted as "findings," does not represent a valid approach to meaning as produced by audiences. Instead, the meaning of the constitutive elements of audience discourses should be interpreted with constant reference to context, both that of the media discourses in question and the broad social context of historical and psychoanalytic circumstances. The steps of such an analysis-cum-interpretation may be illustrated by a concrete case.

CASE: THE VIEWERS' TV NEWS

News is presumably an important *resource* for the political awareness and action of the audience–public. It is for this reason, in part, that the issue of representational accuracy and the problem of propaganda have been debated so fiercely at different historical times and in different cultural settings. However, it is not clear that the news media as currently organized and operated facilitate any significant participation by the public in political processes. Whereas much previous research has examined news with reference to its institutional origins, the biases of its contents, and its impact in terms of basic recall of information or voting decisions (for a survey, see Jensen, 1986, Ch. 6), drawing on the reconceptualization of audience research it becomes possible to examine whether the audience's reception of news items confers any political relevance on the information received. This is by and large an empirical question, and the answer has far-reaching political and ideological implications.

Design. The study summarized here examined viewers' decoding and evaluation of Danish television news (see Jensen, 1988). Television, in Denmark and several other countries, over the last two decades has grown to become a cultural common denominator or a forum (Newcomb and Hirsch, 1984) for consideration of national and international political issues and events. Taking as the point of departure a randomly selected broadcast from the autumn of 1985 in what was still a one-channel public-service system, the study conducted thirty-three in-depth individual interviews about the program within a 24-hour cycle. The respondents, who had watched the program in their home and were subsequently interviewed there, had been selected by a polling firm with the aim of procuring a range of respondents from different age, sex, and socioeconomic groups and from different regions of the country. Though responses could not be considered representative of these groups in the population at large, the specific lines of reasoning can suggest differences in the modes of reception which may then be examined in further, qualitative as well as quantitative research.

The interviews followed a semi-structured guide, focusing on the ten stories of the program. In each case the respondent was asked to recount the subject matter of the story, which was identified by the interviewer with a cue word. Only then did the interviewer begin to probe for specific items of information, and in conclusion respondents were asked for their general assessment of the relevance, bias, and presentational form of each story and later of the program as a whole. Verbatim transcripts of all the interviews as well as of the news program were subjected to a linguistic discourse analysis.

Discourses of news. Leaving out here most of the discourse-analytical detail (see Jensen, 1988: 282–6), the present account focuses on the *themes* of news content and their reception. It is through reference to certain unitary themes that both journalists and viewers are able to arrive at a global understanding of a news story. One important conclusion of the study was that there may be major differences between the journalists' and the viewers' themes referring to a given story. Journalists, in order to establish a "peg" or coordinating principle in a story, tend to draw on a relatively fixed repertoire of issues, events, and actors. Much previous research has shown how a particular conception of news thus grows out of specific journalistic practices and criteria (see Gans, 1979; Golding and Elliott, 1979; Tuchman, 1978 and in this volume). The journalistic pegs are comparable to the notion of theme in linguistics, and were established in a discourse analysis of the news content. The list of ten stories in the broadcast studied, as characterized in standard journalistic terms (Table 7.1), suggests the kinds of political and economic themes (apart from a final, "cultural" feature) that are carried by the agents, issues, and events reported in the news.

Table 7.1 The journalists' news stories

Item number	Characterization
1	Nuclear test by France at Mururoa
2	Change in environmental policy (DK)
3	Theory vs practice in medical training (DK)
4	New plant for recycling paper (DK)
5	East–West relations
6	State of emergency in Argentina
7	Exchange of hostages in El Salvador
8	Business practices of undertakers (DK)
9	The Royal Mint moves abroad (DK)
10	Medieval ballads reinterpreted (DK)

Note: DK indicates a domestic story.

In this context, it is of special interest to note the potential variation of themes in two stories which may serve as examples. In the story about *El Salvador*, reporting an exchange of hostages between the government and the insurgents, it probably was of added news value from the journalistic perspective that one of the hostages was the president's daughter, whose release was depicted in the visuals. Thus, there were both political and personal dimensions to the story. Both these dimensions were in evidence in the decodings as themes, so that the respondents either emphasized that this was "an exchange of hostages," or they characterized the event as "a reunion" of family members. Most interesting, perhaps, is a third theme which some respondents identified, namely social privilege or class difference. Explaining how the exchange came about, one respondent noted that "when it's people high up, things can always be arranged." Here, a highly generalized theme of class difference serves to explain the concrete case by linking the personal level of one family's reunion with the political level of a national conflict over social privileges. Class difference may be a familiar aspect of viewers' daily life which, through reference to the news discourse, relates politics to the everyday.

A second, domestic story addressed a proposal by the Danish National Bank to move its production entity, *The Royal Mint*, abroad. Whereas statements on the concrete dispute by politicians, the National Bank, as well as an employee are included, respondents organize their interpretation around the two more general principles at stake in the dispute. The Mint may be seen as a private enterprise, which, unless it can operate most efficiently at home, should be allowed to move abroad. Or, the Mint may be treated as a public institution affiliated with the National Bank that is responsible for the stability of the national economy as a whole, and hence it should not be allowed to lay off workers and contribute to unemployment. It can be noted in passing that some viewers here engage in sophisticated reflection about issues of national economic theory, while others note the symbolism of surrendering the national currency to a foreign producer. Again, a third, highly generalized theme is introduced by some respondents who see the Mint, above all, as a source of jobs for its employees. For them, (un)employment, being a real threat to many viewers, becomes the focus of the story as received, even to the exclusion of the principles of economic policy:

> . . . it's terrible. They are closing down a place of work, you know, and moving because they want it to be cheaper, you know, and leaving a lot of people unemployed, and that seems crazy – that people who have been happy with their job for many years suddenly haven't got anything.

The themes of the two stories, El Salvador and The Royal Mint, are presented in Table 7.2.

Table 7.2 The viewers' news stories: two examples

Item	Themes
7 El Salvador	(a) Exchange of hostages
	(b) Family reunion
	(c) Social privileges: case
9 The Royal Mint	(a) Mint as private enterprise
	(b) Mint as public institution
	(c) Mint as source of jobs

Super themes. Both "unemployment" and "class" are examples of what will be called super themes. Table 7.3 notes the occurrence of five different super themes in the sample, and indicates their relevance for the ten news items. They may be conceptualized as interpretive procedures which are employed by the audience for the reconstruction of meaning in the news genre. In discourse-analytical terms, a super theme can be defined as a proposition entailed by a set of propositions summing up a news story (or another text) from the recipient's perspective, thus resembling the psychological schemata found by some other studies of news (Graber, 1984; van Dijk, 1988a; but see Crigler and Jensen, forthcoming, on distinctions). As such, super themes, rather than being structuring features of news as formulated by journalists, may be considered as characteristics of the very process of reception. In sum, super themes represent an example of how qualitative research, starting from the respondents' conceptual categories, may identify certain

Table 7.3 The super themes of news reception

Items	Super themes				
	War	Environment	Unemployment	Government role and cutbacks	Class
Nuclear test	×	×			
Environment		×	×	×	
Medical education				×	
Recycling		×	×	×	
East–West	×	×			
Argentina	×				×
El Salvador	×				×
Undertakers				×	
Royal Mint			×	×	
Ballads					×

general processes which are constitutive of mass communication. The systematic study of discursive structures of reception, accordingly, offers a promising approach to theory development in communication research.

The super themes also hold implications for politics and policy. The preliminary findings suggest that respondents with a relatively shorter education are more likely to rely exclusively on super themes in their understanding of news items, whereas respondents with a longer education may reproduce the political themes of the journalistic discourse on a concrete case alongside the super themes. For a *politics* of reception, then, it is important not to romanticize super themes and audience activity generally. On the one hand, super themes are useful mechanisms for understanding news content because they establish a meaningful relationship between the world of politics and the world of everyday life. On the other hand, the fact that some groups of viewers may be unable specifically to associate the generalized themes with the pros and cons of a particular political case is a real problem, not least since these viewers, in referring to super themes such as class, unemployment, and social cutbacks, begin to identify fundamental political and economic conflicts in society. Unless the news empowers the audience to reflect and act upon such conflicts, it falls short of the implied promise to provide a social resource in the form of politically applicable information. In this respect, in-depth studies like the present one can bring forward the audience's perspective on how well media institutions fulfill a public-service mission in the sphere of political information. Similarly, such studies can provide new insights into processes of communication and reception which are important for curriculum development as media literacy increasingly becomes a central element of modern education (see Masterman, 1985; also Chapter 12 in this volume).

For media *policy*, finally, qualitative research may also become increasingly significant. It can be mentioned here that the study was conducted jointly by the University of Copenhagen and the Media Research Department of the Danish Broadcasting Corporation, which at the time of the study operated the only national television channel in Denmark, being a public-service institution comparable to the BBC. Such studies appear to be of interest both for product development by media practitioners and for long-term planning of image or house style (Ellis, 1982: 219) by upper management. Indeed, at a time when new terrestrial and satellite television channels are being introduced in Denmark and elsewhere, research that examines the audience experience and uses of television content may be especially relevant for policy issues. An alternative concept of television news, employing super themes that are linked explicitly to specific political issues in a more integrated visual and verbal narrative, could provide meaningful information and hence could also have significant audience appeal in the more competitive media environment of the future. Reception analysis, thus, addresses a strategically important aspect of mass media at a time when these must legitimate themselves in relation to audiences by serving a complex, negotiated range of interests and needs. The negotiation and social construction of reception raise important issues both for the politics of communication and for further research.

PERSPECTIVES: RECEPTION IN CONTEXT

After a decade when reception analysis has developed new theoretical and methodological approaches to the field, at present there is a call for consolidation, both through more focused empirical projects and through reconsideration of the place of reception in the communication process as a whole. With respect to *further empirical research*, at least three types of endeavor suggest themselves. First, there is a need to build a cumulative research tradition of reception analysis, replicating as well as differentiating the relatively few and small studies so far. As part of this effort, it will be fruitful to undertake multimethod studies combining several forms of scholarship (qualitative and quantitative; theoretical, empirical, and historical), perhaps in research groups, since it is the field rather than the individual researcher that is interdisciplinary. The aim would be to consider concretely the complementarity of different modes of inquiry also at a meta-theoretical level, with reception serving as a test case that has implications for the field generally (Jensen and Rosengren, 1990).

Second, comparative studies across cultures lend themselves particularly well to qualitative, contextualized observation and interaction with audience respondents (Liebes and Katz, 1990; Lull, 1988a). It is far from well understood how the reception and everyday uses of mass communication enter into the specific social practices of different cultural and historical contexts. Qualitative methodologies, in the process, may also serve to assess the degree to which dominant research designs, most of which embody a specific form of Western rationality, apply meaningfully to the reception and impact of media in other cultures. Third, because mass media are increasingly interrelated, both institutionally and through their discursive forms, it will be important in the future to study the social contexts of media use as whole *media environments* (for a research survey and discussion of this development, see Jensen, forthcoming). The mass media exert whatever impact they have, not singly but in concert, in ways that require contextual and discursive modes of analysis. As the "what" (the object of analysis) of mass communication research and, perhaps, the "why" (the knowledge-interests) change, then so may the "how" (Lang and Lang, 1985).

Furthermore, reception analysis, in referring to the dual, social and discursive nature of communication, has identified an important area of further *theory development*. Beyond a conception of the social structures in which media and audiences are embedded, and of the sociocultural identity and subjectivity of media users, a comprehensive theory of communication requires a third element: namely, a theory of discourse which can account for the role of different media (print, aural, visual), genres, and other specific forms of representation in processes of reception and impact. Much theoretical work remains to be done on the specific interconnections between the social and discursive domains of analysis for a social semiotics of mass media to be realized (see Chapter 1).

In the end, politicians, programmers, and probably the public will want to know whether and how the mass media do have effects. Reception analysis, in accounting for the conditions and processes of meaning production, may offer part of the answer. In response to a recent trend in research which exults, echoing a postmodernist position, that media discourses are open or polysemic and may be opposed by audiences who thus become powerful cultural agents (see especially Fiske, 1987; for a critique, see Jensen, 1991), it is important to specify the social level at which such opposition may be enacted. One should recognize, of course, the general finding of reception analysis that audiences reconstruct the meaning of media discourses, to a degree asserting their opposition or difference in discursive terms. But, whether this discursive difference will make a social difference in terms of cognition or action depends crucially on the given historical and cultural context: the genres of communication and their implied social uses, the interpretive repertoires of the audience, and the social reality of institutions that persists outside of reception. The meaning of mass communication as received is constantly in question; so are its social implications. How discursive difference may become social difference is perhaps the key question for further theoretical as well as empirical work on the audience.

It may be surprising to learn in Table 7.3 that respondents associated the super theme of class with the story of Danish medieval ballads. To explain, the news text mentioned that the ballads were written by itinerant bards and not by noblemen, as had previously been thought. This was interpreted by several respondents as an indication of how class differences influence the way history is written. Like news and other stories, then, history may be seen as a construction. Whether this implies a reconstruction of history in the future by the audience–public, is indeed the question.

Chapter 8

Media audiences
Communication and context: ethnographic perspectives on the media audience

David Morley and Roger Silverstone

INTRODUCTION

We all watch television at different times, but with how much attention and with what degree of commitment, in relation to which types of programs and occasions? Only if these kinds of qualitative distinctions are established, can the aggregated statistical results of large-scale survey work be broken down into meaningful components. We need to focus on the complex ways in which television viewing is inextricably embedded in a whole range of everyday practices, and is itself partly constitutive of those practices (Scannell, 1988). We need to investigate context – the specific ways in which particular communications technologies come to acquire particular meanings and thus come to be used in different ways, for different purposes, by people in different types of households. We need to investigate television viewing in its "natural" settings.

The limitations of quantitative techniques for these purposes are by now well established (Ang, 1991; Morley, 1990). Statistical techniques are by their very nature disaggregating, inevitably isolating units of action from the contexts that make them meaningful. Audience measurement is not audience research (Wober, 1981). And, although statistical techniques can establish empirical connections between "facts" of different orders, such connections do not provide a basis for prediction or theory.

This chapter, accordingly, addresses the potential contribution to the study of media audiences offered by *ethnographic* methods of investigation with special reference to television. Traditionally associated with anthropology, these approaches may be defined as the analysis of multiply structured contexts of action, aiming to produce a rich descriptive and interpretive account of the lives and values of those subject to investigation. While, since Malinowski (1922), ethnographic approaches have depended, methodologically, on participant observation, the techniques have themselves developed as the settings in which they are applied have made new demands on research. (See also Chapter 7 in this volume on approaches to the reception of specific media discourses.)

We will argue that television viewing has to be understood within the structure and dynamics of just such a context of actions – the domestic environment. We will also argue that an anthropological perspective allows the researcher to focus on television viewing in the broader context of processes of both material and symbolic consumption. The objective of this kind of qualitative research is to develop a close understanding of the processes through which television and other communication and information technologies acquire meaning.

TELEVISION AND EVERYDAY LIFE: THE CONTEXT OF VIEWING

One of the most important advances in recent audience work has been the growing recognition of the importance of *the context of* reception, specifically, in the case of television, the domestic context. Despite frequent moral panics about television and the family, we still know very little about how families as distinct from individuals (who, after all, mostly live in families or households of some kind) interact with and use television in their everyday lives, engaging in rule-governed activity. As we have argued elsewhere (Morley and Silverstone, 1990), the household or family, as the basic unit of domestic consumption offers the most appropriate context for the naturalistic investigation of the consumption and production of televisual (and other) meanings. In common usage, "watching TV" is the ill-defined shorthand term for the multiplicity of situated practices and experiences in which TV audiencehood is embedded. Moreover, we already know, for example, that "pure" television viewing is a relatively rare occurrence. Thus, Gunter and Svennevig (1987: 12–13) quote surveys showing variously 50 and 64 per cent of viewers as reporting that they usually watch television while doing something else at the same time. Equally, having the set on, or the presence of people in front of the set can mean "a hundred different things" (Towler, 1986). In a similar vein, Bryce (1987) notes that "television viewing" is only "one possible label for a variety of family activities" (Bryce, 1987: 137).

Drawing on the work of Michel de Certeau (1984), Silverstone (1989: 77) has argued elsewhere that   ·

> television is everyday life. To study the one is at the same time to study the other. There are TV sets in almost every household in the western world. . . . Their texts and their images, their stories and their stars provide much of the conversational currency of our daily lives. TV has been much studied.
>
> Yet it is precisely this integration into the daily lives of those who watch it which has somehow slipped through the net of academic enquiry.

Our premise, therefore, is that the analysis of broadcasting must be reformulated to take into account its inscription within the routines of everyday life and the interweaving of domestic and public discourses, which calls for the use of qualitative techniques. Both Bausinger (1984) and Grossberg (1987) offer useful general insights into the ways in which media content is integrated into everyday communication practices in complex forms of interdiscursivity. In particular, Bausinger (1984) reminds us that our analysis needs to deal not with any given medium in isolation, but rather with the "media ensemble" of the household. Moreover, he notes, any given medium is rarely used with full concentration. The media, in general, are an integral part of the everyday, so that the process of viewing or reading (beyond the immediate moment of consumption) is extended into a longer process of conversation and social dialogue through which media materials are "digested."

Among previous empirical studies, Lindlof (1987) offers a fascinating collection of materials on media consumption from a naturalistic perspective (see in particular the articles by Bryce, Traudt and Lont, and Anderson). Brodie and Stoneman (1983) and Wolf *et al.* (1982), further, develop a contextualist perspective on television viewing within family interaction. Goodman (1983) develops a rules-based analysis of viewing from a "family systems" perspective derived from family therapy. Lull's (1980; 1988a) work on family viewing, similarly, follows a rules-based perspective, analysing viewing selection procedures and family communication patterns as part of a broad analysis of the social uses of television. From a feminist perspective, the work of Hobson (1982), Ang (1985),

Brunsdon (1981), Radway (1984), Seiter *et al.* (1989a), and Gray (1987) pursues the gendering of media consumption practices in relation to various forms of feminine subjectivity. Morley (1986) offers an analysis of gendered viewing practices and family dynamics, which, while not using strictly ethnographic techniques, begins to explore the context of family life within which viewing practices must be understood. In our present research (Morley and Silverstone, 1990; Silverstone *et al.*, 1989), repudiating technologically determinist arguments about the impact of new communication technologies on "society," the questions include how household structure and domestic culture affect the perceived salience of these technologies, how these technologies are domesticated by their users (Bryce, 1987), and how the uses of technologies are shaped by the exigencies of their "local" environment (Lindlof and Meyer, 1987; see also Lull, 1988a, for an analysis of cultural differences in international television viewing practices).

If the activity of television viewing is a *rule-governed* process,[1] the primary concern of the ethnographer becomes one of explicating the rules which govern and facilitate this process. As Anderson (1987a: 164) puts it, "family viewing, for example, is no more casual and spontaneous than the family dinner. It is accomplished by competent actors with great improvisational skill." Family behavior around the dining table has long served as the focal point for an understanding of family functioning (Goodman, 1983). Thus, eating habits have been analysed in terms of the rules governing how people are organized around the table, the regulation of manners, the questions of who cooks, prepares, and serves different categories of food, and how meal-time conversations are managed. Goodman's point is that, given the centrality of television in many homes, we can usefully make a parallel study of the rules governing family viewing – how the seating pattern is arranged, who watches what with whom, who chooses programs, and what kinds of talk are defined as appropriate during viewing.

The rules perspective returns us to the focus on everyday communication practices. Following Schutz (1963: 59), we suggest that "the exploration of the general principles according to which man [*sic*] in daily life organises his experiences . . . is the first task of the methodology of the social sciences." Such a phenomenological perspective implies systematically addressing audience activity in its natural setting, using qualitative methods as tools for the collection of naturalistic data, and giving priority to the analysis of categories that can be derived from the respondents' own conceptual frameworks. The rules or logics-in-use of situated everyday behavior must be studied to understand how the various media are incorporated into, and mobilized within, private worlds. An understanding of family dynamics, of the structures of daily life, and of the family system (Gorrell-Barnes, 1985) is a necessary precondition for understanding the place of television (or any other communication technology) in the household.

The material and symbolic dimensions of television, thus, come together in the practices of everyday life which serve to display both goods and cultural competence, both in private and in public. If we are to make sense of the significance of such media-related activities, which, after all, are key to understanding contemporary culture, then we have to take seriously their varied and specific forms. From this follows the case for an anthropology of the television audience, and for a commitment to ethnography as an empirical method.

ETHNOGRAPHIC APPROACHES

Morley (1980) has argued that the relation of audiences to television must always, in principle, be formulated as an empirical question, and that the significant challenge is to develop appropriate methods. In our current research, we have adopted a largely ethnographic approach, the prime requirement being to provide an adequately "thick" description (Geertz, 1973) of the complexities of domestic viewing.

According to Hammersley and Atkinson (1983: 2), ethnography can be understood as

> simply one social research method, albeit an unusual one, drawing on a wide range of sources of information. The ethnographer participates in people's lives for an extended period of time, watching what happens, listening to what is said, asking questions ... collecting whatever data are available to throw light on the issues with which he or she is concerned.

At its simplest, it has been argued that the ethnographer's task is to "go into the field" and, by way of observation and interview, to attempt to describe – and inevitably interpret – the practices of the subjects in that cultural context, on the basis of his or her first-hand observation of day-to-day activities. As Hammersley and Atkinson further argue, in this respect "there is no escape from reliance on commonsense knowledge and on commonsense methods of investigation. All social research is founded on the human capacity for participant observation" (p. 25). The researcher, being an active participant in the research process, is "the research instrument par excellence" (p. 18), and rather than "engaging in futile attempts to eliminate the 'effects' of the researcher, we should set about understanding them" (p. 17; see below on the consequent problems of interpretation and reflexivity in research).

Ethnographies, by their very nature, then, are grounded in the realities of other people's lives, what Geertz calls the "informal logic of actual life" (1973: 17). The problems of doing ethnography – problems of description and understanding – are those of social research as a whole. From a naturalistic perspective, participant observers aim to learn the rules of the culture (or subculture) of the people they are studying, and to learn to interpret events and actions according to those rules, whether implicit or explicit. From this perspective, the objective is not to identify universal laws, but rather to produce "detailed descriptions of the concrete experience of life within a particular culture and of the social rules and patterns which constitute it" (Hammersley and Atkinson, 1983: 8).

Notes of caution are certainly in order here. First of all, self-consciousness (or *reflexivity*) is needed regarding the inevitable partiality of any analysis. Moreover, as Lull (1988b) argues, rigorous and *systematic forms of data collection* and interpretation are just as necessary in qualitative as in quantitative research. Lull notes that in audience studies of recent years, the term "ethnography" has become totemic (a ritual genuflection toward a newly instituted tribal deity?). Suddenly everyone is an ethnographer (the ethnographer as fashion victim?). Yet, as Lull points out, "what is passing as ethnography in cultural studies fails to achieve the fundamental requirements for data collection and reporting typical of most anthropological and sociological ethnographic research. 'Ethnography' has become an abused buzz-word in our field" (Lull, 1988b: 242). Instead, Lull points to the particular responsibilities and requirements that attach to ethnographic practice. Once we invoke the importance of the context of actions and their embedding in the fabric of everyday life, as researchers we then operate under a specific set of responsibilities to do the following:

(1) observe and note routine behavior of all types characteristic of those who are being studied, (2) do so in the natural settings where the behavior occurs, and (3) draw inferences carefully after considering the details of communication behavior, with special attention paid to the often subtle, yet revealing, ways that different aspects of the context inform each other.

(Lull, 1987:320)

The emphasis on the context of actions raises considerable problems concerning the delimitation of the field of research and of establishing which elements of the (potentially infinite) realm of an action's context are going to be relevant to the particular research in hand. This returns us to the familiar debate about the relative advantages and disadvantages of open-ended and closed research strategies. An illuminating example is offered by Gray (1987) who, when researching women's relations to video technology, found that very often the women she interviewed wanted to tell her stories ("their" stories) and that, at first, she was anxious lest they should be "getting away from the point" (their uses of video) in telling stories which often involved extended narratives of family history. However, as Gray herself suggests, the great value of this open-ended approach lay in the fact that in allowing respondents to "tell it their way" with a minimum of direction, she in return received their own understanding of their video (non-)use in the context of their own understanding of their social position. Whatever they might have said in answer to direct questions would have been relatively insignificant, as it was "how they saw their lives" that explained the extent to which they did or did not use the video technologies.

The issue is not only a pragmatic one, of which elements of the context are necessary to understand any given action. It is also a theoretical and epistemological question of the relation between the particular and the general, the instance and the category. Ang (1991) argues that, given the dominance of the generalizing/categorizing tradition in much previous audience research and its acknowledged epistemological limitations, in, for example, the categorizations of "viewer types," it is time for this emphasis to be complemented by the opposite concern with particularization (see also Billig, 1987). As Ang puts it (1991: 160),

rather than reducing a certain manifestation of "viewing behaviour" to an instance of a general category, we might consider it in its particularity, treat it in its concrete specificity,

differentiate it from the other instances of the general category.... Only then can we go beyond (statistical) "significance
without much signification."

THE PROBLEM OF INTERPRETATION

We all know from our everyday existence that the communication
procedures of quotidian life can be deceptively complex, at times
treacherously so. This is because of their vagueness, resulting from
the absence of explication procedures between people who are
already familiar with each other:

> Much of our ordinary communication behavior ... *demands* a
> certain amount of vagueness which further impairs [the research-
> er's] ability to assess what is occurring and why. Ironically, vague-
> ness is the arch villain of positivist science, where clarity and
> objectivity of interpretation are the embraced ideals. But vague-
> ness is essential to daily patterns of social interaction. Without it,
> or worse, with the pursuit of scientific clarity, social interactions
> as we have come to know and experience them would be nearly
> impossible.
>
> (Lindlof and Meyer, 1987: 25)

By its very nature, ethnography attempts to explicate the (often
unspoken) informal logic of communication and other everyday
practices.

Qualitative research strategies such as ethnography are princi-
pally designed to gain access to naturalized domains and their
characteristic activities. The strength of these approaches is that
they offer a *contextual understanding* of the connections between
different aspects of the phenomena being studied. Yet, as qualitative media researchers, we face the difficulty of finally telling stories
about the stories which our respondents have chosen to tell us.
These problems are both irreducible and familiar. As Geertz (1973:
15) remarked, long ago, "we begin with our own interpretations of
what our informants are up to, or think they are up to, and then
systematize those." The analyst's account is, necessarily, an interpretation (and, notes Geertz, often a second- or third-order
one).

However, as Geertz (1973) also suggests, rather than giving up
and going home, the ethnographer's alternative is to try to pick his
or her way through the structures of inference and implication

which constitute the discourse of everyday exchange. For the researcher to attempt to enter this natural world, where communication is vague and meanings implicit, is inevitably to go skating on thin ice. Nonetheless, corresponding claims can then be made in terms of data validity, since, unlike disaggregated forms of statistical knowledge, ethnography allows us to produce knowledge in contexts where the significance of the data can be more readily ascertained. Of course, we never simply describe a social setting, but necessarily interpret to make sense of our respondents' words and actions in our research reports. Ethnographic accounts are essentially contestable, just as cultural analysis is a necessarily incomplete business of guessing at meanings, assessing the guesses, and drawing explanatory conclusions from the better guesses.

Ethnographic analysis is dependent on various techniques of "triangulation" (see also Chapter 2 in this volume for a discussion of triangulation). Triangulation may involve "the comparison of data relating to the same phenomenon but deriving from different phases of the fieldwork, different points in the temporal cycles occurring in the setting, or, as in respondent validation, the accounts of different participants in the setting" (Hammersley and Atkinson, 1983: 198). Ethnography's characteristic use of multiple data sources thus guards against the risks of ecological invalidity which always pertain to any research method that is reliant on a single kind of data, posing the danger that the findings may turn out to be method-dependent. The multi-stranded character of ethnography, produced by different techniques (observation, interview, self-report, etc.), which can then be systematically compared, is a further advantage of the ethnographic approach.

To be sure, our knowledge remains partial, in more ways than one. In the case of research into the domestic consumption of television, access to the private sphere of the household is always a matter of degree; there will almost always be some areas of the household which are "forbidden" (see Bourdieu, 1972) to a stranger. Equally, as Anderson (1987a) notes, some social action will never be displayed in the presence of an outsider. The ethnographer's account, then, must be *reflexive* about its own partiality, incompleteness, and structured gaps. Whereas what we describe is not raw social discourse, to which we do not have full access, "this is not as fatal as it sounds, for ... it is not necessary to know everything in order to understand something" (Geertz, 1973: 20).

A CASE STUDY IN GROUNDED METHODOLOGY

In order to illustrate the theoretical argument concerning a broadly ethnographic approach to the media audience – though one that both expands the definition of ethnography and reconstructs the definition of the audience – we offer now a brief account of the methods employed in our current project, "The household and the domestic consumption of information and communication technologies" (see Morley and Silverstone, 1990; Silverstone *et al.*, 1989; Silverstone *et al.*, 1990a, 1990b, for fuller accounts of this research in progress). Our concern here is not with the substantive "findings" of the research, but with explicating the rationale for the particular methodological choices we have made as this study has progressed. Overall, the study involves detailed work with twenty different families concerning the range of information and communication technologies (ICTs) used in their homes.

The research is designed to explore the fine grain of the relations between domestic culture and the uses of ICTs, among which we include pre-eminently the television, the VCR, the telephone, and the computer. The task is both deceptively simple and terribly ambitious: to understand how families in households live with these technologies and how they are incorporated into their domestic lives. Our premise has been (Morley and Silverstone, 1990; Silverstone, 1990) that television should not be studied in isolation, neither from other technologies nor from the structures of family life. We wanted to understand the processes and dynamics involving families, media, and technologies as systems, both intrinsically (with regard to the internal structure of family life) and extrinsically (with regard to the relations between families, neighborhoods, work, and kin-based networks of friendships and other relationships in the wider society). We were interested to study ICTs as integrating or isolating families and households into or from the world beyond their front door, as well as the role of ICTs in mediating the public and private spheres.

The methods have emerged and evolved as a result of a dialogue with the subjects and subject of the research, the methods themselves being grounded (Glaser and Strauss, 1967) in the activity of research. Likewise, we have attempted not just a multiple triangulation, but also a kind of reflexivity through which the methods would complement each other when subjects comment on the research process and on their own involvement in it as it progresses.

Each of the inputs has a specific function in the research; each also has a secondary reflexive or triangulatory significance in the construction of the overall "methodological raft"[2] on which the research process is placed.

In the first stage of the research (with the first four of the twenty families) our principal commitment was to participant observation supplemented by time-use diaries, focusing on one family at a time. The participant observation, in particular, aimed to provide a plausible and coherent account of family life which went beyond the limitations of the self-reporting techniques employed in much previous audience research. However, it also became apparent that this approach would not readily provide either the basis for a systematic analysis of the key issues of media use or a secure enough basis for any systematic comparative work between families. Nor would it enable us satisfactorily to contextualize families historically and geographically in relation to their pasts, their futures, and their neighborhoods – within time and space relations.

With respect to participant observation, we concluded that, while it was a necessary component of the overall methodology, it was not a sufficient source of data. It did, however, supply valuable data, not only in terms of our observation of the people concerned, but also in terms of our observation of the household's aesthetic and domestic culture as expressed in the furnishing of the rooms to which we had access. Finally, participant observation offered a continuing and necessary check on family members' own accounting of domestic relations and technology use, thus providing one of the many levels of triangulation in the study.

In recognition of these limitations, we redesigned our methods to supplement participant observation with a number of further research inputs. In the first place, we began to give more weight to the time-use diaries, because this record of activities which we could not directly observe (either because they took place outside the home or when we were not present), offered us both an extension of our data set in space and time and a valuable and reflexive basis for interviews with each family member. The time-use diary provided a framework for understanding domestic temporality.

However, we needed an equivalent method to approach the spatial relations of the household. We therefore introduced a "mental mapping" exercise in which each member of the household was asked to draw a map of the internal space of the house and all its rooms. Initially this had the purpose of supplying us with information on those rooms to which we did not have direct access. However, it soon became clear that this technique offered valuable data in quite another way, since respondents' maps differed, often quite considerably, in respect of the presence, absence, or signifi-cance of the different ICTs in their homes. This mapping exercise was supplemented by the use of two network diagrams which each household was asked to complete, showing their geographical and affective distance from relatives and friends as well as showing the modality (from letter writing to face-to-face interaction) of the communication process through which each relationship was princi-pally sustained.

These techniques have allowed us to complement our participant observation and thus to contextualize our observational findings in more meaningful ways. At the same time, we have also developed a technique for contextualizing our observational work with refer-ence to the family's past. Thus, in each family we have organized a "viewing" and discussion of the family's photograph album(s) (or video-tape collection of the family) which makes the family's image of its own "story" or history available to us.

Taken together, these and other interview-based research inputs (for an extensive discussion, see Silverstone *et al.*, 1990b) have allowed us to contextualize our participant observation and to triangulate the findings of one procedure against others. Together the inputs offer, we suggest, both the richness of a participant observation study and the rigor of systematically comparative anal-ysis. For us, ethnography is a multifaceted process in which the requirements of detail and richness, rigor and systematicity, have to be carefully balanced, and where there is no single adequate meth-odological procedure.

POSTMODERN ETHNOGRAPHY?

In conclusion, it is necessary to take note of the serious debates (Clifford, 1986; Marcus and Fischer, 1986) which have developed in recent years about the epistemological and moral/political issues of empirical audience research. Hartley (1987) and Ang (1989) have addressed the difficulties arising generally from the constructivist nature of any research project, and have warned against the dangers of failing to see that our data are, inevitably, products of the research process. Further, Feuer (1986) has pointed to a tendency in empirical audience research to displace questions of meaning from the text (or the critic) onto the audience, only succeeding in producing a new text to be interpreted – that of the audience response (for a critique of Feuer, see Morley, 1989).

In short, what are the *politics* of audience ethnography? Ang (1989) rightly insists that doing research is itself a discursive practice which can only ever hope to produce historically and culturally specific knowledges through equally specific discursive encounters between researcher and informants. Research is thus, from her and our point of view, always a matter of interpreting, indeed constructing, reality from a particular position, rather than a positivist enterprise seeking a "correct" scientific perspective which will finally allow us to achieve the utopian dream of a world completely known in the form of indisputable facts.

It is around these issues that recent debates concerning *postmodern* (or poststructuralist) anthropology and ethnography have centered, especially in the USA. The central issue has been the relationship between the observer and the observed and the basis of the ethnographer's authority to convey the cultural experiences of others. Fiske (1990: 90) refers to "the imperialist ethnographer who descended as a white man [*sic*] into the jungle and bore away back to the white man's world, 'meanings' of native life that were unavailable to those who lived it." Among other commentators, Marcus and Fischer (1986) have talked of a crisis of representation, and Said (1978) has cogently argued for a more reflexive analysis of the process of "Orientalization" – the process of imaginative geography which produces a fictionalized Other as the exotic object of knowledge. In these debates, the object of criticism is a form of naive empiricism or ethnographic realism which would remain insensitive to issues of reflexivity, instead presuming both a transparency of representation and an immediacy of the problematic category of "experience" (see Althusser, 1965). For critics like Clifford (1986: 22) there can be no "place of overview [mountain top] from which to map human ways of life, no Archimedean point from which to represent the world. Mountains are in constant motion . . . we ground things, now, as a moving earth." This, then, requires also media researchers to specify who writes, about whom, and from what positions of knowledge and power.

In response, Geertz (1988) has referred to what he calls the "pervasive nervousness" and "moral hypochondria" engendered by poststructuralist and postmodern writing about ethnography.

These "Jesuits of the Future" or "diehard apostles of the hermeneutics of suspicion" (Geertz, 1988: 86) start from a quite proper suspicion of the Malinowskian ideal of "immersionist" ethnography and of the naive invocation of the ethnographer's sincerity and authenticity – Being There as the founding authority of the ethnographic account. The point for Geertz, however, is that if the traditional anthropological attitude to these questions ("Don't think about ethnography, just do it") is the problem then, equally, to fall into a paralysing (if vertiginously thrilling) trance of epistemological navel-gazing ("Don't do ethnography, just think about it") is no kind of answer for anyone with a commitment to empirical work. Even Clifford (1986: 7) himself has expressed the hope that this "political and epistemological self-consciousness need not lead to ethnographic self-absorption, or to the conclusion that it is impossible to know anything certain about other people."

For Geertz, and for us, there is an important limit to what can be conceded to the poststructuralist argument. To recognize the subjective component of ethnography is no more than common sense; the burden of authorship is inescapable. In Geertz' (1988: 140) words, "to argue . . . that the writing of ethnography involves telling stories" could only ever have seemed contentious on the premise of "a confusion . . . of the imagined and the imaginary, the fictional with the false . . . making things out with making them up." For us, the value of ethnographic methods lies precisely in their ability to help us to "make things out" in the context of their occurrence – in helping us to understand television viewing and other media consumption practices as they are embedded in the context of everyday life.

NOTES

1 Commentators on television viewing speak of it as being "rule-governed," "patterned," or part of the "logic" of daily life. Although strictly speaking each of these terms can, indeed ought to, be understood slightly differently (they imply different ways of understanding the social process), we use them here as broadly synonymous.

2 We use the term "methodological raft" in a specific sense. It refers to the particular lattice of core research methods which have emerged in the study as a way of describing the location of each family–household in space and time. The methodological raft provides a base on which to develop other aspects of the research design and a base for constructing a conceptual model of the household and technology use which has come to inform the research as a whole.

Chapter 9

Media contexts
Qualitative research and community media

Nicholas W. Jankowski

INTRODUCTION

Community studies have traditionally made important and respected contributions to sociology, in part because of the qualitative orientation of their empirical approaches. From the perspective of mass communication, moreover, community studies have helped to explore and specify the relationship between *communication* and *community*, as suggested by several book titles in the area (Halloran, 1975; Schulman, 1988; Thayer, 1982). One particularly salient essay suggests that "the central significance of the concept of community in sociological thought . . . stems from a moral commitment to relationships as dialogue rather than exchange" (Chaney, 1982: 28). Communication, in other words, can be seen as one of the conditions for community.

While a few classic studies have highlighted the place of media within communities (see especially Janowitz, 1952), the attention given to community media has increased substantially since the 1960s, when cable and video technologies made it technically possible to produce and distribute television at the local level. These technological developments were matched by a resurgence of empirical work on small-scale media. Although many small-scale media have been investigated, the emphasis has been on electronic media in the community setting, with empirical work being undertaken in diverse countries and cultures. Thus, there have been studies of satellite-relayed educational television to remote Indian villages (Sinha, 1985); listener-sponsored radio programming in California (Hodel and Chappelle, 1979); participatory radio stations in Ecuador (Hein, 1988) and Costa Rica (Coesmans and van den Goor, 1990); community radio and television stations in the

USA (Barlow, 1988; Fuller, 1984; Schulman, 1985); and the use of radio and video as tools for political and community development (see Wright, 1979; also the special issue of *Media Development* 36, 4, 1989).

In the following pages, I examine some prominent European publications on community radio and television and their elements of qualitative research. In the next section, I discuss two examples in more detail – a study of the British community television station Swindon Viewpoint (Croll and Husband, 1975; Halloran, 1975) and my own investigation of a community television station in Amsterdam (Jankowski, 1988). Finally, I consider areas for further qualitative work on small-scale media, including the introduction of interactive media at the local level.

PREVIOUS RESEARCH

Examining the literature as a whole, one is struck by its diversity. There are reports of very narrowly defined audience surveys and long-term process-oriented studies considering many media within a particular locality. Much of the work is not "scientific" in the narrow sense of a systematic collection and analysis of data related to an explicitly stated problem. It does, however, address general scientific concerns of understanding and theorizing about developments as well as considering consequences for policy, sometimes through qualitative inquiry. The literature can be clustered into three groups: studies which are empirically oriented; reflective essays, often intended for policy discussions; and popular works which seek to inform and sometimes mobilize a wider audience.

Empirical research

During the mid-1970s, several European governments (in the Netherlands, Germany, Denmark, Sweden, Norway, and Great Britain) funded research on experiments with community radio and television (see the review of these and other community radio and television developments in Jankowski *et al.*, 1991). Much of this work, with a few commercial exceptions (see, for example, Young *et al.*, 1979), was conducted by academic institutions. Most of the studies emphasized quantitative data. The studies conducted in Denmark are something of a prototype which employed a panel survey design (Prehn, 1986), as did the main research project in the Netherlands (Stappers *et al.*, 1977). Generally speaking, research in this category was directed at traditional issues: awareness of, attendance to, and opinion of the new media – and any "effect" on resident involvement in the community.

Few qualitative empirical studies have been conducted on the European experiments. However, two examples suggest the explanatory value of a qualitative perspective, and are discussed in detail in the next section on cases. Even in these examples of qualitative research, surveys were a major component in the overall design. Also in a more recent study on the introduction of interactive cable services in a Dutch community (Stappers *et al.*, 1989), the national government insisted that a panel survey be the primary research activity. Thus, there is normally a preference for "hard" quantitative data among government policymakers (for the social and historical background of this quantitative bias, see Chapter 12 and the Introduction to this volume). The empirical literature is, furthermore, largely atheoretical and, in Lazarsfeld's (1941) terms, "administrative" (see also Melody and Mansell, 1983). It reflects, in part, the constraints of contract research investigating narrow problem statements.

Nevertheless, empirical studies have been a stimulus for theoretical work. Heyn's (1979) study of British local media, for one, represents a detailed analysis of documents and secondary sources, which further theorizes about possible forms of media participation generally. Hollander's (1988) examination of local communication with reference to the concept of a public sphere, for another, is the result of nearly a decade of empirical research on small-scale media. Starting from the German concept of *Öffentlichkeit* ("public sphere"; see Habermas, 1989), the author develops the concept of a local public sphere comprising the "totality of communication and information processes in the local setting" (Hollander, 1988: 257). Like other chapters in this handbook, one notes here the emergence of an integrative, contextual perspective on the communicative practices of specific social and cultural communities.

Reflective essays

Literature in this second category is often sponsored by special-interest organizations and institutions such as the Council of

Europe and the National Film Board in Canada, both of which devoted considerable resources to documenting small-scale media in the 1970s and early 1980s. There are literally dozens of Council of Europe studies on, among other things, the financing of public-access channels (Ploman and Lewis, 1977), local radio in Italy (Faenza, 1977), and cable projects in France (Dubois-Dumée, 1973). The reports describe developments and explore policy options, but generally do not have a theoretical objective. Instead, they were intended as materials for policy debate and decision-making by European governments. Since the early 1980s, the Council has ceased supporting studies of small-scale media.

The Canadian National Film Board was active during the same period and published the magazine *Access* (now defunct), which promoted the use of audiovisual media by community groups. One issue, for example, was devoted to a video and film project with Eskimos in Alaska. The main article (Kennedy, 1973) describes in detail how villagers in the Yukon region were involved in the shooting, editing, and distribution of the film, suggesting the emancipatory potential of the medium: "It [the film] has been a very powerful thing ... they [the villagers] have let their feelings be known, and it's the very first time that that kind of pressure has ever been applied from rural Alaska" (Kennedy, 1973: 9). Such work is sometimes referred to as participatory research, which is a form of qualitative research. The objectives may include both concrete political action and general emancipation of project participants. Servaes (1989: 6) characterizes this type of research as an educational process for all involved, a "dialectical process of dialogue between the researcher and the community" (see also Chapter 12 in this volume).

A third example of reflective policy research has made a particular contribution also to theory development. During a major assessment of media policy in the Netherlands in the early 1980s, Hollander (1982) was commissioned to chart the development of small-scale broadcasting in western Europe. The country-by-country overview is now dated (for more recent overviews, see Browne, 1988; Crookes and Vittet-Philippe, 1986; Kleinsteuber and Sonnenberg, 1990), but the theoretical chapter remains an important source of inspiration. Different concepts of community and media from German and Anglo-Saxon traditions are compared and synthesized with reference to the descriptive studies. Hollander in conclusion lays out issues relevant to policymakers: station financing, the regulation of access to and participation in the stations, and the relation between small-scale and other media. The study, in short, exemplifies the contribution that qualitative studies can make simultaneously to theory and policy formulation.

In addition to such explicitly reflective work, special-interest groups have developed activities and publications comparable to those of the Council of Europe and the Canadian Film Board. These groups include the World Association of Community Radio Broadcasters, the National Federation of Local Cable Programmers in the United States, the Dutch Organization of Local Broadcasting, and the British local radio association Relay. Whereas their main objectives are to inform members and lobby in political arenas, their publications include an element of qualitative research, to the extent that political strategies emerge from an analysis of events by participants.

A comparable type of qualitative research is the essays published by station managers, staff, and journalists, which, while based on first-hand experience, tend to be partisan; description hence takes a secondary role to argument. One useful exemplar is a monograph on the Bristol community television channel written by the then station manager, what he calls "a retrospective account by a participant observer who, as station manager, was indeed the 'arch-participant'" (Lewis, 1976: iv). After the station was shut down, Lewis was granted a fellowship by the Independent Broadcasting Authority to reflect on the project. This allowed him "to rescue some of the history, read relevant literature in an attempt to set the experience in some sort of context, and follow up the consequences of [the cable company] Rediffusion's legacy of portable equipment to the community" (Lewis, 1976: vi).

A final example of theoretical reflection by involved actors is *Local Television: Piped Dreams?* (Bibby *et al.*, 1979). As former staff members of the British community television stations Swindon Viewpoint and Channel 40, the authors, like Lewis, were able to write from the insider perspective. Importantly, they provide examples of how the "neutral" access policy of the two stations was, in fact, biased toward middle-class residents and the maintenance of status quo on a variety of community issues. Their work thus has contributed to expanding the theoretical concept of access to include "affirmative access" (see Jankowski, 1988: 169).

Popular publications

Literature in this final category is directed at a wider audience, either academic or lay readers, and is frequently based on material from the first two categories. One of the most influential publications here is Frances Berrigan's (1977) review of access models and community media. The volume combines descriptive cases of access to media in the USA and western Europe with analytical treatment of the concepts of access and participation. Even though it is not based on long-term participant observation, it does make use of case studies to develop its concepts. A similar volume is *Radical Media* (1984) by John Downing, who provides us with descriptive case studies of media around the world practicing self-management. Further, there is overarching reflection on some core elements of radical media in the final chapter. Compared to Berrigan, Downing takes an explicit political stance supporting the ideals of the radical media.

Lastly, many valuable titles on alternative media have been brought out by the activist London-based publisher Comedia. Partridge's (1982) *Not the BBC/IBA: the Case for Community Radio* both charts the development of community radio in Britain and provides concrete organizational and technical information for community groups interested in establishing their own radio stations. Similar information is available for other countries (de Bruin *et al.*, 1983; Jarren and Widlok, 1985; Shamberg, 1971), representing efforts to popularize both the concept and experience of community media. Two academic case studies may illustrate the specific potentials and problems of community media.

TWO CASE STUDIES

Swindon Viewpoint

The Leicester University study of the British community television station Swindon Viewpoint has served as a model for much qualitative research on small-scale media. It comprises the elements of qualitative research which I would consider essential: employment of participant observation, compilation of descriptive case studies, theoretical discussion, and contribution to policy debate.

The research took place during the 1970s, when the British government had authorized five sites for experimentation with local cable programming. The station in Swindon was the only one monitored by an independent research project; other stations were documented by participants (Bibby *et al.*, 1979; Lewis, 1976; 1978). The Swindon design consisted of both a qualitative and a quantitative component. A member of the research team thus spent nine months living in Swindon as a participant observer. The purpose of his presence was "to allow for intensive observation of the production process at Swindon Viewpoint, and for contact with local community activity" (Croll and Husband, 1975: 18).

The qualitative section of the report begins with a case study of a community group producing a television program. The process is charted from the initial formulation of program ideas to scripting and filming, and concludes with the cable transmission of the program. Next, an analysis of the experience of the community group in that process is presented. Another case study was conducted on the development of station policy regarding access and the use of technical facilities by individuals, groups, and community organizations. Here, evidence from station documents and citations from interviews with staff and volunteers are added to the researcher's own observations. Tabular data are also integrated into this discussion to assess a major objective of the station: community participation in television programming.

The qualitative fieldwork was complemented by two audience surveys providing quantitative data on the information needs of city residents, and on their awareness, use, and opinion of the station and its programming. A third survey was held under another sample of cable households to provide supplementary evidence on the impact of cable television in the town. The surveys followed handbook guidelines for such quantitative research, with sampling procedures, data collection, analysis, and presentation of findings all done according to the "rules." Interestingly, however, the quantitative material does not dominate the report in terms of space allotted or substantive treatment. Thus, the qualitative fieldwork was not relegated to the role of prescientific exploration.

The results of the qualitative and quantitative research activities are woven together in the conclusion of the report. Yet, there is limited theoretical discussion other than a brief reference to the sociological concept of community. In a subsequent publication, however, the director of the research project has explored theoretical issues of community media. Halloran (1975) reviews the main findings from the empirical studies and assesses the limitations of media access as practiced in Swindon. While acknowledging that the station was open in principle to all sectors of the community, he notes that predominantly middle-class residents engaged in programming activity. In sum, the form of access practiced in Swindon, a relatively small town with particular informal communication networks, "may not be universally appropriate, especially with a larger station and larger town where a more formal system of guaranteeing access may be needed" (Halloran, 1975: 57).

Community television in Amsterdam

Our project in Amsterdam was influenced considerably by the Swindon model. During preparation for the project, I visited Swindon Viewpoint and spoke at length with the Leicester researchers. Many of the qualitative elements in the Swindon study were incorporated into our work: a combination of participant observation with survey research, contextual analyses of station development, and a theoretical emphasis on the concept of community. Perhaps the most fundamental difference was our effort to include a component of action research into the design; partly as a result of this, we experienced problematic relations with both research funders and members of the station. It is these problems – additions to the Swindon experience – which are elaborated here.

The "Lokale Omroep Bijlmermeer" (LOB) was one of six community television organizations in the Netherlands which had been selected to participate in a government-funded experiment with cable transmission of locally originated radio and television programming. The experiment, held in the mid-1970s under supervision of the Ministry of Culture, was broadly conceived to examine the role that electronic media might play within communities. It was monitored by three independent research teams (Jankowski, 1977; Koole et al., 1976; Stappers et al., 1976; 1977). The LOB community television station had existed as a formal organization since early 1972. During the first three years, however, it produced and transmitted only a handful of programs on the cable system in the housing estate in which it was located. With approval of funding in 1975, the LOB began cablecasting programs on a weekly basis, a frequency maintained until the end of 1978, when funds were exhausted and the station closed down.

The research project was established in cooperation with the LOB station. Although the Ministry of Culture required that stations participating in the experiment be receptive to researchers, most members of the LOB were already convinced of the value of a systematic study of the station and its place within the community. The general research strategy was discussed and determined in consultation with the LOB. The central objective of the project was to examine the station as a resource for community development in the housing estate. Hence, it was decided that I should, much like a cultural anthropologist, live in the housing estate in order to experience at first hand both the community and the station. Participant observation became the primary method and was performed over a four-year period.

The consultation with station representatives was based on the premise that the results should be of service to the LOB itself. Specifically, we wanted to conduct a form of action research, in which the results contributed to improvement of the organization. We were especially concerned with channeling social and political activity in the housing estate into LOB programming, with particular attention to social welfare institutions.

A number of subprojects, rooted in different disciplines, were designed to address these concerns. Our assumption was that a multidisciplinary approach, as outlined by Webb *et al.* (1966), would increase our understanding of the station. In addition, we intended to employ a diversity of methods for collecting and analysing information: participant observation of organizational activities, formal and informal interviews with LOB volunteers, case studies of program development, content analysis of broadcasts, and surveys of community residents. Finally, qualitative methodology within an interactionist perspective (Blumer, 1969; Denzin, 1970a; Glaser and Strauss, 1967) was to guide the project as a whole.

Shortly after the onset of the project, several conflicts developed – between the funders of the research and the researchers and between station personnel and researchers. The government had financed the research project on the condition that an interim report would be produced to facilitate formulation of government policy on the development of cable television. This report, it turned out, was the primary interest of government representatives in the advisory commission of the project, because local governments were expected to finance the stations after the experimental period. The Amsterdam government, however, had no interest in that report; it had not been involved in the experiment and was not willing to consider financing the station. Though the research team hence felt it inappropriate to produce the report, ultimately we agreed to write a policy document, provided it could also discuss the predicament of preparing such a document for an uninterested governmental body.

There were also tensions between station personnel and the research team – problems which indicate the generally delicate relationship between researcher and researched in qualitative studies, not least for action research. The conflicts arose from the presentation of research findings to outsiders, such as a lecture given in the presence of representatives from government and other cable television stations as well as the publication of a subproject. The problem was not so much the critical remarks about the LOB, but the fact that there had been no opportunity for the LOB to comment on the material. Because of the uncertain future of the LOB, the station staff seriously considered legal steps to prohibit further research activity. The crisis was resolved, however, by recalling the report and including LOB commentary in subsequent research documents.

Also from a scientific perspective, the integration of findings from subprojects employing different methods and theoretical perspectives posed problems. It was particularly difficult to reconcile the action research projects providing training in television production and the traditional audience surveys. The theoretical notions guiding this project were originally formulated as "sensitizing concepts" in an effort to ground the study in the actual community (Glaser and Strauss, 1967), but the daily activities of contract research severely limited the time to "discover" theory. Nevertheless, one important contribution of the project was to document comprehensively the dynamics, potentials, and problems of community media, including the interaction between different professional and interest groups, through action research and other qualitative methodologies.

A second outcome of the project was a theoretical typology of community media, later developed in an academic dissertation (Jankowski, 1988). Inspired in part by earlier statements of the mobilizing power of media (Brecht, 1932; Enzensberger, 1970), the typology categorized community stations along three dimensions: access to, participation in, and use of station programming (Jankowski, 1988: 174). So-called "community action stations," it was suggested, devoted more energy to recruiting and training residents outside the middle class, encouraging participation in program production, and providing programming on community issues.

CONCLUSION

The course of the Amsterdam project, then, was similar to that of the Leicester study: theoretical reflection was largely developed after the empirical fieldwork had been documented. In both cases, however, and in both theoretical and empirical inquiry, qualitative methodologies were the foundation of a better understanding of what community media are – and might become.

The meta-theoretical problem of integrating different approaches and methods is critical for further qualitative research (see also Chapter 2 on triangulation). The epistemological difficulty of reconciling different findings or different analytical perspectives cannot, in fact, be eliminated by any amount of "cross-checking." Still, multiple methods and multidisciplinary research can increase the richness and completeness of our understanding, as suggested by the Swindon and Amsterdam experiences.

Most of the qualitative empirical research on community media remains to be undertaken. There is a great need for research within station organizations, for example, on the tension between professional media routines and "ordinary" citizens seeking a medium and a form of expression for their concerns. Similarly, the audience use of community programming is not well understood, in part because it has been almost exclusively studied with quantitative methodologies. The qualitative approaches to audiences' needs and experiences of mass communication, as elaborated in Chapters 7 and 8 of this volume, will be highly relevant in the context of community media.

Moreover, much theoretical work needs to be undertaken, most significantly within the perspective of a democratization of communication of, for, and by communities of different kinds (see the discussions from MacBride, 1980, through Splichal et al., 1990). Access and participation are two central concepts for the democratization of communication (Jankowski and Mol, 1988); one current issue is how these basic principles may fare in an increasingly commercial media environment. Following pioneering theoretical work in this area (Matta, 1981; White, 1984), qualitative case studies may help in determining under what conditions community media can provide a specific alternative.

Finally, new communication and information technologies, such as interactive videotex services and computer conferencing, lend themselves to qualitative research (Jankowski and Mendel, 1990).

Access by the general public and the local community to these interactive media is an important component in a democratic vision of the so-called information society. Qualitative methodologies can help communities to understand not only how new communication technologies are being introduced at present, but also how the emancipatory potential of new media may serve community in the future.

Chapter 10

Media contexts
Historical approaches to communication studies

Michael Schudson

INTRODUCTION

"Communication systems have a history," Robert Darnton has recently observed, "although historians have rarely studied it" (Darnton, 1990: xvii). This echoes Elizabeth Eisenstein's complaint a decade earlier that, despite historians' assertions about the power of the printing press, no systematic study of the impact of printing on culture had ever been undertaken (Eisenstein, 1979: 6). Even the concepts for doing such a study were lacking; major transformations in human communication – in this case, from "scribal" to print modes for publication and distribution of written things – were elided altogether in discussions of a general shift from oral to written cultures.

The writing of communication history is woefully underdeveloped. In part, this is because communication media are to a large extent, as the name declares, the carriers rather than creators of the causes and effects historians normally attend to. Certainly, there are respects in which the medium becomes the message, and certainly, there are moments, especially as mass media institutions differentiate from church or state and attain a degree of autonomy, that the media exert independent influence on politics, society, and culture. But generally speaking, the media develop in the background, not the event-filled foreground, of mainstream historical subjects.

This is not to say the background is unimportant. On the contrary, as Charles Tilly (1989: 690) has recently observed, students of human behavior necessarily try to balance treating people as "objects of external forces" and as "motivated actors." The trouble for the history of communication, however, is that historians are trained to hunt for the actions of motivated actors, and so they neglect topics that are viewed as background factors or external forces. Professional historians are by training resistant to epistemologies of historical method or practices of historical research that would place the background in the foreground.

In the study of communication, the one important exception to historical neglect is "the history of the book" (see Darnton, 1990, for a review of this field). There is now a sophisticated literature about the history of the book, book reading, literacy (see Graff, 1987), and the reading public from the early modern era on, particularly in western Europe. In no other area of communication history have history departments themselves, at least in the USA, taken any organized interest. In no other area of communication history has there been such a systematic gathering of archival sources, piggybacking on the work of bibliographers and bibliophiles. In no other domain of communication history have the various workers in the field had enough common interaction to establish a critical community.

The history of the book is also notable in its self-consciousness about the difficulty of "audience" or "reception" studies. If the study of communication is taken to be a three-part study analysing the production of messages, interpreting the messages or texts themselves, and examining the reception of messages by audiences, the history of reception is by far the most elusive of the three. Historians of the book at least recognize the importance of learning about audiences and the difficulties of doing so (see also Chapter 1 in this volume on literacy). For all these virtues, the history of the book may become all too successful as a "subdiscipline" of history proper and fail to exploit the bolder vision of communication history that comes from its more adventurous proponents in cultural and literary studies and anthropology.

Of the work that has been produced in communication history, there have been, generally speaking, three sorts. These are what I will call macro-history, history proper, and institutional history. I will focus on the general, theoretical frameworks of previous historical research on communication, much of which may be considered qualitative. While addressing some specifically methodological issues, I argue in conclusion that the main problems facing communication history lie not in its methods, but in the scope of its ideas.

PREVIOUS RESEARCH

The *macro-history* of communication is the most widely known of the three types of communication history. It considers the relationship of the media to human evolution and asks the question: how does the history of communication illuminate human nature? It has been very influential in legitimating the field of communication itself as an area of study. The key figures here are the Canadian thinkers Harold Innis (1951) and Marshall McLuhan (1962; 1964). They have left a curiously mixed legacy, on the one hand attracting interest to communication by the sweep of their vision, but on the other hand raising skepticism about the seriousness of communication history by the grandiosity of their claims. While both thinkers have been treated reverently by some, Carolyn Marvin's (1983) evaluation of Innis is little short of scathing and, of course, McLuhan has been widely savaged – not to mention lampooned.

Innis and McLuhan have not been alone in their interest in the transformation from oral to written culture. Jack Goody and Ian Watt (1963), Walter Ong (1982), and Eric Havelock (1986) have contributed important work. And others have written recently with some of the same encyclopedic reach to organize the whole history of communication. Donald Lowe (1982) has essayed a "history of bourgeois perception," and James Beniger (1986) an ambitious survey which argues that an information-based control revolution of the twentieth century has had effects as far-reaching as the industrial revolution of the nineteenth. Works of this broad compass are not the main subject of this essay, but they are still its touchstone.

The *history proper* of communication is, in my view, the least developed of the three types. It considers the relationship of the media to cultural, political, economic, or social history and addresses the question: how do changes in communication influence and how are they influenced by other aspects of social change? Where macro-history is interested only in what communication tells us about something else (human nature, "progress," "modernization"), history proper addresses either what communication tells us about society or what society tells us about communication or both. In its broader strokes, it is exemplified by Elizabeth Eisenstein's (1979) study of the shift from scribal to print culture and the impact of that transformation on politics, science, and social thought. It is represented by Chandra Mukerji's (1983) study of print as a vehicle of, and impetus to, capitalist development, rather than as a superstructural after-effect. It is represented also in Jürgen Habermas' (1989) discussion of the role of communication in the rise of a democratic, bourgeois public sphere.

While Eisenstein's attention to what print does to the character and quality of human thought gives it a kinship to the macro-historical works, these other studies stick more closely to the relationship of a change in communication patterns to changes in social, political, and cultural institutions. My history of the emergence of an ideal of objectivity in American journalism, for instance, seeks to explain this occupational ideology in terms of changes in American politics, economy, society, and culture (Schudson, 1978). Unlike the most widely read, standard histories of American journalism (Emery and Emery, 1988, for instance), I take important internal changes in journalism to be explicable only with reference to broader social change encompassing journalism.

A strategy Eisenstein (1979) used deserves special mention. She devotes her work to the impact of printing on elites, not on masses. This makes the problem of evidence in studying reception more tractable. It is a fruitful approach often overlooked in the fashion of recent historiography to attend to "history from the bottom up" and to seek, in looking for "a history of readers," for new readers. Yet, the history of television and politics, for example, is as much a history of the impact of television on politicians as on the audiences politicians seek to woo. Indeed, I suspect the evidence is clearer that television has influenced the thought of politicians than that it has directly influenced the relation of the general populace to politics. I have made a similar argument regarding the influence of advertising, which may influence investors, salespeople, and retailers more than consumers (Schudson, 1986: xiv).

The third type of communication history is *institutional history*. It considers the development of the media – in the sense primarily of media institutions, but also the history of language, the history of a particular genre of print (the novel) or film (the screwball comedy) – for their own sake. It asks the question: how has this (or that) institution of mass communication developed? It is primarily interested in social forces outside the media institution or industry under study only as they affect that institution or industry; any impact of the institution or industry on society is generally taken for granted, not investigated. Institutional histories of communication are, of course, legion. There are hundreds of histories of individual newspapers, magazines, and publishing companies and dozens of histories of broadcasting corporations and authorities and film companies. This includes some very distinguished works like Asa Briggs (1961–79) on the BBC or Erik Barnouw (1966–70) on American broadcasting. There are also hundreds of memoirs and biographies of individual reporters, editors, publishers, entrepreneurs, advertising agents, filmmakers, poets, novelists, actors, and actresses. These are necessary building blocks of a history of communication, but they do not ordinarily advance a general understanding of the place of communication in human experience or in social change, and I will leave them aside.

This may be the place to observe, however, some typical strengths and weaknesses of institutional history which have general implications for the *methodology* of communication history. Institutional histories, good and bad, often rely on the records and archives of business and government organizations. Institutional histories thus take advantage of their sources to emphasize the internal concerns of media producers and the dynamics and consequences of organizational growth and change. However, organizational records may reveal little about the wider impact of the media on individual consciousness or political and social structures. Institutional histories too often become a parade of personalities and organizational reshufflings; the institutions studied might as well have produced ball bearings as books or mufflers instead of movies, for all the difference it makes to the analysis.

Seeking to establish something about the wider cultural impact of media institutions, where survey data are generally lacking (and are inadequate even where available), is no easy matter for any kind of communication history. Take just the most basic question of who in the past read what. Historians are often left to attend closely to literary sources. Who, for instance, read New York's penny papers in the 1830s? There is no contemporary sociological study to give us clues. We have the claims of penny-paper editors about who read their papers, but these claims were of course promotional efforts, to be taken with a grain of salt. We have the counterclaims of rival editors, to be taken just as skeptically. We have the diary of Philip Hone (1889), the prominent New Yorker who recorded so much about the daily life of his city, and this offers some help. We have stray remarks from other sources like P. T. Barnum (1871: 67), noting in his autobiography that he picked up the *New York Herald* to read the classified advertisements when he came to New York to look for a job. We have James Fenimore Cooper's fictional newspaper editor in his novels *Homeward Bound* (1838) and *Home As Found* (1938) and his anti-newspaper polemics (Cooper, 1838/1969). But we have no comprehensive portrait of who read the penny papers in the 1830s.

Recently, historians have made some methodological advances in getting a sense for the reading public in this period. Richard Brown's *Knowledge Is Power* (1989) looks at a small number of Americans in the eighteenth and early nineteenth century for whom there is a fair amount of information available, in many cases detailed diaries, and extracts from diaries and related documents offer a kind of life history of the individual's reading fare and, to the extent that the information is available, responses to the reading. William Gilmore (1989), rather than focusing on individuals, centers his attention on a geographical area, a rural section of Vermont, and seeks to be as comprehensive as he can for the period 1770–1830 in documenting family library holdings, newspaper subscriptions, and bookstore inventories for towns of different sizes and different degrees of economic development and families of different levels of wealth. Tracking the use of newspapers for him is, however, much more difficult than detailing the use of books because newspapers were passed on or thrown out while books tended to be preserved and accounted for in family inventories and wills. For a later period, David Nord (1986) has learned something of working-class readers by making use of individual family data from a social survey of the US Commissioner of Labor in 1891. He can point to regional, ethnic, and income correlates of reading as well as evidence that families better integrated into *Gesellschaft* institutions read more than those devoted to *Gemeinschaft* institutions. Other evidentiary sources may also be tapped. The depiction of reading in paintings and other art works has been analysed by historians of the book (Darnton, 1990: 167–8) with, again, sophisticated self-consciousness about the value and limitations of such evidence.

Another problem with institutional history, or any history, of communication is the *evanescence* of the fundamental materials for study. In the USA, little national television news is available before 1968, when Vanderbilt University set up the Vanderbilt Television Archives and began taping each evening newscast. Even then, getting materials from Vanderbilt is somewhat costly and cumbersome. If a researcher wants a shortcut, printed news transcripts exist on microfilm for CBS News from the 1960s to mid-1980s, but not for the other networks. If a researcher wants to explore popular fiction, popular phonograph records, movies, or small-town news-papers, much of the record is gone forever. John MacKenzie's (1984: 174) impressive survey of the media through which British imperial propaganda spread from 1850 to 1950, found school text-books very hard to locate. Older films are disintegrating worldwide – the historical record disappearing before our eyes (Kaufmann, 1990).

METHODS AND CASES

I turn now to specific, well-executed examples of the *history proper* of communication. This kind of history draws our attention to the place of communication (in its various guises and dimensions) in human experience. It takes from macro-history its dramatic ques-tion: how do communication media constitute the human charac-ter? But it takes this question of philosophical anthropology to an historically situated place – how do specific changes not only from one medium to another, but transformations in organization, ideol-ogy, economic relations, or political sponsorship within a given medium relate to changes in human experience? Where macro-history asks primarily how the media shape the capacities of the human mind, the history of communication as I am describing it asks how media constitute and are constituted by the self, the experience of time and space, the notion of the public, the concept and experience of politics and society, and the languages through which people understand and experience any part of the world.

Michael McGerr's (1986) study of the transformation of Ameri-can political campaigning in the late nineteenth century is an ex-emplary work in two respects: first, it examines the relationship of a medium to the changing constitution of a field of human experience – politics; second, it refuses to confine its understanding of "medium" to the usual trio of oral, written, and electronic media. The communication medium McGerr is interested in is the cam-paign – part oral and participatory ritual, part printed exhortation, part party-organized mass spectacle. (Interestingly, it is a medium that symbolically characterizes American culture as a whole: Jules Verne's Phileas Fogg's first experience in the USA as he disembarks in San Francisco is to be jostled by people in the streets for a campaign rally.)

McGerr's intent is "to explain why politics no longer excites many Americans." He argues that the USA had a very lively political life in the mid-nineteenth century, characterized by a vividly and sometimes viciously partisan press, powerful allegiances of citizens to parties, and "spectacular" political campaigns in which vast numbers of citizens participated. By the 1920s (long before television, one might note), he finds that this "popular politics" has been replaced by "a more constricted public life, much like our own" (McGerr, 1986: vii).

While others have tried to explain the decline in voter turnout and political involvement in the USA after the 1890s, McGerr is original in emphasizing how a new ideology of political elites, concerning what kind of communication an electoral campaign should use, engendered new campaign practices. Urban liberal reformers in the 1870s found fault with the strong party system and the fierce loyalty citizens showed their parties. They initiated independence movements breaking from parties and founded extra-party organizations like good government clubs and municipal reform organizations. As they promoted ballot reform and civil service, they began to create "an alternative political style" (McGerr, 1986: 66). They invested not in uniforms and torches for parades as in the past, but in educational pamphlets for widespread distribution. The political campaign, in their model, was an indoor event, centered on reading, not an outdoor carnival. By 1888 a Wisconsin Democratic leader promised "to abstain from such methods of campaigning as address themselves to the excitement of the emotions rather than educating or convincing the intelligence of our citizens" (McGerr, 1986: 87). The *New York Times* praised candidate Grover Cleveland's emphasis on the tariff issue because "it makes no appeal to the emotions" (McGerr, 1986: 89). What contemporaries aptly called a "political Protestantism" set in as campaigning shifted from parading to pamphleteering.

McGerr's work is instructive for communication studies on several grounds. First, McGerr offers historical perspective that forces a more complex understanding of contemporary life than we sometimes get, demonstrating, for instance, that the decline of voter participation in the USA did not begin with television and TV-centered campaigning. Second, McGerr's examination of political communication is free from the institutional narrowness of much media history. That is, while he takes the press to be a vital actor in the story he tells, the chief agents in his drama are the leaders of political party organizations. The political party, in McGerr's work, is itself a medium of communication. If a communication medium is an agency for transmitting information from one person or group of people to another, then surely a party is, among other things, a communication medium. (Again, contemporary lessons are easy to draw: in 1990 the political parties are still more agenda setters than the media will ever be in most parts of the world, even in a system with traditionally weak parties as in the USA.) Third, McGerr is also unconstrained by the common distinction in the field of communication between transmission models of communication and ritual models of communication. When he examines the political campaign, he obviously sees both models at work. We could characterize the transformation he documents as a shift from the campaign as a communal ritual, "a process of communal self-revelation," to the campaign as information transmission, or, in McGerr's (1986: 149) terms, the "educational" and "advertised" rather than "spectacular" campaign styles. This gives the two models of communication a genealogy; abstractions, in McGerr, take on flesh. Finally, of course, his approach integrates the media of communication into a broader political, economic, and social history.

A study of theater as communication has been undertaken by Lawrence Levine (1988) with interestingly parallel results. Levine examines the reception of Shakespeare's plays in the USA to show that, early in the nineteenth century, Shakespeare was a part of the common culture, the popular culture, not something set aside for educated tastes. In the late nineteenth century, however, Shakespeare was appropriated as "high culture," taken to be intellectually beyond the reach of the masses. At the same time, theater-going became a more rigidly controlled public behavior. Entertainment as well as politics underwent a protestant reformation, in this case, under the tutelage of an anxious, defensive upper class.

The broader framework for a work like McGerr's or Levine's is that of Jürgen Habermas, although there is no indication that McGerr or Levine, situated in independent traditions of American political and cultural history, were influenced by Habermas. The translation of *The Structural Transformation of the Public Sphere* into English in 1989 was an important event, even though the outlines of the book were available to English-speaking scholars earlier from a capsule summary in *New German Critique* (Habermas, 1974) and from Alvin Gouldner's (1976) stimulating rendition.

Habermas outlines what is probably the single most important model available for placing the media in a larger framework of modern world history. Rejecting the conventional liberal theory that the growth of new communications media is necessarily a force for increased human liberty, Habermas is interested in both the emergence and decline of what he calls *"the public sphere."* If one believes that human beings should organize their societies so that all people can participate in decision making, with decision making arranged so that communication is as free, full, and fair as possible, then a history of the constitution of the public sphere, coterminous with the emergence of publicly available news media, representative democracy, and limitations on secret proceedings in government, becomes a central subject for modern history.

Habermas (1989) traces the rise of the "bourgeois public sphere" in the seventeenth and eighteenth centuries and its decline from the mid-nineteenth century on. In the earlier period, the bourgeois attack on feudal society and absolutist state power was fueled by a belief in principles of rational public discussion and freedom of speech. In the new bourgeois order, newspapers and public discussion carried on in coffeehouses and elsewhere established a public sphere, that is, a physical and discursive space between the state and its agencies, on the one side, and private enterprise and family life, on the other.

In the later period, the bureaucratization of politics and the commercialization of the media repressed the emancipatory possibilities of the bourgeois public sphere (however compromised they were from the outset by confinement to white, propertied males). Public opinion, once arrived at dynamically and authentically in public places, became more and more engineered by bureaucrats, advertisers, and propagandists. James Curran's (1977) influential essay on capitalist control of the British press offers for one country a concrete illustration of how capitalist expansion in the late nineteenth century repressed radical expression even after direct state controls on the press were repealed. This is consistent with the general position Habermas outlines, although, in recent work, Curran is sharply critical of Habermas and holds that the Habermasian notion of the early public sphere is flawed in part because it neglects the importance and virtues of the radical press (Curran, forthcoming).

Habermas' work does not adequately address how limited the bourgeois public sphere was in what was (for Habermas) its heyday. The glowing image of the democratic London coffeehouse, where people from all walks of life stopped to read the newspaper and argue with leading intellectual lights of the day, is hard to reconcile with what we know of the small size of the voting public, traditions of deferential voting, and the relative secrecy of governmental proceedings. The historical evidence in support of the Habermas view is all too scanty: "So far, historians using the Habermas model usually talk about the public of journalism without ever actually coming into contact with it" (Dooley, 1990: 473). Moreover, as John Keane (1984) observes, Habermas also paints too bleak a portrait of contemporary culture, seeing little room for contradiction or resistance in the administered society.

Even so, Habermas offers communication history a persuasive rationale. It is too little rationale to study communication institutions for their own sake – that is a kind of antiquarian motive; and it may be too much to study communication history as the central constitutive feature of human nature. This latter rationale is indeed a legitimate scientific motive, in my view, but so encompassing as almost to defy actual research and so grand as to dwarf differences among media that make a difference, differences worth talking about and fighting about, say, between a relatively free and relatively closed press.

PERSPECTIVES

Insofar as communication history has had an implicit structure, it is very nearly what Garth Jowett (1975: 36) observed in his review fifteen years ago: "the central problem confronted by communications historians is what takes place when a new medium of communication is introduced into a society." This should no longer be taken as "the" central problem. Putting the central question of communication history this way directs attention to discretely defined technologies. We know enough now to be skeptical of this orientation. Particularly if we take "technologies" to be the broadly defined realms of oral, print, and electronic communication, we are in deep trouble. Eisenstein's (1979) close attention to the differences between two forms of written communication – the scribal and the printed – should have permanently settled that issue.

But even within a more precisely defined technology, say, handwritten, alphabetic writing, the political and cultural contexts for the uses of that writing may vary so greatly as to minimize any common social, political, or cognitive consequences of the technology as such. That seems to me a vital lesson of the anthropological studies of literacy in North African and West African cultures conducted by Jack Goody and independently by Michael Cole and Sylvia Scribner (see Goody, 1987; Scribner and Cole, 1981). Communications media must be understood as *social practices* and cultural affordances, not distinct technologies. Raymond Williams (1974) makes this distinction clearly in his book on television, defined as a technology and a *cultural form*. Indeed, it is misleading to assume that we can even identify a technology apart from the cultural forms in which it is employed. In any event, the evolution and impact of new cultural forms is just as important as the evolution and impact of new technologies and just as amenable to study. Ian Watt (1957), among others, has studied the history of the novel as a cultural form; I have studied the history of the "inverted-pyramid" news story as a cultural form (Schudson, 1982); Daniel Hallin (forthcoming) and Kiku Adatto (1990) have both examined changing television broadcasting editorial practices as a cultural form, Adatto characterizing them as literary fashions or styles, Hallin as occupational assertions of professional power.

Speaking more generally, the organization of communication history according to a sequence of technical inventions, as Raymond Williams calls them, prejudges the history of communication in favor of some sort of technological determinism. It is difficult to avoid structuring histories of communication in a way that privileges the moment of invention of a new technical device. At the same time, the limitations of this technological model should be kept clear. Raymond Williams (1983a: 20) observes, just as one example, that in the 1880s and 1890s, as film technology emerged and made possible "new kinds of mobile and dynamic composition," in the arts August Strindberg was writing a new kind of stage drama with rapid shifts of location, sequences of images, and what we would now call "dissolves." And yet, there is no reason to believe either that Strindberg influenced early film workers or that early film experiment influenced Strindberg; both, instead, were part of, and responding to, a deeper cultural movement.

As the macro-historians insist, communication has to do with the underlying organization of *time and space* in a society. This is the peculiar complication for the study of communication of received ideas, Marxist or otherwise, of "base" and "superstructure." Communication practices are both base (we might even say fundamental) and primary shapers and carriers of superstructure. There is an opportunity here to link the heritage of Marx and Weber, on the one hand, with that of the anthropological Durkheim (1915/1965), on the other, who wrote of the social structuring of each human culture's concepts of time and space. There is also an opportunity to integrate into communication history the subject matter of geographers. The railroad is as much a medium of communication as the telegraph (though it carries goods as well as messages), the automobile as much a medium of communication as the radio, the airplane as much as television.

Alfred Chandler's work (1977), for instance, makes the case that the development of railroads in the nineteenth-century USA forced and provided opportunity for new management styles, new consumer habits, and ultimately new ways of being in the world, not only because the railroads reduced the effects of distance on human interaction, but because they were able, through new forms of coordination, predictably to reduce the effects of distance. Society was changed not only because you could move more speedily from A to B than before, but because goods started moving in large quantity from A to B and new systems of coordination and communication were developed to control this leap in the quantity of circulating objects. If innovations in communication and transportation provided an opportunity for denser human interaction (as did urbanization, a crucial change in human "communication"), they did so through the medium of increasingly sophisticated human organizations. So the history of communication is not just the history of technological changes that reduce the impact of time and space on human interaction, but social-organizational changes that make altering the coordinates of time and space desirable and manageable. This is the other side of the point James Carey (1967) made long ago in his criticism of Marshall McLuhan: that the direct effect of a new communication technology is not on "cognition" or "the mind" so much as on patterns of social organization and social coordination through which cognition is organized. Cognition itself is not an individual property, but a socially (and not just technologically) constructed phenomenon. Communication history will improve when the implicit psychology of the field of communication becomes less behaviorist, more Vygotskyan (1962).

"Time" and "space" are organized not only technologically and conceptually, but politically and linguistically. If there is an unjustly neglected work in the history of communication, it may be Benedict Anderson's book-length essay, *Imagined Communities: Reflections on the Origin and Spread of Nationalism* (1983). This is Anderson's confrontation with the almost total neglect of the problem of nationalism in the Marxist tradition. One might add that nationalism has been largely neglected in classic social theory in general; Weber and Durkheim offer no more insight than Marx. Anderson (1983: 15) offers less a fully developed argument than a strikingly developed insight – that nationhood is an "imagined political community." Nationhood, for Anderson, is an imaginative act. The cultural carriers of the national idea are the novel and the newspaper, and Anderson (1983: 39) borrows from Hegel to describe the reading of the daily newspaper as a mass ceremony, the modern person's substitute for morning prayers. For Anderson the convergence of capitalism and print technology, superimposed on the diversity of human languages, created the basis for a new form of imagined community, the nation-state.

If this is correct, then communication as a field has a historical subject which other disciplines have tended to neglect and which communication has all but totally ignored: the emergence of the nation-state and the system of nation-states that is the background assumption, the taken-for-granted of most social science of our day, not to mention the chief source of most of the major horrors of the twentieth century. Philip Schlesinger (1987) has recently called to the attention of communication scholars the problem of national identity. He correctly holds that most research on communication and nationhood takes the nation-state, national culture, and national identity for granted as unproblematic terms. He suggests, instead, that we "begin with the problem of how national identity is constituted and locate communications and culture within that problematic" (Schlesinger, 1987: 259).

In conclusion, I should note what by now is obvious – that in an essay purportedly about methodology I have said very little about methodology. The trouble with communication history is not that it lacks methodologies or that it abuses them. The trouble is that (a) there is so little historical writing that takes communication issues as central or problematic; (b) there is so little writing within communication history that recognizes the inseparability of technology and cultural form; and (c) there is so little sense of how to integrate an understanding of communications media with the central issues of social, economic, political, and cultural change that are at the heart of most historical writing. Rudimentary ideas, not faulty methods, betray communication history. What is unsatisfying is the floating between provocative, but abstract grandiosity and narrowly conceived, institutional histories. There is not nearly enough middle-range communication history. As for Jürgen Habermas and Benedict Anderson, I offer them not as exemplary methodologists, but as two thinkers who have offered compelling ideas about which an agenda of research in communication history could be developed. In the case of Habermas, the research agenda is under exploration in a variety of fields, including history, sociology, and communication. In the case of Anderson, I think the opportunities remain largely untapped.

In any event, there is plenty of room for historical research more theoretically informed and more linked to other features of history – history proper. Communication must be analysed with reference to the organization and social uses of technologies in specific historical settings; the technologies themselves must be seen as social and cultural practices. As always, this is as true from the side of reception as of production. If the production of cultural objects incorporates assumptions about how people make meaning and why they want information and in what forms they would like to receive it, so does their reception. "Reading," as Robert Darnton (1990: 171) observes, "is not simply a skill, but a way of making meaning, which must vary from culture to culture." When we understand this, I think, we will be much closer to developing communication history as a coherent field of study.

Part III

Pragmatics

The third and last part of the Handbook takes up the "pragmatics" of qualitative methodologies – how may qualitative approaches be applied for various purposes of research; what are the social uses and political implications of qualitative work; and what might be the perspectives for further theoretical and empirical development?

As in the introduction to Part I, we refer here to a few general reference works which may be useful to students and scholars in further work; the works cited in Part I remain relevant for this purpose. Two dictionaries of media studies which give attention to qualitative perspectives should be mentioned: *Key Concepts in Communication* (O'Sullivan *et al.*, 1983) and *A Dictionary of Communication and Media Studies* (Watson and Hill, 1989). In addition, the Sage series on "Qualitative Research Methods" and "A beginner's guide to doing qualitative research in mass communication" (Pauly, 1991) may be helpful. A volume surveying the main models of communication in the social sciences may also provide a point of departure for critique and for further work developing theories and models of communication which consider both its social-scientific and its humanistic-discursive aspects: *Communication Models for the Study of Mass Communications* (McQuail and Windahl, 1981).

The two chapters in Part III each represent a specific perspective on pragmatics. Chapter 11 explains the relevance of qualitative research for *theory development* with illustrations from some of the authors' own classic studies. Several other chapters in this handbook, of course, provide examples of theory development through qualitative inquiry. Chapter 11 documents, moreover, that qualitative research may be conducted systematically and has explanatory value beyond that of pilot studies. One important challenge for further work in this area is to develop the kind of *meta-theory*, mentioned in the introduction to Part II, which will enable research-ers to weigh different kinds of evidence with reference to a common standard cf analysis.

Chapter 12 brings in the relationship between qualitative re-search and its objects of inquiry – culture and society. The chapter thus poses a number of issues concerning the *social uses* and *contexts* of research, particularly in education and community life. One key argument is that various educational and political contexts lend themselves to *meta-communication*, or reflexivity about the pur-poses and structures of mass communication. Qualitative metho-dologies may help to empower the audience-public in such contexts by developing media literacy curricula and by involving the audi-ence in an assessment of the media's service to the public.

In conclusion, Chapters 11 and 12, like other contributions to the Handbook point to possible avenues for *further research*. The Handbook as a whole suggests that qualitative and quantitative methodologies are different, but complementary modes of inquiry, both of which have explanatory value in their own right. It remains for further studies to elaborate the distinguishing features of the two modes of inquiry and, more generally, their relevance for particular cultural contexts and social uses of research. Mass communication researchers need to consider not only why the mass media work as they do, but also the second-order why: *why* researchers want to know.

Chapter 11

Theory development
Studying events in their natural settings

Kurt Lang and Gladys Engel Lang

INTRODUCTION

If a guy brought an elephant through that door and one of us said, "that's an elephant," some of the doubters would say, "that's an inference – that could be a mouse with a glandular condition."

This remark, coming at a critical moment in the televised debates of the House Judiciary Committee over the impeachment of Richard M. Nixon, caused the hearing room to break into uncontrolled laughter that carried over, no doubt, to viewers as well. Representative William L. Hungate, the speaker, was nevertheless trying to score a serious point against die-hard supporters of the President, who kept insisting that anything less than a "smoking gun" was purely inferential. No court would ever accept it as evidence.

How do we indeed tell the difference between an elephant and an oversized mouse? Certainly not just by taking measurements. Nor would one have to examine hundreds of mice to rule out that a particular elephant was a highly improbable aberration of a diminutive mammal. Rather, our determination follows from what we already know, from what we take for granted within our universe of discourse. It depends, in short, on context.

Knowing the context is likewise the only way to infer the meaning read into more complex social situations. Such meanings do not exist as "givens"; they can be contested as heatedly, and frequently are, as the question of presidential complicity in Watergate. Nor can we ever accept without some probing the reasons persons offer as "explanations" of their behavior. One interprets or infers from what one hears and observes.

In what follows, we show how to plan direct observation in a natural setting and how one can draw inferences about the motives of participants from such data. The method is compatible with rigorous analysis; it is pre-eminently suited for on-site observation of public behavior at odds with the conventions by which people order their lives. The method also yields data with which to challenge the dominant "outsider" view typified in the big news stories carried by the media. Insofar as we seek to clarify meanings, our approach can be characterized as "interpretative."

An original version of this paper was presented at a Conference on Alternatives to Survey Methods (Santa Fe, New Mexico, 1975) examining "alternative" methods of attitude assessment. Surveys are also widely used in communication research as sources for quantitative measures of media penetration, of audience behavior, of general preferences, and of perceptions, knowledge, and opinion through which one can gauge the magnitude of media effects, or, by looking at the patterns of correlation, infer the underlying processes. No longer need we rely on personal impressions or evidence of a purely anecdotal sort. Telephone surveys, launched on almost a moment's notice, have greatly augmented our knowledge of short-term change in response to particular messages or events, while the longer time series available allow us to track shifts in knowledge, opinions, behavior, and social values and to relate these to other indicators, including measures of media content. These data consist of what people say to an interviewer, not on how they conduct themselves or what they produce, two equally important components of culture. What respondents tell interviewers about themselves does not always accord with their behavior in circumstances they cannot fully anticipate.

Everyone acknowledges that no method can deal with more than a tiny fragment of reality. Thus, survey texts focus on sampling, on how to select respondents sufficiently representative to reflect the distribution of responses in the society at large. But we also sample what is in the respondents' minds and insofar as our queries grow out of concerns previously made focal, the survey is less than a fully neutral instrument (see, for example, Phillips, 1971). Pollsters often present issues to which respondents have given little thought. And, in terms of the general movement of public opinion, as opposed to changes in individual feelings or beliefs, changes in the questions asked (not just how questions are worded) can be as useful an indicator of issues that occupy public attention as the changing distribution of responses to a question repeated over time.

Direct observation also has its drawbacks. Here, too, as in other methods of inquiry, there are problems of observer bias, of replication, of subject reactivity, and so forth. No observer, or team of observers, can be literally everywhere at once. A field director must station them according to some strategic plan and instruct them on the setting, the actors, and the transactions on which they should focus as well as on background events. This, by itself, is not enough. The more intimate view that "getting close" affords is no guarantor of "objectivity." Entrapped by the "insider's" viewpoint, the observer may accept the participants' own common-sense explanations without checking them through. And lastly, insofar as the observer has actually become a participant, there can be effects on the behavior studied. In at least one instance, such a presence actually became a major influence on the survival of a cult being studied (Festinger *et al.*, 1957). More common is the effect of the press when it manages to get into the thick of things. Turning on its spotlight keeps some things going. To avoid this, social science observers usually keep a low profile, yet, in so doing, forgo data that might be available were they to assume a more active role.

Although direct observation in natural settings is, as we shall argue, compatible with rigor in design and careful analysis, when it comes to the study of the current scene in what Graham Wallas (1915) described as the "great society," referring to the expansion of its horizons, one cannot, even when employing a multitude of observers, simply transpose the methods of descriptive eth-nography. This is what Charles Madge and Tom Harrisson (1939) did in their mass-observation studies of Great Britain in the mid-1930s, with volunteer observers sending in reports on the cel-ebration of Armistice Day, the inauguration of King George VI, the Lambeth Walk as it was danced by young people, and so forth (for recent evaluations of early mass-observation activity, see Clader and Sheridan, 1984, and Finch, 1986). These pioneer studies con-tain much vivid description, but little in the way of analysis beyond the general summary of observer accounts. The authors drew few inferences, most of them *ad hoc* with no effort to put them to any systematic test against their data. Since then, observational studies have advanced some distance beyond these pioneering attempts. No longer can they be dismissed out of hand as "soft" (see Miles and Huberman, 1984).

ENUMERATION

To make an enumeration is to make a record of a predefined category of events. While nearly all enumeration is preceded by some interpretation, however rudimentary, as to whether the event does or does not fit the prescribed category, this objective is secondary to a complete listing of relevant observations.

We distinguish between two different approaches to enumeration. The first has the observer recording "objective" events in a way similar to how interviewers record statements made by their survey respondents. Observers, no less than interviewers, are required to be "neutral," to maintain a psychological distance, and to assume a posture of detachment with but one essential difference: the interviewer controls the situation by soliciting responses, whereas the observer is meant not to intrude at all.

In the second approach, the observer is expected to play a dual role – as observer *and* as participant. The record of observations should include an analysis of one's own experience as well as the interpretations that grew out of them. It is, in short, a variant of participant observation, where the observer doubles as the analyst (Denzin, 1970a).

We shall refer to the first approach as "multiple observation" and the second as "mass observation." As always, the distinction is sharper in theory than in actuality.

Multiple observation

Multiple observation is the more appropriate technique for studying events that occur in well-defined settings, are clearly bounded in time and space, and replicate essentially the same relationship. The exact number of observers does not matter as much as do other conditions that have to be met.

First, observations have to be standardized much in the same way as the interviews in a survey. The dimensions or attributes focal to the investigation need to be specified in advance, so that observation schedules can be drawn up and observers instructed as to what to look for.

Second, the events and occurrences to be enumerated must be accessible to observers from preselected vantage points to which they can be assigned. Again, such assignment to sampling points is broadly analogous to the selection of respondents from lists of individuals or by households but with one significant difference:

events, not individuals, are the units of observation. Hence, sampling strategy must aim at an unbiased selection of stations or situations where the relevant encounters, transactions, or behavioral responses are likely to be found with acceptable frequency.

Insofar as there is a predictable pattern of physical movement, one can sample by locale, stationing observers at sites where people normally pass in their rounds of daily activity (a marketplace or a railroad station), in centers of certain institutional activities (a cathedral or a lecture hall), or at sites where particular kinds of transactions typically take place (a check-out counter or a hiring hall). Any of these qualify as strategic vantage points from which to observe particular kinds of behavior. This is also how many organizations generate their own records, usually on standardized forms, by focusing on points of routine contact with their public or clientele. But their procedures do not of themselves ensure that the observations are standardized. They may ask for information about which the record keepers are sensitive, or the record itself may be used to measure administrative performance. Sometimes definitions and/or baselines are changed for reasons that have nothing to do with research objectives. As everyone knows, unless an enumeration stands in a constant relation to the phenomenon it is meant to track, the cross-group and time-series comparisons based on it lose much of their value. Indeed, they may actually obscure the true state of affairs.

When it comes to events that have no distinct locale but are clearly linked to role behavior, observers have to follow their subjects in their normal round of activity. This is what Reiss (1971) did in studying police–citizen encounters. Latane and Darley (1970) went even further in studying bystander behavior in simulated attacks against persons in public places. Such contrivance increased their control over the stimulus event. The recording procedures were, of course, the same as in autonomously generated situations.

Although one suspects that the presence of "outsiders" in circumstances as touchy as law enforcement and crime would have some influence on police behavior, this may be less than expected. As time passed, so Reiss (1971) maintains, the scientific observers became part of the team, and officers ceased to accord them any undue attention. There are, nevertheless, limits to the utility of observations conducted in a "natural" setting. For one thing, it creates a dependence on what one can see and is able to overhear. It precludes statistically random selection. Replication with comparable samples is difficult. Researchers are also deterred by its high cost. The use of administrative records that cover long time spans and the time-series data produced by surveys are so much more economical. When both are lacking, knowledgeable information can fill the gap. Yet, systematic observation, even when confined to a single point in time, can be a useful supplement, even an indispensable corrective, to more conventional methods of social research.

Mass observation

Our own interest has been in the more elusive outpourings of sentiments and shifts in public mood. Events of this sort are neither as circumscribed nor as closely tied to routines as the recurrent and repeatable incidents that have been the subject of multiple observation. Usually they follow a build-up in which the mass media have come to play an increasingly important role. Because of its greater flexibility, mass observation is the more suitable technique for collecting fugitive data that are likely to be lost irretrievably unless recorded as things happen. When it comes to riots, acts of insurgency, hostile outbursts, collective expressions of euphoria, devotion, or fear, social scientists all too often are forced to rely on press accounts and such official sources as the police or a government inquiry supplemented by such eye-witness accounts as one is able to dredge up afterwards. How much better to have reports from trained observers at the scene, who are free to roam, to vary their mode of observation, to track down whatever leads they find, and generally to use their ingenuity though guided by some prior notion of what is relevant to the study objective. Each works much as an ethnographer would, playing a dual role as "outside" observer and as participant in the event.

Unlike the ethnographer in the field, observers of the urban scene will often, by the nature of the situation, be moving among complete strangers. Their identity remains unknown, forcing observers to fall back on appearances just as most of us do in everyday life. Erving Goffman (1959: 3) formulated the general paradox as follows: "The more the individual is concerned with reality that is not available to perception, the more he must concentrate his attention on appearances." The statement is an implicit guide to what an observer should enumerate.

The first and most obvious among these enumerations are visual cues as to the identity of participants. An on-the-spot survey might be too distracting. But estimates of age, sex, and racial compositions can be made at a glance. They are gross but nevertheless useful indicators, especially when supplemented by further clues about identities from the badges and uniforms people wear; still more subtle indicators can be found in the manner of dress and how people generally comport themselves. Appearances can also reveal how people come to be where they are, but obviously do not suffice insofar as in the urban setting the "appearential" order has been partly replaced by spatially segregated activity (Lofland, 1973).

Additionally, one can look at patterns of traffic to understand where participants come from. During our observational study of the religious crusade Billy Graham conducted in New York (Lang and Lang, 1960), our observers systematically surveyed the number of chartered buses and their places of origin, which media reports of the crusade usually overlooked. In another study (Lang and Lang, 1953), we were greatly helped by the statistics of the Chicago transport authorities and commuter lines, which bolstered our confidence in the generalizations based on direct observation of the throngs that lined the streets of Chicago on the day of General Douglas MacArthur's triumphal return to receive his hero's welcome in what was then America's second city. Our statistics were a corrective to the live coverage and the blown-up media reports of the welcoming crowds.

A second and altogether different kind of "appearance" are the chance remarks and conversations reaching the ears of observers. Revealing of the prevailing climate as such "overheards" often are, one can hardly accept them as representative of everyone's view. Much is therefore to be gained by an observer who takes a more active role by engaging others in conversation or, occasionally, by interviewing them openly. The latter method was used with some success in studies of participants in several political demonstrations – such as the 1965 civil rights demonstration along US Route 40, the interstate highway that led into Washington (Pinard et al., 1969); the Vietnam Day march in London in 1969 (Barker et al., 1969); and the Washington March for Victory (Lin, 1974; see also Hadden and Rymph, 1966). Unfortunately, these interviews did no more than probe backgrounds and motivations; they failed to take full advantage of the observers' presence at the scene.

Observers who are focused on head counts and on other things demanded of them, may be too busy to note less tangible cues about shifts in mood or the signs and symbols that force themselves into the focus of attention. They are unlikely to involve themselves sufficiently to adopt the perspective of other participants necessary for the kind of "thick description" advocated by Clifford Geertz (1973).

This is one reason for instructing observers to include in their record what they themselves are experiencing. We try to control for subjectivity by two procedures: observers are requested to keep this information separate from their descriptions of the behavior of others; they are also given pre-observation questionnaires that ask about what they themselves expect and for what they prepare themselves. With these two sets of information, we can look upon our observers as respondents. Their accounts help to illuminate from "within" what others have merely viewed from the outside.

Finally, we acknowledge that the study of an event by mass observation remains incomplete unless placed in a more general symbolic (political or religious) context. Public pageantry, insignia, leaflets, or any activity in support of a particular image is yet another field on which observations must focus. Equally relevant are the surrounding commercial activity and the visible presence of police, ushers, ambulances, and other social control agents. Together, with assistance from the press, they set the stage. The public recognition granted by the news media can make a national spectacle out of a purely local event.

The news media have a key role in shaping our ideas of the world. They tell us not only what is important, but they also shape our expectations of things to come and disseminate an image of what the public mood is (McCombs and Shaw, 1972). Press statements concerning an impending event exemplify press intervention. Other relevant media content are media portrayals of tension and tranquillity, of public euphoria and dismay, of heroes and villains and the degree to which they, and the groups they may represent, are consistently cast into unambiguously positive (or negative) stereotypes or depicted in a more or less balanced manner (see, for example, Turner and Surace, 1956).

So ubiquitous have the media indeed become that sometimes they steal the show. To cite just one example, during the Paris student disorders in May 1968, radio reporters with open microphones were instrumental in bringing a student leader into negotiations with the French minister of education. Later the rejection by the student leader of a proposal to end the strike was heard live by a national television audience, later becoming part of the lore of 1968 (for a good English summary of these incidents, see Singer, 1970). Since then, audiences all over the world have been witness to revolutionary events played out live on television, often with that larger audience in mind. In 1989 English-language banners were carried by Chinese students in Tiananmen Square and in several demonstrations in eastern Europe.

The possibility of such interplays between on-the-scene and media activity force mass observers to be on the lookout for any presumably spontaneous activity generated by, or staged for, the benefit of the television camera as well as for evidence of feedback. To cite another French example: in 1961 draftees among the troops in Algiers defied orders to launch a revolt after appeals of the civil government and estimates of the situation by journalists reached them via the transistor radios many of them had (Ambler, 1966; Kelly, 1965). And in postwar Germany, media recognition of their "heroic struggle" during the Berlin blockade of 1948–9 was a real morale booster which made the inhabitants of that besieged city more determined to hold out in the face of Soviet threats to close out this outpost of the West completely isolated within Soviet-controlled territory (Davison, 1956).

INFERENCES

Regardless of what method of enumeration is used, the principles embedded in the methodology for drawing inferences remain essentially unchanged. In mass observation, as in sociological research generally, two logically distinct, though pragmatically overlapping and hence complementary, steps are involved: inferring the subjective mental states that underlie the social behavior of actors, and constructing a more abstract theoretical model of the causal relationships that underlie the pattern, the equivalents of Max Weber's meaningful interpretation and causal explanation (Weber, 1964: 88). To be sure, each step has its pitfalls, and one can draw false inferences from even the most painstakingly accurate enumerations. But the legitimacy of these complementary approaches has been recognized by methodologists as different in orientation as Karl Popper and Aaron Cicourel (see Cicourel, 1964, and Popper, 1952, which discusses the logic-of-the-situation approach).

We shall briefly address four issues related to the analytical procedures of inference. They are: (1) imputing meaning from observations of the behavior of others; (2) analysing situations so as to infer the meanings others read into them; (3) constructing a model of the process through which diverse perspectives develop into public definitions; and (4) checking out such inferences for their consistency with the data and their fit with the model.

1 *Imputation of meaning.* As a rule we are prepared to accept verbal statements as valid expressions of opinion. We take them, as one says, at face value; only statements that for some reason are implausible will be discounted. But we also know that people do not always mean what they say. Sometimes they consciously dissimulate. On sensitive subjects especially, they may be unwilling to reveal their "real" thoughts. Where public and private opinion diverge, it is not always clear which of the two governs behavior.

That there are problems, is dramatized whenever one encounters the phenomenon of "pluralistic ignorance": most residents in a community may declare themselves personally willing to admit minority-group members as close neighbors and friends, but simultaneously may consider progress hampered by strongly contrary feelings that they ascribe to many other residents in their community. In this instance, the group opinion, summed by what respondents individually convey to the interviewer, contradicts the perception of public opinion, of what people in general believe. But how does one determine where the "real" opinion lies? Did respondents, not wanting to appear "bigoted," rationalize their behavior by imputing to others the feelings they hesitated to voice to the interviewer? Or did they unthinkingly assume that the prevailing state of affairs had to be sustained by community opinion, as the analysis by Fields and Schuman (1976) suggests? Such misreading, if that is what it is, becomes an obstacle to change.

One can go further and argue that, in situations like the above, behavior is a more valid indicator of the willingness to desegregate than opinion on hypothetical situations. But as to the true feelings of respondents or how they will respond when the issue becomes acute, one can never be sure. Respondents themselves will be making inferences about the concrete consequences of desegregation and adjust their "opinions" to what they perceive to be the community interest as conveyed to them both by persons with whom they converse and through the news media.

2 *Interpretation of how others see a situation*. Many standardized enumerations do no more than measure behavior against some standard and do not, in fact, involve any inference at all. To illustrate, we draw once again on the enumeration by Reiss (1971) of police behavior, especially when making arrests. During some 5,000 transactions observed, all in urban high-crime areas, police were judged to have exhibited "antagonistic" behavior toward citizens in about 8 per cent of the incidents; there were only fifteen instances (less than one-third of a percent) of "excessive force." Taken at face value, these figures belie the deterioration of police–civilian relationships in black ghetto areas, on which charges of police brutality and demands for more civilian oversight had been based.

The enumerations also contained evidence that police actually tended to be less restrained when dealing with citizens of their own race. But provocative conduct by police officers in only a diminutive proportion of encounters may nevertheless suffice to set off a storm of protest. The point here is not, however, the frequency with which such police offenses must occur before they arouse generalized hostility, or whether the enumeration is a statistically accurate estimate of overall "incivility." Observation needs to clarify how police conduct is defined by citizens in the kind of incident in which police normally intervene. The broader sociological issue is that police authority, even when exercised in a lawful manner, as it seems to be in the overwhelming number of cases, often enjoys no legitimacy.

What makes police intervention controversial and provokes interference from bystanders and resistance to arrests – behaviors which, in their turn, impel behavior through which the police assert their authority – is a chain of events most often set off by an arrest for a minor violation, where citizens proclaim their innocence and thereby make the police action appear arbitrary, regardless of whether or not it is justified. This sequence is even more likely when a police officer intervenes on his own authority, coming upon a situation by chance rather than in answer to a call. In these circumstances, there is no "complainant" to defend the legitimacy of police intervention. The emergency aspect also keeps the police officer from making the usual queries through which he establishes his rightful authority.

The enumerations of these more or less routine encounters begin to form a picture. They suggest how divergent definitions of police conduct develop. Bystanders, not knowing the reason for police intervention, or perhaps knowing themselves to be as guilty as the person being apprehended, are aroused to protest against treatment perceived as unjust. To them it appears that the offender is picked up solely on grounds of class, race, age, or other prejudice (Reiss, 1971: 55–9). One can test this inference with further enumerations of "overheards," through which more general political currents can be identified. Police coping with potential disorder in political demonstrations are especially vulnerable to charges that, instead of intervening on the side of justice, they are in fact preserving the power of privileged groups. As Peter Manning (1977: 10) points out, "potential discrepancies between public and private meanings [in police work] have not been sufficiently attended to."

3 *Public moods.* Persons consciously associate themselves with certain symbols which, so to speak, become extensions of their selves. One's personal make-up, mode of dress, recreational and artistic preferences, and so forth reflect the urge, not necessarily conscious, to present oneself as a particular social type along with the complementary urge to differentiate oneself from those of a different type. This duality – cited by Simmel and others as the essential moving force behind fashion (see Simmel, 1957) – states an important sociological principle.

The long hair, the beards, the distinctively casual costuming which became popular among American youth in the late 1960s, the emergence of "alternative" publications, the partial displacement of the more conventional themes of love and courtship in popular music by lyrics openly challenging establishment values – have been among the visible expressions of social ferment. Can one accept these indicators at face value? Some caveats are in order.

One should not jump to the conclusion, accepted by so many authorities, that there is an *intrinsic* connection between a style and the ideology propounded by its early proponents. The odd assortment through which disaffected youth in the 1960s chose to present itself were as much Edwardian as Fidelista. And while hairstyle was partly modeled after the Beatles, the preferred attire was a strange mixture of conventional work clothes, US frontier dress, and Third World styles. Before long, emblems associated with social protest and the peace movement were being commercially marketed like any other fashion. Two sociologists found that the overwhelming number of teenagers, exactly when protest in America was nearing its height, were unable to give a correct rendering of the main themes in Top Ten protest songs. They had no clear awareness of the deviant message carried by the lyrics (Robinson and Hirsch, 1969). Consequently, the popularity of this type of song in the late 1960s (see Cole, 1971; also Carey, 1969; Denisoff and Peterson, 1972; Horton, 1957) cannot, despite all other appearances, be taken as an accurate indicator of anti-establishment sentiment, but has obvious links to a whole series of changes, particularly in sound broadcasting, which had lost its mass audiences to television and now had to be content with winning listeners from the remaining minorities. This opened new opportunities for small record companies, prepared to give writer–performers more leeway than the industry giants. Meanwhile, court decisions weakened the power of official censors and undercut the *de facto* monopoly of ASCAP (the American Society of Composers and Performers) over all music that went on the air. Purveyors of protest music were freed to serve a growing and increasingly affluent youth market.

Although there is, no doubt, some relationship between cultural trends and the standards that managers of media organizations consider acceptable or desirable, exploitation by the media of the more sensational aspects of the ferment associated with the 1960s exaggerated the extent to which these expressions enjoyed general acceptance. They obviously found more favor within the cultural and artistic establishment than in the population at large. Many of us, including reporters and researchers, become entrapped in the reality the news media collectively construct. This is evident even in projects intended to "correct" press bias. Thus, the study by a group at Leicester University of the anti-Vietnam demonstration held in London in 1969 (Halloran *et al.*, 1970) instructed observers stationed along the line of the march to enumerate all manifestations of violence as a basis for comparison with the attention violence received in news reports of the event. By this measure, the coverage, governed as it was by certain news values, greatly overplayed a small number of incidents in a march which, except for a clash between demonstrators and police at Grosvenor Square, site of the US Embassy, was basically peaceful.

The criticism of the coverage may be valid. What it overlooks is how much not only the press but also the marchers, and certainly the researchers themselves, were focused on the possibility of violence. The *New Statesman*, for example, devoted considerable attention to the prospects for a violent clash between police and demonstrators (see, for instance, Jones, 1968). Queried about their expectations, the majority of a representative sample of 270 participants in the march, two-thirds of whom were veterans of prior demonstrations, said that they had indeed expected violence, but coupled this, in almost all instances, with declarations that they personally would do their utmost to keep things peaceful. When a small minority, bent on provoking an incident, broke away from the main line of the march to head in the direction of the US Embassy where, true to form, they tried to break through police cordons, police and TV cameras were there – the one to prevent, the other to record and transmit the inevitable clash.

4 *Checking out inferences.* We now briefly describe, in more general terms, how one infers the fabric of meanings. The utility of some quantitative procedures is by no means ruled out. Enumerations of indicators found in records are, as we shall show, often indispensable in the management of vast amounts of qualitative description. But these operations are no more than a prelude to the construction of richer interpretations, which then need to be tested for their consistency with data in observer reports. There is no mystery about this. Analysis of a psychological experiment or a field survey also goes beyond internal validity checks to develop the more general implications underlying the hypothesis subjected to a strict quantitative test. Moreover, the form in which mass observation material is recorded forces one to make some inferences, however low-level, at every step along the way. The continuous checking of tentative inferences against data, some of which may have appeared irrelevant in prior scannings, makes it difficult to separate theory testing from theory construction (see, for example, Glaser and Strauss, 1967).

None of this implies that one conducts a mass observation study or embarks on the analysis of mass observation data without preconceptions. Haphazardly planned fishing expeditions rarely yield interesting results. But there should be no premature closure even if this means less than absolutely systematic data collection. The inventive researcher, using a trained imagination and drawing on the existing body of social science knowledge, may find other sources of evidence to complement and fill some of the gaps in observer reports.

How inferences derived from observations in a microcosm can clarify trends in the larger surrounding world will now be illustrated with two of our own mass observation studies – of the Billy Graham religious crusade to win new souls for Christianity and of the reception which General Douglas MacArthur, the last of the World War II heroes to return to the continental USA, received on his visit to Chicago following his abrupt dismissal by President Truman for insubordination.

BILLY GRAHAM

It was in the summer of 1957, years before the heyday of the TV evangelists, that Billy Graham took his crusade to New York, the reputed city of sin, provoking much media fanfare and many comments about the revival of religion in the USA. In a reversal of a previous trend away from religiosity, church attendance in recent years had been going up. Third-generation Americans, so it was said, were once again returning with enthusiasm to forms of worship and practices which their parents had been all too ready to abandon in their haste to become part of the mainstream. Certainly, the 56,246 "decisions for Christ" among the estimated two million who came to hear the famous evangelist in Madison Square Garden seemed to attest to the success of his three-and-a-half months' effort.

Its advance billing practically mandated that the event be televised. And so it was. We, for our part, wanted to improve our understanding of what such decision making meant for the individuals and for the future of organized religion (Lang and Lang, 1960). About the middle of the crusade, when it was running full steam, we sent forty-three students to observe. They were to blend with the crowds while observing as best they could *who* was moved by Graham's appeals, and *how* – by what techniques and what symbols – he made his appeal. Each student filled out a pre-observation questionnaire about his or her religious orientation, church affiliation, views on the crusade, and feelings about participating in the study. They also handed in detailed written accounts of their observations together with a personal evaluation of the experience.

Even without direct questioning, simply by noting how people looked, how they dressed, how they were seated, the way they raised their hands in response to the queries about where they had come from, and the signs on charter buses parked nearby, observers were able to establish without much difficulty that the audience was not even remotely representative of the New York City population. Observers agreed that on the day they made their observations, nearly one-half the audience definitely came from outside the city, from the ring of suburbs and exurbs within commuting distance and even beyond. As to the sections predominantly occupied by local residents, observers uniformly remarked on the small number of blacks and Puerto Ricans, who were living near Madison Square Garden. Lower middle class was a label that would have fitted the majority of attendees.

Some other readily accessible quantitative measures: women predominated by a ratio between five to one and eight to one. Most visible among them was the middle-aged, middle-class woman wearing her summer hat, many of whom were also carrying small bibles or other religious artifacts. And, judging by the show of hands when asked "who has been here before," men far more than women turned out to be first-nighters. Conversations and interviews held as spot checks confirmed these observations.

Observers were also able to differentiate between the organized "flocks," who mostly sat in the reserved sections downstairs, and the unorganized "flotsam," mostly loners who had found their own unshepherded way into the Garden and typically found seats in the open sections upstairs. These included a fair number of "regulars." From where they sat observers found it difficult to estimate just how many these were, because they did not stand out in any way by their appearance from the rest. Those that observers were able to engage in conversation typically disavowed any intention to heed Graham's call to step forward; having repented long ago, a number of them explained to observers, they saw no reason to heed the call to step forward. They had come to watch others find their salvation and thereby to assure themselves that these people believed as they did themselves.

Observers did, however, agree that the proverbial middle-aged, lower-middle-class woman with her hat was much less in evidence among those who came forward in answer to Graham's call. Now family groups (often with children), teenagers, and young adults, either in couples or alone, predominated, and there were proportionately many more men than in the audience as a whole. They consisted overwhelmingly of people attending for the first time.

We had two competing explanations for what had moved people to make a "decision for Christ." One was predicated on the assumption that the setting in which Graham issued his appeal had breached the resistance of some who normally would have held back. Observers instructed to remain aware of and to record their own reactions to things that might even have moved them cited Graham's unobtrusive entrance on the stage, his voice – soft to begin with but gradually rising, while still soothing, as he issued his invitations – the way in which, with assistance from the lighting, he managed to monopolize attention, and the care taken to control all outbursts of emotion, even religious ecstasy, or behavior that might detract from the solemnity of the scene. The setting did indeed evoke some analogies to how hypnotists work.

Alternatively, we could work with the hypothesis that most of those making their decision that night had at least been strongly disposed to do just that. First-nighters in a flock with persons who already had made their decision would be under some pressure from those who now wished to see the group of converts enlarged. Flotsam who joined them may have included some regulars – apparently people who needed time to overcome a sense of their own unworthiness or finally screwed up their courage, in a few instances by returning in the company of a partner.

The second interpretation is consistent with certain themes in Graham's appeal. Lacking recording equipment, we were unable at the time to undertake a systematic content analysis, and must rely on the allusions in observer reports to the all too obvious effort to create a familiar setting, to put the audience at their ease (including jokes), to keep them involved by inviting them to join in the singing and other familiar forms of worship, and to maintain a highly respectable decorum. When it came to the decisions, which Graham described as "hard," everything in the power of the managers was done to make them as "easy" as possible. The sins explicitly mentioned by Graham were mostly nominal and vague enough to be defined however one wished. The hell-fire appeals of old-fashioned revivalism were totally lacking. No one was called upon to make a public confession and, so Graham assured his audience, it would not take very long or be the cause of any undue embarrassment.

The demographic characteristics of the audience, insofar as these could be inferred, together with the emblems people carried, also suggest a strong prior identification with Protestantism. And, looking at the subjective reactions of our own observers, we found that practicing Catholics described themselves as least "moved" by Graham's exhortations. On the other hand, several Jewish observers had felt personally touched, but would have gone forward only, so they said, if the decision had been presented as being "for

God." (The one person who did step out recanted soon after.) In other words, reactions were pretty much in accord with previous religious orientations and practice, and did not represent either new commitments or changes in attitude toward religion.

What the crusade succeeded in producing is what Johnson (1971: 887), in a truly ingenious experimental replication of our study, calls a "normatively prescribed 'religious experience' for urban individuals already socialized into this form of religious experience." Except for the term "urban," which may apply to the subjects in his study of the Seattle crusade, this finding accords with our inferences about the small number of converts won by Graham and the even fewer souls he wrested from the claws of the devil.

This last point could have been substantiated directly had we been able to conduct a survey of the converts or at least been given a breakdown of how frequently each of the five alternatives given on the "decision cards" were recorded by Graham's assistants. The choices for those who stepped forward ranged from "acceptance of Christ as Saviour and Lord" and "an assurance of salvation" to "restoration," "dedication," and "reaffirmation of faith." At the time, the Billy Graham organization refused to release such information; it was also too soon for a follow-up to the churches to whom "converts" were being referred. Some information published since then essentially bears out the conclusions from our own "soft" data (McLoughlin, 1960). Having risen for a decade, church attendance peaked in 1957 before beginning a slow downward glide (Gallup, 1972).

MACARTHUR DAY IN CHICAGO

The ticker-tape reception given to General Douglas MacArthur on his return to the USA in April 1951 was an opportunity to revive the custom of honoring returning heroes, last practiced six years before when other military leaders back from World War II were given enthusiastic welcomes by a population still jubilant over their victories. Times had changed. American troops in Korea, after a forced retreat from advanced positions near the Chinese border, had managed to organize an effective defense near the thirty-eighth parallel, the originally agreed-upon boundary between South and North Korea. For several months, the two armies had been facing each other in an apparent stalemate, leaving Americans divided over the wisdom of Truman's policy to fight a limited war.

MacArthur from his position as supreme commander in the Far East had, on several occasions, publicly spoken out in harsh criticism against presidential policy.

It is against this background that we need to understand the rush by the mayor of Chicago, along with those of other cities, big and small, to extend an invitation for a hero's welcome. There were obvious political overtones to the general's triumphal return. In the two weeks between the dismissal and the reception in Chicago, MacArthur dominated the news. Statements of support and expressions of public indignation at the treatment meted out to him were prominent. Our own open-ended study of MacArthur Day (Lang and Lang, 1953) was designed above all as a first-hand exploration of outbursts described by some as bordering on hysteria. We used some thirty-one observers, and two persons monitored the TV coverage to supplement observations made on the streets.

Our first, and perhaps most dramatic, finding was that MacArthur Day as experienced by participants differed from MacArthur Day as it appeared to those who watched the live coverage on television. This finding was entirely serendipitous. Our study had *not* been planned as a quasi-experimental comparison of a sample of participants with a control group of television viewers limited to vicarious participation. We had included the home screen only because we wanted the fullest picture. Using the reports to seek the reasons for the unanticipated contrast between the two perspectives came only as an afterthought. Our first hint that the television perspective gave a less than authentic view of reality came from a telephone conversation right after the event between an observer and one of the television monitors. It was sustained and sharpened by systematic content analysis of all observer reports and of that section of the audio tapes of the television available to us. (There were as yet no VCRs, and our incomplete audio tapes were borrowed.)

Our analysis led us to identify three factors in the television coverage responsible for the creation of an image of the event which was profoundly different from that of the people in the crowds lining the streets of Chicago. These factors were: the consistent pointing of cameras toward the most spectacular, dramatic, and "interesting" aspects of the welcome; a commentary that raised expectations even when ostensibly nothing was happening; and "reciprocal effects" in the form of crowd responses to the television cameras. The televised spectacle, as seen from the perspective of mobile cameras and roving reporters, stood in sharp contrast to the more mundane experience of those lining the streets. They had a long wait with little to do. Reaction to MacArthur, when he finally showed up, was remarkably restrained.

Tabulation of "overheards" and conversations with observers showed us that a plurality of attenders had been looking forward to something wild, even mildly threatening. These allusions, taken together with those that emphasized spectacular aspects of the event, made up well over half of the remarks relevant to our assessment of why people had come. A still more encompassing tabulation of every suggestion in the records, including badges and behavioral cues, about what had brought out the crowds, yielded the following rank order: interest in seeing a celebrity like MacArthur turned out to have been the prime attraction with "interest in the spectacle" a close second. Only a minority of the statements coded as evidence pointed to such other motives as "rendering homage to MacArthur personally" or "support of his political cause."

That observers no less than spectators were reacting to expectations derived from the media build-up, is evident from information elicited before the event. Both groups had been more or less primed by the press to expect something dramatic, and so drama it had to be, at least for television, even if the reality did not quite live up to the billing. This inference was backed up by interviews with TV producers. The welcome was depicted almost entirely in terms of unifying patriotic rather than potentially divisive symbols. The coverage steered clear of any reference to the political controversy that was coming to a head. Expressions of dissent, such as a critical banner that greeted the parade as it passed near the campus of the University of Chicago, were passed over lightly. Nothing was allowed to mar the occasion. But given the background of controversy, the picture of the public response conveyed by the coverage, intentionally or not, left an impression that the public had rallied behind MacArthur against the President who had dismissed him.

It is hard to exaggerate the prominence that the press had given MacArthur in the short two-week interim between word of the abrupt dismissal and Chicago's red-carpet welcome, thereby establishing the framework for the interpretation of the day's events. Content analysis of the three major Chicago dailies revealed that preparations for MacArthur Day, together with reports of the tumultuous crowds that had turned out in other cities, enjoyed nearly uninterrupted front-page attention during the entire period. Newspapers were also filled with expressions of support for MacArthur in his confrontation with the President and of indignation that he should have been fired quite so unceremoniously.

Although these and other media-built expectations remained unfulfilled, we later learned from other, partly anecdotal, sources that some of the disappointment experienced by spectators on the streets was compensated when they were made aware that they had been present at an event recognized by the media as extraordinary. No matter how much this distorts their actual experience, the media image survives in the collective memory, reinforced by the occasional news story commemorating the dismissal on one of its anniversaries. Of these we have two clippings.

The inferences we drew from mass observation about the temper of the time belie the picture presented by television. The media coverage, with tacit assistance from a temporarily inarticulate opposition, had produced a "landslide effect," an impression of a massive turning-out to support the general against the President, who was deliberately lying low for a time. In fact, there had been a mass exodus from the city by employees given a half-holiday; rush hour had been moved up, as shown by statistics from the local transportation authority.

Our interpretation is consistent with the way that MacArthur quickly "faded away" from the political scene (like an "old soldier," as he himself had predicted). It also receives some support from the polls (Gallup, 1972).

THEORY CONSTRUCTION

How can one build theory from ideographic case studies of fugitive events with mass observation data? Do they amount to no more than descriptive ethnography? We unhesitatingly admit that neither our study of the Graham crusade nor of MacArthur Day was planned to test a specific hypothesis or to identify causal variables that "explained" what happened or why people acted as they did. Nor did we pretend that such ethnographic data as we collected would allow us to make quantitative estimates about the diffusion of religious sentiment or of political support for MacArthur. Rather, we looked upon these two events as strategic research sites in which to explore firsthand and to refine by direct observation our understanding of conversion rituals and of the behavior of crowds. The analysis was to be "from within."

Our point of departure was Herbert Blumer's (1956: 686) exhortation to "look upon human life as chiefly a vast interpretative process in which people, singly and collectively, guide themselves by defining the objects, events, and situations which they encounter." The conceptual structures behind their everyday acts as revealed to observers are not themselves social-scientific explanations. They do, however, provide the raw material out of which theories are constructed. Our procedure of theory development in the empirical studies was that of "analytic induction" (see further Chapter 2 in this volume on that procedure). Our two case studies bear directly on how collective definitions develop in response to the news media.

Mass observation certainly lends itself to a "debunking," a scaling down of what the mass media accounts blow up out of proportion, or as an authentication of the view "from below" against the tide of "pseudo-events." We recall here the discrepancy between our own observations of two noteworthy events and other accounts of these same events. More important is how media recognition feeds on itself. It magnifies and, to some extent, modifies anything that comes into its purview. The coverage of MacArthur Day, even more clearly than the play given to the Graham crusade, documents how the image of events conveyed through the lens of the media is subject to "refraction." Notwithstanding Boorstin (1962: 11), who contrasts "God-made" events, like a train wreck or an earthquake, with non-spontaneous pseudo-events, we see no clear line that sets pseudo-events, largely contrived for the benefit of audiences, apart from other events which are immutably natural but then symbolically transformed into "disasters."

In both cases, our interest was not in the event *per se* but in the process through which such events unfold and enter into public consciousness. Similar processes can be observed in communication networks other than the mass media. Public definitions also develop through oral networks, some of them linked to what the press reports. The generation of rumors exhibits many similarities, as well as some differences, with the way in which reporters produce what is certified as genuine "news" (Lang and Lang, 1961; Shibutani, 1966; for an explicit statement in favor of a "process" sociology, as distinguished from a "unit" sociology, see Bigus *et al.*, 1982).

The two case studies also document the interplay between the media perspective and that of participants in the event. Stepping forward in response to Graham's appeal was more than a strictly private decision. The act was encouraged by companions and by the atmosphere generated through the staging in Madison Square Garden. Beyond that, those heeding the call could not possibly avoid seeing their decision as a statement of support for a religious crusade in which they wanted a part. In the case of MacArthur, the chance to participate in a historic spectacle was equally hard to resist even for people without any further political commitment. Here the two perspectives were merged whenever crowds responded directly to the presence of the TV cameras (see, for example, Dayan and Katz, 1987). Evidence of a more indirect consequence of media recognition comes from surveys of the beleaguered citizens of Berlin during the long months of the Soviet blockade, when they were totally dependent for all their needs on the airlift from the West. Seeing themselves through the media with the attention of the whole Western world focused on their struggle was a real boost to their morale (Davison, 1956).

More generally, we point to the part played by so-called third parties that are somehow perceived, however vaguely, in the transactions between newsmakers and reporters which define what becomes news. The involvement of a large and diffuse public tends to transform ceremonies originally designed only for those present into spectacles. Regardless of what participants may feel, they will be perceived more as performers acting in behalf of "everyone" within an integrated structure of motives. On the other hand, being conscious during a controversy of the presence of a third party usually has a moderating effect. It creates pressure to play by the rules or at least to make it appear so. Such changes as have occurred in electioneering practices over the years might fruitfully be approached with this concept in mind.

In conclusion, we submit that observational techniques combined with informant interviews can be more than a continuous pilot, a grandiose fishing expedition for interesting but impressionistic data. They are especially useful in probing the processes behind the social construction of events and in explaining how things ultimately come to be remembered, that is, how events come to be defined in the collective memory.

Chapter 12

Social contexts and uses of research
Media, education, and communities

Michael Green

INTRODUCTION

Qualitative mass communication research has social concerns and uses whose possibilities have scarcely begun to be realized. This form of research need not restrict itself to a subdivision of a specialist discipline, but can contribute to a sustained, critical development of reflections and conversations about media that are widespread in everyday life. Thus, qualitative work serves to establish contexts in which a thoughtful awareness of current media practices may develop. Such work may include an exploration of the procedures by which we, the audience-public, are represented and of the alternative ways in which the different interests and purposes of diverse social and cultural groups might be communicated in a public form. To put on record means more than putting findings into scholarly debate. If the research community is to become at least in some ways the community's research, then this work must constantly assess its own sources, contexts, and spheres of influence.

This chapter, therefore, looks at qualitative research particularly as it arises from and in the growing media education movement. Furthermore, the chapter addresses other social uses and implications of this research as it has been taken up and developed in arguments and campaigns by various groups across society. What connects these areas of activity is a common concern with *meta-communication*: one shared purpose is to establish the contexts in which the users and audiences of media are empowered to communicate *about* mass communication and its social purposes. Media develop, and are developed by, changing publics and needs. In this conception, then, media are examined not as a branch of the leisure industries whose consumers' private tastes must be understood, but as cultural forms in which groups, communities, and societies articulate their diversity and point in the direction of imagined horizons. Qualitative research becomes a social resource, not only through its specific methods, but by initiating, organizing, and directing its inquiry in relation to the interests and needs of specific social groups. It will be argued below that local contexts and networks of communication provide an opportunity for qualitative research to register publicly and substantiate movements toward change, hence contributing to fulfilling the media's emancipatory potential.

THE STATE OF MEDIA EDUCATION

By the 1990s, media education has a status and strength in many countries which was not anticipated even a few years ago. While a detailed account of the theoretical and pedagogical developments and debates falls outside the scope of this chapter (see the helpful surveys in Masterman, 1980; 1985; 1988, and UNESCO, 1977; 1984), it also remains difficult to chart the current international position. It is encouraging to hear, as this chapter is in preparation, that the major conference on media education held in 1990 at Toulouse and organized with UNESCO support, is to be reported in a book, emphasizing work in developing countries. For one thing, the practice of media education is deeply embedded in the specific circumstances of the particular educational systems of different countries. For another, much of the good pioneering work in pedagogical practice by teachers at various levels of the school system, has gone unrecorded, is passed on through personal communication, and remains underresearched. (The International Association for Mass Communication Research convenes a continuing working group on Media Education at its biannual conference which is of interest to both researchers and teachers.) What appears evident from the documentation that is available is the rapid growth of interest and of educational innovation in the field of media education (Alvarado *et al.*, 1987; Drummond and Lusted, 1985).

This development is taking place despite conflicting motivating impulses. While the massive presence of mass media in everyday life might in itself motivate general training about, through, and for the media at all levels of the educational system, there are at least two distinct positions with respect to the purposes of such training.

On the one hand, media education has tended to be promoted anxiously as a form of damage limitation or inoculation in response to various proclaimed effects of media and hence causes for social concern. The concerns arise from a realization of the very scale of media reading, listening, and viewing; they include the fear that perceptions by social groups of themselves and of the world are now crucially formed by and through media rather than through parents or schooling; worries about exposure to undesirable (including foreign) values; a sense that new, transnational technologies are rapidly, and adversely, affecting culture and tradition; and a belief that individual growth or social order would be enhanced by other, "better communication." It was such concerns which, in part, motivated the federally funded projects developing media literacy curricula in the USA a decade ago (Corder-Bolz, 1982). In addition, there has been a sometimes reluctant concession on the part of educational authorities that media texts deserve analysis if only to point up by contrast the more fundamental aesthetic or human values of great literature. A recent example is the English National Curriculum, pointedly retaining a distinction between literary and non-literary texts. All these concerns situate media education nearer to topics such as health education than to fundamental analytic disciplines such as history, mathematics, or geography. The familiar issue among researchers of whether communications constitute a field or a discipline remains an unanswered question also in the educational sector as mass communication is being introduced into the curriculum in a variety of ways.

On the other hand, the teachers who have generated the growth of media education were typically formed by the new social movements of the 1960s and 1970s and by the experience of media responses to the innovations of that period. Their motivations, accordingly, have emphasized the development of a critical awareness of media as cultural industries (Adorno and Horkheimer, 1977). Media education originally gave priority to notions of partial representation or misrepresentation; to the restricted agenda of news and the moral panics in media creating their own accounts and momentum; and to stereotypes, absences, and the extraordinary attention given to news of the male public domain. Teaching often took its concrete point of departure in concepts of ideology, perhaps first in the idea of mass media as an ideological state apparatus (Althusser, 1971), and in an understanding of dominant worldviews in the media as active in the negotiation of hegemony (Gramsci,

1971). Later work began to give serious attention to the pleasure and entertainment related to the more private spheres of leisure, exploring forms of popular culture as modes of celebration and perhaps of resistance for subordinate groups in society (see, for example, Hall *et al.*, 1980). Later still, further political developments have put feminist, anti-racist, and perhaps now also "green" priorities at the center of media education, as currently witnessed in critiques of dominant media representations of these priorities and in the proliferating activities of alternative media production to be examined further below. At the same time, more general critiques of the education system itself, particularly of the institutionalized, segregated forms of disciplinary knowledge and of the hidden agendas and selection mechanisms operating in learning situations, have produced a determination also among some media teachers to work with students and colleagues in more collaborative and democratic ways, across departments, and in an exploratory manner.

From these rather different starting points, over time a certain stability regarding the ends and means of media education is being reached. "Media literacy" is often advanced as a goal for teaching about the media, not just in the American media literacy curricula, but in different cultural contexts. This is in spite of the ambiguity of that concept and the very different ways in which it may be promulgated (Buckingham, 1989; Foster, 1979). A further element of consensus refers to media comprehension in a broader sense, including the use of media as means of creative expression and as part of "a preparation for responsible citizenship" (UNESCO, 1982: 340). A more radical inflection of citizenship would see both critical analysis of media and public participation in production and decision making as constitutive elements of a democratic empowerment that should be open to all. It has been argued that democracy in mass communication implies a right to transmit as well as to receive (Brecht, 1932; Enzensberger, 1970; Williams, 1962). However, less radical perspectives also concur in seeing the aim of media education as cultivating life-long skills that remain useful in watching the news or considering media policy changes many years after the end of formal schooling. Indeed, media education should not be confined to state education systems ending at the age of eighteen. Whereas currently many forms of work with and debate on the media appear to thrive in adult education and around alternative media production centers, it is interesting to speculate on the possible contribution of media education to forms of life-long education as this concept continues to be implemented and developed in different institutional and cultural contexts over the next decade.

At present, a theoretical and political reorientation is noticeable among media educators. It is now less common for teachers to assume that they are working against the media, in a spirit of adversity. Instead, some would probably see themselves in sympathy with media practitioners in trying to pursue accuracy, variety, and excellence against commercial and competitive pressures (in both education and media institutions). For some scholars, there is a significant scope for creativity within media industries (see the contribution by Newcomb in this volume). Moreover, as noted by much research over the last decade, many forms of popular culture have real utility as a social and cultural resource for their audiences to articulate their difference, pleasure, even resistance in the face of other, dominant representations and cultural practices (for a survey and critical discussion, see Schudson, 1987). The developments in media education, then, may be attributed in part to a reorientation that is simultaneously theoretical and political. When the merit of media products and the power of audiences *vis-à-vis* media are re-evaluated, the educational approach to creating new media and new audiences also may change.

The reorientation may also lead to a more relaxed, pragmatic, and pluralistic view of the place of media in the curriculum. Depending on its context and purpose, media education may find its best home and fullest growth inside a particular subject, either the national language and literature or in sociology/social studies, or as a critical approach to media sources and media representations across and within all school subjects, or, finally, as a curriculum area in its own right. The important challenge will be to establish some form of institutional framework in which students may address mass media as a public good and cultural resource. Mass media – from the press to television and the computer – are general-purpose technologies that may be put to a variety of uses, depending on which social form the technology is given and under what historical circumstances. In contrast to the computer, which is associated with instrumental applications and job opportunities both in public debate and in education, other mass media still are often linked with private pleasures. If the personal computer offers users "a second self" (Turkle, 1984), a forum in which questions of identity are asked, this is even more true of the mass media. Mass communication represents a broad cultural forum (Newcomb and Hirsch, 1984). In order to assess and participate in that forum, media users require the skills of meta-communication that are acquired in educational contexts.

To sum up, media education has now transcended some earlier versions, such as a skills training in media production. As an area of general education throughout the school system, media offer certain intrinsic pleasures and uses from which student interest and a critical sense may flow. Furthermore, the media studied now include not only film, newspapers, magazines, and video, but also tape/slide media, radio, and television, even though a full incorporation of music, popular fiction, and perhaps radio is still to be achieved in many settings. Yet, a comprehensive theory and pedagogical practice of media education is still in the making. For further development, this chapter points to the principles of qualitative research examined in more detail elsewhere in this volume, outlining below some implications of qualitative methodologies for media education practice.

QUALITATIVE PERSPECTIVES ON MEDIA EDUCATION

Three features of much qualitative research are particularly relevant for its practical applications. First, qualitative studies normally attempt to interpret the concrete analysis with constant reference to some comprehensive theoretical framework. This has been a major aim of the cultural studies tradition (for a statement of this tradition, see Williams, 1977) from which the work reported below grows. One assumption here is that the center of inquiry lies not in the media themselves, their texts or audiences, but in the social and cultural practices in which the media are embedded, and which serve to orient mass communication. For example, media representations of "race," ethnicity, and minorities must be linked to broader issues of migration, racism, and social policy. Similarly, cultural studies address both the dominant and the emerging forms of culture that are articulated in media, as well as the historical and policy changes affecting media over time. The center of media education also may lie outside the mass media.

Second, qualitative research takes an interpretive approach to social and cultural practices, studying the everyday, lived realities of people. Cultural studies specifically draw on both the humanities and the social sciences, because the field is concerned both with the meaning and the power respectively of media and their users. It thus may engage the reality of students who are simultaneously media users and social agents.

Third, and perhaps most important, much qualitative research is committed to making explicit its own political foundations and implications, what Habermas (1971) calls the knowledge-interests of different forms of scientific inquiry. This does not imply that all qualitative research is by definition "critical." Who is researching what on behalf of whom and why, may suggest more salient criteria. Nor is it implied that qualitative research should necessarily move in the specific direction of action research (see the discussion and references in Chapter 2, this volume). However, qualitative methodologies may have a specific explanatory value and utility in the context of education. The following passage may suggest the predicament that qualitative researchers and students of media education share:

> What we are reaching for is a mode of work which will acknowledge a complex situation that can be simply stated: cultural studies is a reflection of the fact that the culture we study is our own and, because of that, we are responsible for making it as well as analyzing it.
>
> (Cook, 1986: 136)

A simple statement of a complex situation in media education is to say that it asks children to talk, for example, about what they see in a photograph; how it comes to appear in the media; what differences might arise in other photos of the same subject; how captions suggest a variety of meanings; and why some people might enjoy the picture or find it offensive. Such critical discussion can be, first, collaborative, and, second, it can suggest alternative ways of representing people and ideas (for concrete examples, see Development Education Centre, 1989, and Building Sights, 1989). Interviewing offers special possibilities for developing reflexive and collaborative activities in media education.

INTERVIEW PRACTICES

Interviews and interviewing are essential to contemporary life, not least in mainstream media texts. The examination of different genres of interviewing in the classroom may suggest how interviewing, other interpersonal communication, as well as mass communication contribute to the social construction of reality (Berger and Luckmann, 1966). Interviewing by students, possibly as young as thirteen or fourteen, further, can be a feasible, enjoyable, and useful way for them to ask questions about media, audiences, communities, themselves. In essence, interviewing provides an opportunity for combining practical, analytical, and interpretive approaches to media.

It should be emphasized that the primary purpose of such media education is not to convey or teach research findings to students, but crucially to involve them in a practice of inquiry that is grounded in their own social and cultural context. This may be conceived theoretically as education-through-research or research-as-education, thus underscoring the origin of both these activities in social practice. Education, in other words, is not just a matter of learning to read, but of reading (listening, viewing) to learn (Heath, 1980: 130).

This section presents a brief characterization of key elements of media educational practice with reference to interviewing, and draws examples from the author's own work with media education and educators over several years. The purpose will not be to provide a typology of media education, but to suggest some practical implications of the state of media education reviewed above. Like mass communication, media education represents not a steady state, but a practice and process of making sense.

Production

Three elements of media education, while interrelated, may be distinguished for analytical purposes: production, analysis, and interpretation. Production, first of all, presents an opportunity for students to deconstruct the techniques and codes of mass communication. Having mastered the production perspective, the reception perspective also becomes less opaque for the student-audience. Conversely, students have been able, certainly from the late primary or early secondary levels, to apply critical insights gained in reception and analysis to the production of specific genres, for example in reconstructing melodramatic and crime series in video productions that question the conventions of such genres.

For production purposes, interviewing may serve at least two different functions. First, interviewing is central to the re-enactment of specific media contents through various forms of role playing which consider alternative representations of the events and issues. Role playing and similar group dynamic techniques have recently been employed in qualitative audience research to consider alternative ways of organizing media (Jensen, 1990b). In addition to their own experience as audience members, students will be able to draw, in such role plays, on first-hand observation during visits to media institutions, for instance, a television production set.

Second, and more importantly, student productions particularly of news can draw on interviews with different types of "sources" in the process of investigating and researching a "story." Such interviewing raises classic issues of news criteria, bias, and the reliability of sources of news that may feed into analysis and discussion of news as a specific social construction. Concrete suggestions for analysis are available in a number of media textbooks (see, for instance, Hartley, 1982).

This form of interviewing in journalism blends into the use of interviewing in research. As witnessed also by work in oral history (Thompson, 1978), interviewing is a primary mode of access to both past and present.

Analysis

It has, indeed, proved possible for students to carry out series of open-ended interviews as well as combining these with other forms of analysis of media use. Projects may include elements of interviewing, textual analysis, as well as participant observation, with interviewing being perhaps the most manageable approach. Again, there are two interview types: role-played interviews that are conducted as practice in the classroom, and research interviews that are relatively focused on a particular purpose of inquiry.

Research interviews lend themselves to a combination, for example with diaries, suggesting to students the limits and strengths of each source of information as well as raising more substantive issues of how people represent and legitimate their own media use, also in the discourses of research. A further source of comparison with diaries and interviews lies in the available statistics concerning the town's or the nation's consumption patterns (with some guidance statistics are accessible for students in secondary school). Moreover, a modest version of participant observation among friends and family or of media use in public places, noting content selection, duration, and related conversation, can also more generally encourage observational skills of "reading" social reality that may have been neglected in educational cultures founded on the written word.

The interview texts themselves obviously deserve detailed analysis: of the linguistic registers and the forms of speech used, of the rhythms, pauses, and awkwardnesses of the interview situation, and of the pleasures and positions expressed. Even the writing-up of the interviews or their presentation in public raises questions about selection and editing, questions which are of equal relevance to students, teachers, and media professionals. Conceiving interviews as texts, then, these texts call for the kind of comparative textual or discourse analysis that is also taught in language and literature classes. Textual analysis allows students to identify a traditional discursive feature such as point of view, whether that of the interviewee at different points of the interaction, of the interviewer's implicit agenda, or of the media contents referred to. Thus, textual analysis enables students to begin to address and assess the discourses both of media and of research.

Interpretation

Ultimately, the implications of mass media for students and other audiences are established in a process of interpretation that is situated in a specific social context. Media education may empower students to raise questions about the role of media in processes of social conflict and historical change, ideally also outside the particular forum of reflexivity that education represents. Both in educational and other contexts, such meta-communication may promote a critical awareness of the ends and means of mass communication in society.

Students are similar to media audiences in the sense that they are the product of a specific social institution. In other words, students are constitutive of educational practices, whereas audiences are constitutive of communicative practices, the difference being the social purpose of each set of practices. Notwithstanding McLuhan's (1964) dictum that the medium is the message, it may be true that the audience is the message – or product, particularly of the television medium (Smythe, 1977). What media education may produce is an audience with a difference or, perhaps, a vengeance.

Finally, the process of meta-communication can feed back into the media through various forms of public debate. In concrete terms, some interviewees do prove willing to come and discuss a project in the school or college context. Similarly, media professionals as well as professional researchers may be engaged in such dialogues. This four-way approach to meta-communication, involving educational institutions, community groups, media workers, and researchers, represents an intermediate level between mass and interpersonal communication that may be perceived as relevant by all groups.

OTHER CONTEXTS OF QUALITATIVE RESEARCH

What happens in classrooms, then, should be conceptualized with reference to other media-related institutions and practices. In particular, the various forms of professional mass communication research call for analysis and discussion here, since research traditions lend orientation to much media education, sometimes implicitly, and have other important social uses, as well. The issues include the knowledge interest and epistemology of particular studies, but it may be as important in this context to consider the institutional and economic origins of the theoretical orientations. Three types of qualitative research, accordingly, can be specified.

First, there exists a large body of sophisticated and expensive market research, employing qualitative methodologies, which offers detailed examination of changing social patterns and tastes to business clients, especially advertisers and product designers. At least in the development of products and advertising, qualitative methodologies may outdistance some quantitative forms of research. Much of this work is proprietary information because of its commercial relevance, though there are also commercial research journals that discuss approaches and findings in the public domain (see especially the *Journal of Consumer Research*). It is interesting to note that recent work on marketing and on organizations has incorporated elements of semiotics to account for the structures and functions of commercial operations as well as to suggest instrumental solutions (for an overview, see Umiker-Sebeok, 1987; also the theme issue on marketing and semiotics of the *International Journal of Research in Marketing* 4, 3–4, 1988). Whereas some critics may deplore this use of semiotics as a technique for commercial ends, such uses follow from the fact that most scientific theory is and presumably should be public. It is surely one responsibility of critical researchers to keep up with the substance and methods of this work in order to make it available for alternative uses and to discuss its social implications.

A related variety of research is the kind of studies that have been regularly conducted or commissioned also by media institutions with public-service obligations. A primary example is the research activity of public-service broadcasters in the European countries (see Docherty *et al.*, 1988, and Gunter and Svennevig, 1987; also the publications of PUB, the research department of the Swedish Broadcasting Corporation, some of which are available in English). While much of the work of these research departments, traditionally and now increasingly in a more competitive media environment, has been preoccupied with audience ratings, other studies have had the sort of general implications normally associated with basic, academic research. One important use of the latter type of studies is in product development. Thus, in-house research may provide new knowledge that is relevant not just for the decisions of upper and middle management, but also for journalists, producers, scriptwriters, and other media professionals. This recalls the reorientation of media education noted above which leads some researcher-teachers to seek allies among media professionals in order to reform media and their social uses.

The third type of qualitative research is mainly generated from academic institutions of research and higher education, and is the core of the developments documented in this volume. One limitation of this work traditionally has been its restricted circulation and impact outside the academic context. The audiences of this research tend to be either students at the institutions or the international networks of research, both of which have limited public access. However, the social impact of research findings may also be of a more indirect, long-term, and systemic nature, being communicated to other social agents (including students) and media that enact the impact in practice. For example, Janice Radway has interestingly discussed her attempt to "make use of any opportunity that comes my way through the media themselves to discuss my findings and interpretations for wider audiences . . . generate more serious public discussion about the mass media and their ability to speak to very real problems in the lives of Americans" (Radway, 1986: 116). Even so, some of the most cogent and valuable work suggests a picture of rather solitary researchers seeking to make connections from a research activity that is somewhat lost in its own isolation.

That is why important opportunities arise for a fourth form of research which springs from and speaks to local contexts and circumstances. Such research would seek to transcend the notions of "communities" and "campaigns" as these are normally defined in the context of mass media.

COMMUNITIES AND CAMPAIGNS

It has perhaps been too common to think of the social groups that organize campaigns through the media as being sporadic and limited, though intense, in their concerns, and to conceive of the communities embedding media and campaigns as relatively homogeneous, whether their cultural identity is currently threatened or secure. Indeed, this way of conceiving culture and communication may be an effect, in part, of the way in which campaigns and communities have been represented by media themselves. Moreover, campaigns may have been associated particularly with commercial marketing or with specific issues such as health education. In truth, campaigns represent a general structural or organizational resource for placing particular issues on a public agenda. Such issues proliferate as societies less readily map onto classic, social and political divisions of interest (Castells, 1983). More accurately, campaigns are a way of opening up and addressing more complex aspects of society through the vantage point of that issue. At the same time, communities themselves, both of place and of interest, have become more various and complex in view of migration and the general tendencies of postindustrial or, better, post-Fordist societies (Harvey, 1989). If contemporary social conflicts are increasingly acted out in a complex cultural domain, it becomes crucial for critical research to explore how the "campaigns" of "communities" may be, and are in fact, processed through the media.

In doing so, research may depart from the commitments and energies of various local and national organizations and institutions as these engage in a sustained and public form of dialogue through periodicals, conferences, and other means, which could hardly be considered spasmodic irruptions of a transient public opinion. It is an important feature of current political cultures that interest groups of all kinds have become much more aware of the importance of the ways in which they are represented, both to themselves and to others. This is witnessed by some previous research in several countries (see Beharrell and Philo, 1977; CCCS Media Group, 1982; Gitlin, 1980). In addition, there have developed organizations which distinctively concentrate on media such as, in the USA, Action for Children's Television and Viewers for Quality Television (see also Simpson, 1987) as well as the British Campaign for Press and Broadcasting Freedom. Among the independent film and video production centers, community presses, and radio stations which are proliferating in many countries (Berrigan, 1977), there are also some that focus specifically on the representation of local groups and concerns.

More generally, the expectations among the audience-public of what media should accomplish for communities, are likely to change as part of the social-structural developments outlined above. The young people who are today's children in front of the television screen, and today's students in media education classes, may conclude that, as they become adult "citizens," they are both more and less than that. Less, because citizenship, in mass communication as elsewhere, implies rights of knowledge, of access, and of participation which are not widely granted; more, because these citizens do not make up a homogeneous formation which, in converging on a consensus, addresses a shared agenda. This conclusion implies reconsidering the ends and means of mass communication. The determining factors of the whole process are likely to arise less from the media themselves, than from the social, contextual uses to which they are applied; these factors carry an agenda for further qualitative research.

FURTHER RESEARCH

After at least two decades of qualitative research on mass communication, while many studies particularly of how media represent groups and studies of how groups perceive media are available, these two bodies of research appear somewhat disconnected and are not always simultaneously known. This may explain, in part, why the social uses of media by specific audiences and the possible reforming impact of audiences on processes of mass communication, remain underresearched. Qualitative methodologies, as applied also in media education, offer a framework for examining media use in broader contexts of social action. The question is not only what audiences do with media, but how they apply media contents in the context of their social and cultural practices.

Because qualitative research, as defined here, examines the lived reality of audience-publics in a comprehensive social context with reference to an explicit purpose or knowledge interest, it may be perceived as both relevant and accessible by these audience-publics. It may, therefore, be an opportunity for qualitative researchers in the coming period to focus research projects on the social uses of media with reference to the specific issues and campaigns of particular communities involved.

Three efforts suggest themselves in this area of qualitative media research, building on the interest and activity in media education. First, what began at school in "the lesson" may become a right and a pleasure which can continue in the community. There appear to be innovations under way in the activities generated in and through public libraries, arts centers, and new media centers, in part encouraged by a new climate of support for cultural policy in major cities (see Bianchini *et al.*, 1988), and these institutions may in fact be converging institutionally and technologically. In addition to the development of more and more specific media curricula, then, research projects, in combining a pedagogical component and a research and assessment component, may explore a range of possibilities for learning and creative expression through such media-related institutions. While similar to educational research on media-aided instruction, such projects would examine schools and media centers as different, but complementary institutions in the community, asking which kinds of institutional cooperation and educational practice yield what results and for whom. A second, related area of mass communication research also takes an action perspective and asks to what extent particular local media represent and serve community interests and needs. Research, further, may support the access of community groups and institutions to media, for instance by documenting the viability of a local newspaper or the organizational structure of a community radio station.

Third and finally, it may be possible, with the cooperation of local media, community groups, and teachers, to develop historical projects on media in relation to social change and the specific transformation of neighborhoods and communities. Such a project, in addition to representing audience interests and concerns, could create a fund of knowledge that would be made available to the community as a whole through various print and electronic media forms. The project would constitute a cultural resource facilitating meta-communication on media past and present, ideally feeding back into the media in the form of discussions, repeat screenings, and other formats. While some previous studies have produced this type of materials (Day-Lewis, 1989; Richards and Sheridan, 1987; see also Chapter 11 in this volume on mass-observation research), it will be especially important to make this kind of cultural resource generally available as the media of communication increasingly serve to construct community.

CONCLUSION

Media education has developed over the last two decades from a fringe tendency toward becoming a constituent element of the curriculum in a number of contexts. What media education may offer throughout the educational system is a forum in which students acquire and exercise skills of meta-communication, critically examining the ends and means of mass communication. Qualitative research may be especially relevant both in the development of curricula and as a method of education-through-research. A related social use of qualitative research lies in organizing community access to and uses of mass media and assessing their place in cultural practices from the perspective of the audience-public.

This chapter has emphasized not only the social applications, but also the social origins of research. The two aspects are related, because the knowledge interests of studies tend to decide their applications, methodology being an intervening level of reflection. The essay has suggested the specific relevance of qualitative methodologies for certain social and educational uses of research.

The further implication is that researchers, like media users, need to engage in reflection and meta-communication about the purpose and status of their own discourse. Researchers can sometimes be well placed to help make connections between media users and producers, and between different sectors of media education. It may be useful to remind ourselves from time to time that while researchers do publish their work, they may do so in a variety of forms; and that to publish means to make public, which is a normal and necessary feature of a public cultural life.

References

Abrams, M. (1953) *The Mirror and the Lamp*, Oxford: Oxford University Press.

Abrams, M. *et al.* (1962) *The Norton Anthology of English Literature*, vol. 2, New York: Norton.

Ackroyd, S. and Hughes, J. (1981) *Data Collection in Context*, London: Longman.

Adatto, K. (1990) "Sound bite democracy: network evening news presidential campaign coverage, 1968 and 1988," paper, Cambridge, MA: John F. Kennedy School of Government, Harvard University.

Adorno, T. and Horkheimer, M. (1977) "The culture industry: enlightenment as mass deception," in J. Curran, M. Gurevitch, and J. Woollacott (eds) *Mass Communication and Society*, London: Edward Arnold.

Agar, M. (1980) *The Professional Stranger: an Informal Introduction to Ethnography*, New York: Academic Press.

Agee, W.K., Ault, P.H., and Emery, E. (1985) *Introduction to Mass Communications*, New York: Harper & Row.

Allen, R.C. (1987) "Reader-oriented criticism and television," in R.C. Allen (ed.) *Channels of Discourse*, London: Routledge.

Althusser, L. (1965) *For Marx*, London: Verso. Reprinted (1972), Harmondsworth: Penguin.

Althusser, L. (1971) *Lenin and Philosophy*, London: New Left Books.

Altman, R. (1987) *The American Film Musical*, Bloomington: Indiana University Press.

Alvarado, M. and Buscombe, E. (1978) *Hazell: the Making of a TV Series*, London: British Film Institute.

Alvarado, M., Gutch, R., and Wollen, T. (1987) *Learning the Media*, London: Macmillan.

Ambler, J.S. (1966) *The French Army in Politics, 1945–1962*, Columbus, OH: Ohio State University Press.

Anderson, B. (1983) *Imagined Communities: Reflections on the Origin and Spread of Nationalism*, London: Verso.

Anderson, J.A. (1987a) "Commentary on qualitative research," in T. Lindlof (ed.) *Natural Audiences*, Norwood, NJ: Ablex.

Anderson, J.A. (1987b) *Communication Research: Issues and Methods*, New York: McGraw-Hill.

Anderson, J.A. and Meyer, T. (1988) *Mediated Communication: a Social Action Perspective*, Newbury Park, CA: Sage.

Anderson, N. (1923) *The Hobo: the Sociology of the Homeless Man*, Chicago: University of Chicago Press.

Ang, I. (1985) *Watching Dallas*, London: Methuen.

Ang, I. (1989) "Wanted: audiences," in E. Seiter, H. Borchers, G. Kreutzner, and E. Warth (eds) *Remote Control: Television, Audiences, and Cultural Power*, London: Routledge.

Ang, I. (1991) *Desperately Seeking the Audience*, London: Routledge.

Antaki, C. (ed.) (1988) *Analysing Everyday Explanation*, London: Sage.

Arnheim, R. (1974) *Art and Visual Perception*, Berkeley: University of California Press.

Arnold, C. and Frandsen, K. (1984) "Conceptions of rhetoric and communication," in C. Arnold and J. Bowers (eds) *Handbook of Rhetorical and Communication Theory*, Boston: Allyn & Bacon.

Ashworth, P.D., Giorgi, A., and de Koning, J.J. (eds) (1986) *Qualitative Research in Psychology: Proceedings of the International Association for Qualitative Research*, Pittsburg, PA: Duquesne University Press.

Austin, J. (1962) *How to Do Things with Words*, London: Oxford University Press.

Barker, P., Taylor, H., Kadt, E.D., and Hopper, E. (1969) "Portrait of a protest," *New Society* 318, 12: 631–64.

Barlow, W. (1988) "Community radio in the U.S.: the struggle for a democratic media," *Media, Culture and Society* 10, 1: 81–105.

Barnouw, E. (1966–70) *A History of Broadcasting in the United States*, 3 vols, New York: Oxford University Press.

Barnouw, E. *et al.* (1989) *International Encyclopedia of Communications*, 4 vols, New York: Oxford University Press.

Barnum, P.T. (1871) *Struggles and Triumphs: or, Forty Years' Recollections of P. T. Barnum*, New York: American News.

Barthes, R. (1964) "Introduction," *Communications* 4: 1–3.

Barthes, R. (1973) *Mythologies* (orig. publ. 1957), London: Paladin.

Barthes, R. (1983) *The Fashion System* (orig. publ. 1967), New York: Hill & Wang.

Barthes, R. (1984a) "Rhetoric of the image" (orig. publ. 1964), in S. Heath (ed.) *Image Music Text*, London: Fontana.

Barthes, R. (1984b) "Introduction to the structural analysis of narratives" (orig. publ. 1968), in S. Heath (ed.) *Image Music Text*, London: Fontana.

Barthes, R. (1984c) *Elements of Semiology* (orig. publ. 1964), New York: Hill & Wang.

Bateson, G. (1955) "A theory of play and phantasy," in G. Bateson, *Toward an Ecology of Mind*, 2nd edn 1972, New York: Ballantine Books.

Bateson, G. (1972) *Steps to an Ecology of Mind*, London: Paladin.

Baudrillard, J. (1988) *Selected Writings*, Cambridge: Polity Press.

Bausinger, H. (1984) "Media, technology, and daily life," *Media, Culture and Society* 6: 343–52.

Becker, H.S. (1951) "Role and career problems of the Chicago public school teacher," dissertation, University of Chicago.

Becker, H.S. (1967) "Whose side are we on?" *Social Problems* 14: 239–47.

Becker, H.S. and Geer, B. (1957) "Participant observation and interviewing: a comparison," *Human Organization* 16, 3: 28–32.

Becker, H.S. and Geer, B. (1958) "Participant observation and interviewing: a rejoinder," *Human Organization* 17, 2: 39–40.

Becker, H.S., Geer, B., Hughes, E.C., and Strauss, A.L. (1961) *Boys in White: Student Culture in Medical School*, Chicago: University of Chicago Press.

Beharrell, P. and Philo, G. (1977) *Trade Unions and the Media*, London: Macmillan.

Bellour, R. (1986) "Segmenting/analyzing," in P. Rosen (ed.) *Narrative, Apparatus, Ideology: a Film Theory Reader*, New York: Columbia University Press.

Beniger, J. (1986) *The Control Revolution*, Cambridge, MA: Harvard University Press.

Beniger, J. (1988) "Information and communication: the new convergence," *Communication Research* 15, 2: 198–218.

Bennett, T. and Woollacott, J. (1987) *Bond and Beyond*, London: Methuen.

Benney, M. and Hughes, E.C. (1956) "Of sociology and the interview," *American Journal of Sociology* 62: 137–42.

Bentele, G. (ed.) (1981) *Semiotik und Massenmedien* (Semiology and the Mass Media), Munich: Oelschlager.

Benton, T. (1977) *Philosophical Foundations of the Three Sociologies*, London: Routledge & Kegan Paul.

Berelson, B. (1952) *Content Analysis in Communications Research*, Glencoe, IL: Free Press.

Berelson, B. (1959) "The state of communications research," *Public Opinion Ouarterly* 23: 1–6.

Berger, C. and Chaffee, S. (eds) (1987) *Handbook of Communication Science*, Newbury Park, CA: Sage.

Berger, P.L. and Berger, B. (1976) *Sociology: a Biographical Approach*, Harmondsworth: Penguin.

Berger, P.L. and Luckmann, T. (1966) *The Social Construction of Reality*, London: Allen Lane.

Bernstein, R. (1986) *Philosophical Profiles*, Cambridge: Polity Press.

Berrigan, F.J. (ed.) (1977) *Access: Some Western Models of Community Media*, Paris: UNESCO.

Bianchini, F., Fisher, M., Montgomery, J., and Worpole, K. (1988) *City Centres, City Cultures*, Manchester: Centre for Local Economic Strategies.

Bibby, A., Denford, C., and Cross, J. (1979) *Local Television: Piped Dreams?*, Milton Keynes: Redwing Press.

Bigus, O.E., Hadden, S.C., and Glaser, B.G. (1982) "Basic social processes," in R.B. Smith and P.K. Manning (eds) *Qualitative Methods*.

Vol. II of *Handbook of Social Science Methods*, Cambridge, MA: Ballinger.

Billig, M. (1987) *Arguing and Thinking*, Cambridge: Cambridge University Press.

Blum, R. and Lindheim, R. (1987) *Primetime: Network Television Programming*, Boston, MA: Focal Press.

Blumer, H. (1933) *The Movies and Conduct*, New York: Macmillan.

Blumer, H. (1935) "Moulding of mass behavior through the motion picture," *Publications of the American Sociological Society*, 29, 3: 115–27.

Blumer, H. (1954) "What is wrong with social theory," *American Sociological Review* 19: 3–10.

Blumer, H. (1956). "Sociological analysis and the variable," *American Sociological Review* 21: 683–90.

Blumer, H. (1969) *Symbolic Interactionism: Perspective and Method*, Englewood Cliffs, NJ: Prentice-Hall.

Blumer, H. and Hauser, P.M. (1933) *Movies, Delinquency and Crime*, New York: Macmillan.

Blumler, J. and Katz, E. (eds) (1974) *The Uses of Mass Communications*, Beverly Hills, CA: Sage.

Boas, F. (1940) *Race, Language and Culture*, New York: Macmillan.

Bogdan, R. (1972) *Participant Observation in Organizational Settings*, Syracuse, NY: Syracuse University Press.

Bogdan, R. and Biklan, S.K. (1982) *Qualitative Research for Education: an Introduction to Theory and Methods*, Boston: Allyn & Bacon.

Boorstin, D. (1962) *The Image*, New York: Atheneum.

Bordwell, D. (1985) *Narration in the Fiction Film*, London: Methuen.

Bordwell, D., Staiger, J., and Thompson, K. (1985) *The Classical Hollywood Cinema: Film Style and Mode of Production*, New York: Columbia University Press.

Bourdieu, P. (1972) "The Berber house," in M. Douglas (ed.) *Rules and Meanings*, Harmondsworth: Penguin.

Braber, T. (1989) "Romantiek van binnen uit. Etnografische methoden in het ontvangersonderzoek naar populaire cultuur voor vrouwen" (Romance from the inside out. Ethnographic methods in audience research of popular culture for women), *Massacommunicatie* 17, 3: 253–62.

Brecht, B. (1932) "Radiotheorie 1927–32," in *Gesammelte Werke* (1967) vol. 18, 1–20, Frankfurt am Main: Suhrkamp.

Breed, W. (1955) "Social control in the newsroom," *Social Forces* 33: 326–35.

Brewer, J. and Hunter, A. (1989) *Multimethod Research: a Synthesis of Styles*, London: Sage.

Briggs, A. (1961–79) *The History of Broadcasting in the United Kingdom*, 4 vols, Oxford: Oxford University Press.

Brodie, J. and Stoneman, L. (1983) "A contextualist framework for studying TV viewing," *Journal of Family Issues* 4, 2: 329–48.

Broughton, I. (ed.) (1986) *Producers on Producing: the Making of Film and Television*, Jefferson, NC: McFarland.

Brown, R. (1989) *Knowledge is Power*, New York: Oxford University Press.

Browne, D.R. (1988) *What's Local About Local Radio? A Cross-National Comparative Study*, London: International Institute of Communications.

Bruin, M. de, Doormaal, T. van, and Jankowski, N. (eds) (1983) *Kleine Media: Lokale Omroep en Video* (Small-Scale Media: Local Broadcasting and Video), The Netherlands: Macula.

Bruner, J. (1986) *Actual Minds, Possible Worlds*, Cambridge, MA: Harvard University Press.

Brunsdon, C. (1981) "Crossroads: notes on soap opera," *Screen* 22, 4: 32–7.

Bruyn, S.T. (1966) *The Human Perspective in Sociology: the Methodology of Participant Observation*, Englewood Cliffs, NJ: Prentice-Hall.

Bryce, J. (1987) "Family time and TV use," in T. Lindlof (ed.) *Natural Audiences*, Norwood, NJ: Ablex.

Buckingham, D. (1989) "Television literacy: a critique," *Radical Philosophy* 51: 12–25.

Building Sights (1989) *Whose Image? Anti-Racist Approaches to Photography and Visual Literacy*, Birmingham: Building Sights.

Bulmer, M. (1984) *The Chicago School of Sociology: Institutionalization, Diversity, and the Rise of Sociological Research*, Chicago: University of Chicago Press.

Burgess, R.G. (1982) *Field Research: a Sourcebook and Field Manual*, London: George Allen & Unwin.

Burgess, R.G. (1984) *In the Field: an Introduction to Field Research*, London: George Allen & Unwin.

Camilo, M., Mata, M.C., and Servaes, J. (1990) *Autoevaluación de Radio Enriquillo, informe final* (Final Report of Self-evaluation Research of Radio Enriquillo), Santo Dominico, Dominican Republic: Cebemo & Aler.

Cantor, M. (1971) *The Hollywood Television Producer: his Work and his Audience*, New Brunswick, NJ: Transaction Books. Reprinted (1988) with new introduction, New York: Basic Books.

Carey, J.W. (1967) "Harold Innis and Marshall McLuhan," *Antioch Review* 27: 5–37.

Carey, J.W. (1969) "Changing courtship patterns in the popular song," *American Journal of Sociology* 74: 720–31.

Carey, J.W. (1989) *Communication as Culture*, Boston, MA: Unwin Hyman.

Castells, M. (1983) *The City and the Grassroots*, London: Edward Arnold.

Cavan, S. (1978) Review of *Investigative Social Research: Individual and Team Research*, *American Journal of Sociology* 83: 809–11.

Cawelti, J. (1970) *The Six Gun Mystique*, Bowling Green, OH: Bowling Green University Popular Press.

Cawelti, J. (1976) *Adventure, Mystery, and Romance*, Chicago: University of Chicago Press.

CCCS Media Group (1982) *Fighting over Peace: Representations of CND in the Media*, Birmingham: CCCS.

Certeau, M. de (1984) *The Practice of Everyday Life*, Berkeley: University of California Press.

Chambers, E. (1986) *Producing TV Movies*, Englewood Cliffs, NJ: Prentice-Hall.

Chandler, A. (1977) *The Visible Hand*, Cambridge, MA: Harvard University Press.

Chaney, D. (1982) "Communication and community," *Communication* 7, 1: 1–32.

Chatman, S. (1983) *Story and Discourse: Narrative Structure in Fiction and Film*, Ithaca, NY: Cornell University Press.

Chibnall, S. (1977) *Law and Order News: an Analysis of Crime Reporting in the British Press*, London: Tavistock Press.

Chilton, P. (ed.) (1985) *Language and the Nuclear Arms Debate: Nukespeak Today*, London: Pinter.

Chilton, P. (1988) *Orwellian Language and the Media*, London: Pluto Press.

Chomsky, N. (1965) *Aspects of the Theory of Syntax*, Cambridge, MA: MIT Press.

Christensen, M. and Stauth, C. (1984) *The Sweeps: Behind the Scenes in Network TV*, New York: William Morrow.

Cicourel, A. (1964) *Method and Measurement in Sociology*, New York: Free Press.

Clader, A. and Sheridan, D. (eds) (1984) *Speak for Yourself: a Mass-Observation Anthology, 1937–49*, London: Jonathan Cape.

Clifford, J. (1986) "Partial truths," in J. Clifford and G. Marcus (eds) (1986) *Writing Culture: the Poetics and Politics of Ethnography*, Berkeley: University of California Press.

Clifford, J. and Marcus, G.E. (eds) (1986) *Writing Culture: the Poetics and Politics of Ethnography*, Berkeley: University of California.

Coesmans, K. and Goor, G. van den (1990) *El aire para todos, communicación participativa en tres pequeñas emisoras de Costa Rica* (The ether for everyone: participatory communication in three small local cultural radio stations in Costa Rica), San José, Costa Rica: Instituto Costaricense de Enseñanza Radiofónica.

Cohen, S. and Young, J. (eds) (1973) *The Manufacture of News: Deviance, Social Problems and the Mass Media*, London: Constable.

Cole, R.R. (1971) "Top songs of the sixties: a content analysis of popular lyrics," *American Behavioral Scientist* 14: 389–400.

Colfax, J.D. and Roach, J.L. (eds) *Radical Sociology*, New York: Basic Books.

Cook, J. (1986) "Critiques of culture: a course," in D. Punter (ed.) *Introduction to Contemporary Cultural Studies*, London: Longman.

Cooley, C.H. (1930) *Sociological Theory and Social Research: Selected Papers*, New York: Holt, Rinehart, & Winston.

Cooper, J.F. (1838/1969) *The American Democrat*, Baltimore: Penguin.

Corder-Bolz, C. (1982) "Television literacy and critical television viewing skills," in D. Pearl, L. Bouthilet, and J. Lazar (eds) *Television and Behavior*, vol. 2, Washington, DC: Government Printing Office.

Coulthard, M. (1977) *An Introduction to Discourse Analysis*, London: Longman.

Coulthard, M. and Montgomery, M. (eds) (1981) *Studies in Discourse Analysis*, London: Routledge & Kegan Paul.

Coward, R. and Ellis, J. (1977) *Language and Materialism*, London: Routledge & Kegan Paul.

Cressy, P.G. (1932) *The Taxi Dance Hall*, Chicago: University of Chicago Press.

Crigler, A. and Jensen, K.B. (forthcoming) "Discourses of politics: talking about public issues in the United States and Denmark," in P. Dahlgren and C. Sparks (eds) *Communication and Citizenship*, London: Routledge.

Croll, P. and Husband, C. (1975) *Communication and Community: a Study of the Swindon Community Television Experiment*, Leicester: University of Leicester.

Crookes, P. and Vittet-Philippe, P. (1986) *Local Radio and Regional Development in Europe*, Manchester: European Institute for the Media.

Crystal, D. and Davy, D. (1969) *Investigating English Style*, London: Longman.

Culler, J. (1975) *Structuralist Poetics*, London: Routledge & Kegan Paul.

Culler, J. (1981) *The Pursuit of Signs*, Ithaca, NY: Cornell University Press.

Curran, J. (1977) "Capitalism and control of the press 1800–1975," in J. Curran, M. Gurevitch, and J. Woollacott (eds) *Mass Communication and Society*, Beverly Hills, CA: Sage.

Curran, J. (forthcoming) "Rethinking the media as a public sphere," in P. Dahlgren and C. Sparks (eds) *Communication and Citizenship*, London: Routledge.

Dahlgren, P. (1977) "Network TV news and the corporate state: the subordinate consciousness of the citizen-viewer," dissertation, New York: City University of New York.

Dalton, M. (1959) *Men Who Manage*, New York: Wiley.

Darnton, R. (1990) *The Kiss of Lamourette*, New York: W.W. Norton.

Davis, H. and Walton, P. (eds) (1983) *Language, Image, Media*, Oxford: Blackwell.

Davison, W.P. (1956) "Political significance of recognition via mass media – an illustration from the Berlin blockade," *Public Opinion Quarterly* 20: 327–33.

Day-Lewis, S. (1989) *One Day in the Life of Television*, London: Grafton.

Dayan, D. and Katz, E. (1987) "Televised ceremonial events," in A.A. Berger (ed.) *Television in Society*, New Brunswick, NJ: Transaction Books.

Deleuze, G. (1986) *Cinema 1: the Movement-Image*, Minneapolis: University of Minnesota Press.

Deleuze, G. (1989) *Cinema 2: the Time-Image*, London: The Athlone Press.

Dember, W. (ed.) (1964) *Visual Perception: the Nineteenth Century*, New York: Wiley.

Denisoff, S. and Peterson, R.A. (eds) (1972) *The Sounds of Social Change*, Chicago: Rand McNally.

Dennis, E. (1988) "Whence we came: discovering the history of mass communication research," in N.W. Sharp (ed.) *Communications Research: the Challenge of the Information Age*, Syracuse, NY: Syracuse University Press.

Denzin, N.K. (1970a) *The Research Act: a Theoretical Introduction to Sociological Methods*, Chicago: Aldine; 2nd edn (1978), New York: McGraw-Hill.

Denzin, N.K. (1970b) *Sociological Methods: a Sourcebook*, Chicago: Aldine.

Derrida, J. (1967) *Of Grammatology*, Baltimore, MD: Johns Hopkins University Press.

Deutscher, I. (1973) *What We Say/What We Do*, Glenview, IL: Scott, Foresman.

Development Education Centre (1989) *Get the Picture! Developing Visual Literacy in the Infant Classroom*, Birmingham: Selly Oak Colleges.

Dewey, J. (1925) *Experience and Nature*, New York: Dover.

Dewey, J. (1927) *The Public and Its Problems*, New York: Holt.

Dijk, T.A. van (1977) *Text and Context: Explorations in the Semantics and Pragmatics of Discourse*, London: Longman.

Dijk, T.A. van (1980) *Macrostructures: an Interdisciplinary Study of Global Structures in Discourse, Interaction, and Cognition*, Hillsdale, NJ: Erlbaum.

Dijk, T.A. van (ed.) (1985a) *Discourse and Communication*, Berlin/New York: de Gruyter.

Dijk, T.A. van (ed.) (1985b) *Handbook of Discourse Analysis*, 4 vols, London: Academic Press.

Dijk, T.A. van (1987a) *Communicating Racism: Ethnic Prejudice in Thought and Talk*, Newbury Park, CA: Sage.

Dijk, T.A. van (1987b) *Schoolvoorbeelden van racisme: de reproduktie van racisme in maatschappijleerboeken* (Textbook Examples of Racism: the Reproduction of Racism in Social Science Textbooks), Amsterdam: Socialistische Uitgeverij Amsterdam.

Dijk, T.A. van (1988a) *News as Discourse*, Hillsdale, NJ: Erlbaum.

Dijk, T.A. van (1988b) *News Analysis: Case Studies of International and National News in the Press*, Hillsdale, NJ: Erlbaum.

Dijk, T.A. van (1991) *Racism and the Press*, London: Routledge.

Dijk, T. A. van and Kintsch, W. (1983) *Strategies of Discourse Comprehension*, New York: Academic Press.

Docherty, D., Morrison, D., and Tracey, M. (1988) *Keeping Faith? Channel 4 and Its Audiences*, London: John Libbey.

Dooley, B. (1990) "From literary criticism to systems theory in early modern journalism history," *Journal of the History of Ideas* 51: 461–86.

Douglas, J.D. (1976) *Investigative Social Research: Individual and Team Field Research*, London: Sage.

Downing, J. (1984) *Radical Media: the Political Experience of Alternative Communication*, Boston: South End Press.

Drummond, P. and Lusted, D. (eds) (1985) *Television and Schooling*, London: British Film Institute.

Dubois-Dumée, J. (1973) *Cable Television in France. A New Medium. Structures and Projects*, Strasbourg: Council of Europe.

Durkheim, E. (1915/1965) *The Elementary Forms of the Religious Life*, New York: Free Press.

Eagleton, T. (1983) *Literary Theory: an Introduction*, Minneapolis, MN: University of Minnesota Press.

Eco, U. (1976) *A Theory of Semiotics*, 2nd printing (1979), Bloomington, IN: Indiana University Press.

Eco, U. (1981) *The Name of the Rose*, London: Picador.

Eco, U. (1987a) "Introduction: the role of the reader," in U. Eco, *The Role of the Reader*, London: Hutchinson.

Eco, U. (1987b) "Narrative structures in Fleming" (orig. publ. 1965), in U. Eco, *The Role of the Reader*, London: Hutchinson.

Eisenstein, E. (1979) *The Printing Press as an Agent of Change*, New York: Cambridge University Press.

Eliot, M. (1983) *Television: One Season in American Television*, New York: St Martin's Press.

Ellen, R.F. (ed.) (1984) *Ethnographic Research: a Guide to General Conduct*, New York: Academic Press.

Elliott, P. (1972) *The Making of a Television Series*, London: Constable; 2nd edn (1979), London: Constable and Sage.

Ellis, J. (1982) *Visible Fictions*, London: Routledge & Kegan Paul.

Emery, M. and Emery, E. (1988) *The Press and America*, Englewood Cliffs, NJ: Prentice-Hall.

Enzensberger, H.M. (1970) "Constituents of a theory of the media," *New Left Review* 64: 13–36; reprinted in D. McQuail (ed.) (1972) *Sociology of Mass Communications*, London: Penguin.

Epstein, E.J. (1973) *News From Nowhere: Television and the News*, New York: Random House.

Ericson, R.V., Baranek, P.M., and Chan, J.B.L. (1989) *Negotiating Control: a Study of News Sources*, Toronto: University of Toronto Press.

Eriksen, T. (1987) *Budbringeren* (The Messenger), Copenhagen: Christian Ejlers' Forlag.

Faenza, R. (1977) *The Radio Phenomenon in Italy*, Strasbourg: Council of Europe.

Farr, R. M. and Moscovici, S. (eds) (1984) *Social Representations*, Cambridge: Cambridge University Press.

Farrell, T. (1987) "Beyond science: humanities contributions to communication theory," in C. Berger and S. Chaffee (eds) *Handbook of Communication Science*, Newbury Park, CA: Sage.

Faulkner, R.R. (1982) "Improvising on a triad," in J. van Maanen, J.M. Dabbs, and R.R. Faulkner (eds) *Varieties of Qualitative Research*, London: Sage.

Festinger, L., Riecken, H.W., and Schachter, S. (1957) *When Prophecy Fails*, Minneapolis, MN: University of Minnesota Press.

Fetterman, D.M. (1989) *Ethnography Step by Step*, London: Sage.

Feuer, J. (1986) "Dynasty," paper, International Television Studies Conference, London, July.

Feuer, J. (1987) *Genre Study and Television*, in R.C. Allen (ed.) *Channels of Discourse*, London: Routledge.

Feyerabend, P. (1975) *Against Method: Outline of an Anarchistic Theory of Knowledge*, London: NLB.

Fields, J.M. and Schuman, H. (1976) "Public beliefs about beliefs of the public," *Public Opinion Quarterly* 40: 427–48.

Filstead, W.J. (ed.) (1970) *Qualitative Methodology: Firsthand Involvement with the Social World*, Chicago: Markham.

Finch, J. (1986) *Research and Policy: the Uses of Qualitative Methods in Social and Educational Research*, London: Falmer Press.

Fish, S. (1979) *Is There a Text in This Class? The Authority of Interpretive Communities*, Cambridge, MA: Harvard University Press.

Fisher, B.M. and Strauss, A.L. (1978) "Interactionism," in T. Bottomore and R. Nisbet (eds) *A History of Sociological Analysis*, London: Heinemann.

Fishman, M. (1980) *Manufacturing the News*, Austin: University of Texas Press.

Fiske, J. (1987) *Television Culture*, London: Methuen.

Fiske, J. (1989) *Understanding Popular Culture*, Boston: Unwin Hyman.

Fiske, J. (1990) "Ethnosemiotics," *Cultural Studies* 4, 1: 85–100.

Fiske, J. and Hartley, J. (1978) *Reading Television,* London: Methuen.

Fiske, S.T. and Taylor, S.E. (1984) *Social Cognition*, Reading, MA: Addison-Wesley.

Floyd, P. (1988) *Backstairs with "Upstairs, Downstairs,"* New York: St Martin's Press.

Foster, H. (1979) *The New Literacy: the Language of Film and Television*, Urbana, IL: National Council of Teachers of English.

Foster, H. (ed.) (1988) *Vision and Visuality*, Seattle: Bay Press.

Foucault, M. (1972) *The Archaeology of Knowledge*, London: Tavistock.

Fowler, R. (1991) *Language in the News*, London: Routledge.

Fowler, R., Hodge, B., Kress, G., and Trew, T. (1979) *Language and Control*, London: Routledge & Kegan Paul.

Freire, P. (1974) *Education for Critical Consciousness*, New York: Seabury Press.

Fuller, L.K. (1984) "Public access cable television: a case study on source, content, audience, producers, and rules-theoretical perspective," dissertation, University of Massachusetts.

Gadamer, H. (1975) *Truth and Method*, New York: Seabury Press.

Galbraith, J.K. (1967) *The New Industrial State*, New York: Signet.

Gallup, G.H. (ed.) (1972) *The Gallup Poll: Public Opinion 1935–1971*, New York: Random House.

Gamson, W.A. (1984) *What's News: A Game Simulation of TV News (Participant's Manual)*, New York: Free Press.

Gamson, W.A. and Lasch, K.E. (1983) "The political culture of social welfare policy," in E. Spiro and E. Yuchtman-Yaar (eds) *Evaluating the Welfare State: Social and Political Perspectives*, New York: Academic Press.

Gamson, W.A. and Modigliani, A. (1987) "The changing culture of affirmative action," in R.D. Braungart (ed.) *Research in Political Sociology*, vol. 3, Greenwich, CT: JAI Press.

Gamson, W.A. and Modigliani, A. (1989) "Media discourse and public opinion on nuclear power," *American Journal of Sociology* 95: 1–37.

Gans, H. (1974) *Popular Culture and High Culture*, New York: Basic Books.

Gans, H. (1979) *Deciding What's News*, New York: Pantheon Books.

Garfinkel, H. (1967) *Studies in Ethnomethodology*, Englewood Cliffs, NJ: Prentice-Hall.

Garside, R., Leech, G., and Sampson, G. (eds) (1987) *The Computational Analysis of English: a Corpus-based Approach*, London: Longman.

Geertz, C. (1973) *The Interpretation of Cultures*, New York: Basic Books.

Geertz, C. (1988) *Works and Lives: The Anthropologist as Author*, Cambridge: Polity Press.

Geis, M. (1987) *The Language of Politics*, New York: Springer.

Gerbner, G. and Gross, L. (1976) "Living with television: the violence profile," *Journal of Communication* 26, 3: 173–99.

Giddens, A. (1984) *The Constitution of Society*, Berkeley: University of California Press.

Gilmore, W. (1989) *Reading Becomes a Necessity of Life*, Lexington: University of Kentucky Press.

Gitlin, T. (1978) "Media sociology: the dominant paradigm," *Theory and Society* 6: 205–53.

Gitlin, T. (1980) *The Whole World Is Watching*, Berkeley: University of California Press.

Gitlin, T. (1983) *Inside Prime Time*, New York: Pantheon.

Glaser, B.G. (1978) *Advances in the Methodology of Grounded Theory: Theoretical Sensitivity*, Mill Valley, CA: Sociology Press.

Glaser, B.G. and Strauss, A.L. (1965) *Time for Dying*, Chicago: Aldine.

Glaser, B.G. and Strauss, A.L. (1967) *The Discovery of Grounded Theory: Strategies for Qualitative Research*, Chicago: Aldine.

Glasgow University Media Group (1976) *Bad News*, London: Routledge & Kegan Paul.

Glasgow University Media Group (1980) *More Bad News*, London: Routledge & Kegan Paul.

Goffman, E. (1959) *The Presentation of Self in Everyday Life*, New York: Doubleday.

Goffman, E. (1963) *Behavior in Public Places: Notes on the Social Organization of Gatherings*, New York: Free Press.

Goffman, E. (1974) *Frame Analysis: an Essay on the Organization of Experience*, Cambridge: Harvard University Press.

Goffman, E. (1976) *Gender Advertisements*, London: Society for the Study of Visual Communication.

Golding, P. and Elliott, P. (1979) *Making the News*, London: Longman.

Gombrich, E.H. (1960) *Art and Illusion*, Princeton: Princeton University Press.

Goodman, I. (1983) "TV's role in family interaction," *Journal of Family Issues* 4, 2: 405–24.

Goodman, N. (1976) *Languages of Art*, 2nd edn, Indianapolis, IN: Hackett.

Goodman, N. (1978) *Ways of Worldmaking*, Indianapolis, IN: Hackett.

Goody, J. (1987) *The Interface Between the Written and the Oral*, Cambridge: Cambridge University Press.

Goody, J. and Watt, I. (1963) "The consequences of literacy," *Comparative Studies in Society and History* 5: 304–45. Reprinted in J. Goody (ed.) (1968) *Literacy in Traditional Societies*, Cambridge: Cambridge University Press.

Gordon, P. and Klug, F. (1986) *New Right, New Racism*, London: Searchlight Publications.

Gorrell-Barnes, G. (1985) "Modern systems theory and family therapy," in M. Rutter and L.K. Herzov (eds) *Modern Child Psychiatry*, London: Tavistock.

Gouldner, A.W. (1968) "The sociologist as partisan: sociology and the welfare state," *American Sociologist* 3, 2: 103–16.

Gouldner, A.W. (1970) *The Coming Crisis of Western Sociology*, New York: Avon.

Gouldner, A.W. (1976) *The Dialectic of Ideology and Technology*, New York: Seabury.

Graauw, C. de, Weegh, P. op de, and Hutjes, J. (1986) *Dbase III in Onderzoek: Gebruiksmogelijkheden voor de sociale wetenschappen* (Dbase III in Research: Possibilities for Use in the Social Sciences), Nijmegen: Institute of Applied Sociology (ITS).

Graber, D. (1984) *Processing the News: How People Tame the Information Tide*, New York: Longman.

Graff, H. (1987) *The Labyrinths of Literacy*, London: Falmer.

Gramsci, A. (1971) *Selections from the Prison Notebooks*, New York: International Publishers.

Gray, A. (1987) "Reading the audience," *Screen* 28, 3: 24–36.

Greimas, A.J. (1966) *Semantique structurale*, Paris: Larousse.

Grishman, R. (1986) *Computational Linguistics: an Introduction*, Cambridge: Cambridge University Press.

Grossberg, L. (1987) "The in-difference of TV," *Screen* 28, 2: 28–46.

Gunter, B. and Svennevig, M. (1987) *Behind and in Front of the Screen: Television's Involvement with Family Life*, London: John Libbey.

Habermas, J. (1971) *Knowledge and Human Interests*, Boston, MA: Beacon Press.

Habermas, J. (1974) "The public sphere: an encyclopedia article," *New German Critique* 1: 49–55.

Habermas, J. (1984) *The Theory of Communicative Action*, vol. 1, Boston, MA: Beacon Press.

Habermas, J. (1989) *The Structural Transformation of the Public Sphere: an Inquiry into a Category of Bourgeois Society*, Cambridge, MA: MIT Press.

Hadden, J.K. and Rymph, R.C. (1966) "The marching ministers," *Transaction* 36, 3: 38–41.

Hall, O. (1944) "The informal organization of medical practice: case study of a profession," dissertation, University of Chicago.

Hall, S. (1973) "Encoding and decoding in the television discourse," Occasional Paper No. 7, Birmingham: CCCS.

Hall, S. (1979) "Culture, the media, and the 'ideological effect'," in J. Curran, M. Gurevitch, and J. Woollacott (eds) *Mass Communication and Society*, London: Edward Arnold.

Hall, S. (1980) "Cultural studies: two paradigms," *Media, Culture and Society* 2: 57–72.

Hall, S., Critcher, C., Jefferson, T., Clarke, J., and Roberts, B. (1978) *Policing the Crisis*, London: Macmillan.

Hall, S., Hobson, D., Lowe, A., and Willis, P. (eds) (1980) *Culture, Media, Language*, London: Hutchinson.

Halliday, M.A.K. (1978) *Language as Social Semiotic*, London: Longman.

Halliday, M.A.K. (1985) *An Introduction to Functional Grammar*, London: Edward Arnold.

Halliday, M. and Hasan, R. (1976) *Cohesion in English*, London: Longman.

Hallin, D.C. (1986) *The "Uncensored War": the Media and Vietnam*, New York: Oxford University Press.

Hallin, D.C. (1991) "The rise of the ten second sound bite," *Columbia Journalism Review*, January.

Halloran, J.D. (1975) *Communication and Community: the Evaluation of an Experiment*, Strasbourg: Council of Europe.

Halloran, J.D., Elliott, P., and Murdock, G. (1970) *Demonstrations and Communications: a Case Study*, Harmondsworth: Penguin.

Hammersley, M. (1989) *The Dilemma of Qualitative Method: Herbert Blumer and the Chicago Tradition*, London: Routledge.

Hammersley, M. and Atkinson, P. (1983) *Ethnography. Principles and Practice*, London: Tavistock.

Hartley, J. (1982) *Understanding News*, London: Methuen.

Hartley, J. (1987) "Invisible fictions," *Textual Practice* 1, 2: 121–38.

Harvey, D. (1989) *The Condition of Postmodernity*, Oxford: Basil Blackwell.

Harvey, L. (1987) *Myths of the Chicago School of Sociology*, Brookfield, VT: Gower.

Hauser, A. (1951) *The Social History of Art*, 4 vols, New York: Vintage.

Havelock, E. (1963) *Preface to Plato*, Oxford: Blackwell.

Havelock, E. (1986) *The Muse Learns to Write*, New Haven, CT: Yale University Press.

Hawkes, T. (1977) *Structuralism and Semiotics*, London: Methuen.

Heath, S. (1980) "The functions and uses of literacy," Journal of Communication 30, 1: 123–33.

Heath, S. (1981) *Questions of Cinema*, London: Macmillan.

Heim, M. (1987) *Electric Language*, New Haven, CT: Yale University Press.

Hein, K.J. (1988) *Radio Baha'i Ecuador: A Baha'i Development Project*, Oxford: George Ronald.

Held, D. and Thompson, J. (eds) (1989) *Social Theory of Modern Societies: Anthony Giddens and his Critics*, Cambridge: Cambridge University Press.

Herman, E. S. and Chomsky, N. (1988) *Manufacturing Consent: the Political Economy of the Mass Media*, New York: Pantheon Books.

Heyn, J. (1979) *Partizipation und Lokalkommunikation in Grossbritannien. Video, Fernsehen, Hörfunk und das Problem der Demokratisierung kommunaler Kommunikation* (Participation and Local Communication in Great Britain. Video, Television, Radio and the Problem of Democratic Community Communication), Munich: Minerva.

Hiemstra, R., Esseman, E., Henry, N., and Palumbo, D. (1987) "Computer assisted analysis of qualitative gerontological research," *Educational Gerontology* 13: 417–26.

Hill, D. and Weingrad, J. (1986) *Saturday Night: a Backstage History of "Saturday Night Live,"* New York: Beech Tree Books/William Morrow.

Hobbs, R., Frost, R., Davis, A., and Stauffer, J. (1988) "How first-time viewers comprehend editing conventions," *Journal of Communication* 38, 1: 50–60.

Hobson, D. (1982) *Crossroads: the Drama of a Soap Opera*, London: Methuen.

Hodel, M. and Chappelle, L. (1979) *A Twenty-Year History of KPFK-FM, Los Angeles*, Los Angeles: Pacifica Foundation.

Hodge, R. and Kress, G. (1988) *Social Semiotics*, London: Polity Press.

Hofstadter, D. and Dennett, D. (eds) (1982) *The Mind's I*, London: Penguin.

Hoggart, R. (1957) *The Uses of Literacy*, London: Penguin.

Höijer, B. (1990) "Studying viewers' reception of television programs: theoretical and methodological considerations," *European Journal of Communication* 5, 1: 29–56.

Hollander, E.H. (1982) *Kleinschalige Massacommunicatie: Lokale Omroepvormen in West-Europa* (Small-Scale Mass Communication: Local Broadcasting Forms in Western Europe), The Hague: Government Publishing House.

Hollander, E.H. (1988) "Lokale Communicatie en Lokale Openbaarheid. Openbaarheid als Communicatiewetenschappelijk Concept" (Local communication and local public sphere. Public sphere as a concept in communication science), dissertation, Nijmegen: Catholic University.

Holub, R. (1984) *Reception Theory: a Critical Introduction*, London: Methuen.

Hone, P. (1889) *The Diary of Philip Hone*, New York: Dodd, Mead.

Horton, D. (1957) "Dialog of courtship in popular songs," *American Journal of Sociology* 62: 569–78.

Hughes, H. (1940) *News and the Human Interest Story*, Chicago: University of Chicago Press.

Hughes, R. (1981) *The Shock of the New*, New York: Alfred A. Knopf.

Hycner, R.H. (1985) "Some guidelines for the phenomenological analysis of interview data," *Human Studies* 8: 279–303.

Innis, H. (1951) *The Bias of Communication*, Toronto: University of Toronto Press.

Innis, H. (1972) *Empire and Communications*, Toronto: University of Toronto Press.

Jakobson, R. (1960) "Closing statement: linguistics and poetics," in T. Sebeok (ed.) *Style in Language*, Cambridge, MA: MIT Press.

Jankowski, N.W. (1977) *Lokale Omroep Bijlmermeer in het Proces van Samenlevingsopbouw: Een Beleiedsrelevant Verslag* (Community Television Bijlmermeer in the Process of Community Development: a Policy-oriented Report), Amsterdam: SISWO.

Jankowski, N.W. (1988) "Community television in Amsterdam. Access to, participation in, and use of the 'Lokale Omroep Bijlmermeer'," dissertation, Amsterdam: University of Amsterdam.

Jankowski, N.W. and Mendel, R. (1990) "Public access to telematics: a pilot study of user involvement in the design and implementation of telematics," research proposal, Amsterdam: Centre for Interactive Media Projects.

Jankowski, N.W. and Mol, A. (1988) "Democratization of communication and local radio in the Netherlands," *RTV Theory and Practice* 3: 97–121.

Jankowski, N.W., Prehn, O., and Stappers, J.G. (1991) *The People's Voice: Local Radio and Television in Europe*, London: John Libbey.

Janowitz, M. (1952) *The Community Press in an Urban Setting*, 2nd rev. edn (1967), Chicago: University of Chicago Press.

Jarren, O. and Widlock, P. (1985) *Lokal Radio für die Bundesrepublik Deutschland* (Local Radio in the Federal Republic of Germany), Berlin: Vista Verlag.

Jay, M. (1973) *The Dialectical Imagination. A History of the Frankfurt School and the Institute of Social Research 1923–50*, London: Heinemann.

Jensen, K.B. (1986) *Making Sense of the News*, Aarhus, Denmark: Aarhus University Press.

Jensen, K.B. (1987) "Qualitative audience research: toward an integrative approach to reception," *Critical Studies in Mass Communication* 4, 1: 21–36.

Jensen, K.B. (1988) "News as social resource," *European Journal of Communication* 3, 3: 275–301.

Jensen, K.B. (1989) "Discourses of interviewing: validating qualitative research findings through textual analysis," in S. Kvale (ed.) *Issues of Validity in Qualitative Research*, Lund, Sweden: Studentlitteratur.

Jensen, K.B. (1990a) "The politics of polysemy: television news, everyday consciousness, and political action," *Media, Culture and Society* 12, 1: 57–77.

Jensen, K.B. (1990b) "Television futures: a social action methodology for studying interpretive communities," *Critical Studies in Mass Communication* 7, 2: 1–18.

Jensen, K.B. (1991) "When is meaning? Communication theory, pragmatism, and mass media reception," in J. Anderson (ed.) *Communication Yearbook*, vol. 14, Newbury Park, CA: Sage.

Jensen, K.B. (forthcoming) "Print cultures and visual cultures: a research agenda on new media environments," in J. Stappers (ed.) *Approaches to Mass Communication*, London: Sage.

Jensen, K.B. and Rosengren, K.E. (1990) "Five traditions in search of the audience," *European Journal of Communication* 5, 2–3: 207–38.

Jick, T. (1979) "Mixing qualitative and quantitative methods: triangulation in action," *Administrative Science Quarterly* 24 (December): 602–11.

Johnson, B. (1971) "The religious crusade: revival or ritual?" *American Journal of Sociology* 76: 873–90.

Johnson, J.M. (1975) *Doing Field Research*, New York: Free Press.

Jones, M. (1968) "The police and the militants," *New Statesman* 76: 418–21.

Jowett, G. (1975) "Toward a history of communication," *Journalism History* 2: 34–7.

Junker, B. (1960) *Field Work: an Introduction to the Social Sciences*, introduction by E.C. Hughes, Chicago: University of Chicago Press.

Kaplan, A.E. (1987) "Feminist criticism and television," in R.C. Allen (ed.) *Channels of Discourse*, London: Routledge.

Katz, E. and Lazarsfeld, P. (1955) *Personal Influence*, Glencoe, IL: The Free Press.

Katz, E. and Liebes, T. (1984) "Once upon a time in *Dallas*," *Intermedia* 12, 3: 28–32.

Kaufmann, S. (1990) "Stanley Kaufmann on film: crisis," *The New Republic*, 23 July: 26–7.

Keane, J. (1984) *Public Life and Late Capitalism*, Cambridge: Cambridge University Press.

Kelly, G.A. (1965) *Lost Soldiers*, Cambridge, MA: MIT Press.

Kennedy, T. (1973) "The Skyriver project: the story of a process," *Access* 12: 3–12.

Kirk, J. and Miller, M. (1986) *Reliability and Validity in Qualitative Research*, Beverly Hills, CA: Sage.

Klapper, J. (1960) *The Effects of Mass Communication*, New York: Free Press.

Kleinsteuber, H.J. and Sonnenberg, U. (1990) "Beyond public service and private profit: international experience with non-commercial local radio," *European Journal of Communication* 5: 87–106.

Koole, T., Oorburg, J., and Wartena, W. (1976) *Lokale Televisie in Deventer: een Experiment-begeleidend Onderzoek* (Local Television in Deventer: an Experimental-Advisory Research Project), Groningen: Institute of Sociology.

Kracauer, S. (1947) *From Caligari to Hitler*, Princeton: Princeton University Press.

Kracauer, S. (1953) "The challenge of qualitative content analysis," *Public Opinion Quarterly* 16, 2: 631–42.

Kracauer, S. (1963) "Über Erfolgsbücher und ihr Publikum" (About Bestsellers and their Readers) (orig. publ. 1931), in S. Kracauer *Ornament der Masse* (Ornament of the Mass), Frankfurt am Main: Suhrkamp.

Kracauer, S. (1974) *Kino* (Cinema), Frankfurt am Main: Suhrkamp.

Kress, G. (1985) "Ideological structures in discourse," in T. van Dijk (ed.) *Handbook of Discourse Analysis*, vol. 4 (Discourse Analysis in Society), London: Academic Press.

Krippendorff, K. (1980) *Content Analysis*, Beverly Hills, CA: Sage.

Kuhn, T. (1970) *The Structure of Scientific Revolutions*, rev. edn, Chicago: University of Chicago Press.

Kuper, A. (1973) *Anthropologists and Anthropology: the British School 1922–72*, Harmondsworth: Penguin.

Lacan, J. (1977) *The Four Fundamental Concepts of Psychoanalysis*, Harmondsworth: Penguin.

Lang, G.E. and Lang, K. (1983) *The Battle for Public Opinion: the*

President, the Press and the Polls During Watergate, New York: Columbia University Press.

Lang, K. and Lang, G.E. (1953) "The unique perspective of television and its effect: a pilot study," *American Sociological Review* 18: 3–12. Reprinted in W. Schramm (ed.) (1960) *Mass Communications*, Urbana: University of Illinois Press.

Lang, K. and Lang, G.E. (1960) "Decisions for Christ: Billy Graham in New York," in M. Stein, A.J. Vidich, and D.M. White (eds) *Identity and Anxiety in Mass Society*, New York: Free Press.

Lang, K. and Lang, G.E. (1961) *Collective Dynamics*, New York: T.Y. Crowll.

Lang, K. and Lang, G.E. (1985) "Method as master, or mastery over method," in M. Gurevitch and M. Levy (eds) *Mass Communication Review Yearbook*, vol. 5, Beverly Hills, CA: Sage.

Lasswell, H. (1948) "The structure and function of communication in society," in B. Berelson and M. Janowitz (eds) *Reader in Public Opinion and Communication*, Glencoe, IL: The Free Press.

Latane, B. and Darley, J.M. (1970) *The Unresponsive Bystander: Why Doesn't He Help?*, New York: Appleton-Crofts.

Lauretis, T. de (1984) *Alice Doesn't*, Bloomington, IN: Indiana University Press.

Lazarsfeld, P. (1941) "Remarks on administrative and critical communications research," *Studies in Philosophy and Social Science* 9: 2–16.

Leech, G.N. (1966) *English in Advertising*, London: Longman.

Leech, G.N. (1974) *Semantics*, Harmondsworth: Penguin.

Leech, G.N. (1983) *Principles of Pragmatics*, London: Longman.

Lester, M. (1975) "News as a practical accomplishment," dissertation, Santa Barbara: University of California.

Lévi-Strauss, C. (1963) *Structural Anthropology*, New York: Penguin.

Lévi-Strauss, C. (1967) "The structural study of myth" (orig. publ. 1958), in C. Lévi-Strauss, *Structural Anthropology*, New York: Anchor Books.

Levine, L. (1988) *Highbrow/Lowbrow*, Cambridge, MA: Harvard University Press.

Levinson, R. and Link, W. (1981) *Stay Tuned*, New York: Ace Books.

Levinson, R. and Link, W. (1986) *Off Camera: Conversations with the Makers of Prime-time Television*, New York: American Library.

Lewis, J. (1985) "Decoding television news," in P. Drummond and R. Paterson (eds) *Television in Transition*, London: British Film Institute.

Lewis, P.M. (1976) *Bristol Channel and Community Television*, London: Independent Broadcasting Authority.

Lewis, P.M. (1978) *Community Television and Cable in Britain*, London: British Film Institute.

Lewis, P.M. (1984) "Community radio: the Montreal conference and after," *Media, Culture and Society* 6: 137–50.

Leymore, V. (1975) *Hidden Myth: Structure and Symbolism in Advertising*, London: Heinemann.

Liebes, T. and Katz, E. (1990) *The Export of Meaning*, New York: Oxford University Press.

Lin, N. (1974) "The McIntire march: a study of recruitment and commit-
ment," *Public Opinion Quarterly* 38: 562–73.
Lincoln, Y.S. and Guba, E.G. (1985) *Naturalistic Inquiry*, London: Sage.
Lindesmith, A. (1947) *Opiate Addiction*, Bloomington, IN: Principia
Press.
Lindlof, T. (ed.) (1987) *Natural Audiences*, Norwood, NJ: Ablex.
Lindlof, T. (1988) "Media audiences as interpretive communities," in J.
Anderson (ed.) *Communication Yearbook*, vol. 11, Newbury Park, CA:
Sage.
Lindlof, T. and Meyer, T. (1987) "Mediated communication: the foun-
dations of qualitative research," in T. Lindlof (ed.) *Natural Audiences*,
Norwood, NJ: Ablex.
Livingstone, S. (1990) *Making Sense of Television*, Oxford: Pergamon.
Lofland, J. (1971) *Analyzing Social Settings: a Guide to Qualitative Obser-
vation and Analysis*, 2nd rev. edn (1981) Belmont, CA: Wadsworth.
Lofland, L. (1973) *A World of Strangers*, New York: Basic Books.
Lowe, D. (1982) *History of Bourgeois Perception*, Chicago: University of
Chicago Press.
Lowenthal, L. (1961) *Literature, Popular Culture, and Society*, Englewood
Cliffs, NJ: Prentice-Hall.
Lowery, S. and DeFleur, M. (1988) *Milestones in Mass Communication
Research: Media Effects*, 2nd edn, New York: Longman.
Luger, H.H. (1983) *Pressesprache* (Press Language), Tübingen: Niemeyer.
Lull, J. (1980) "The social uses of television," *Human Communication
Research* 6: 197–209.
Lull, J. (1987) "Audiences, texts and contexts," *Critical Studies in Mass
Communication* 4: 318–22.
Lull, J. (ed.) (1988a) *World Families Watch Television*, Newbury Park,
CA: Sage.
Lull, J. (1988b) "Critical response: the audience as nuisance," *Critical
Studies in Mass Communication* 5: 239–43.
Lynch, J. (1973) "Seven days with 'All in the Family'," *Journal of Broad-
casting* 17, 3: 259–74.
Lynd, R.S. and Lynd, H.M. (1929) *Middletown: a Study in Contemporary
American Culture*, New York: Harcourt, Brace, & Janovich.
Lyotard, J. (1984) *The Postmodern Condition*, Minneapolis: University of
Minnesota Press.
Maanen, J. van (1988) *Tales of the Field: on Writing Ethnography*, Chicago:
University of Chicago Press.
Maanen, J. van, Dabbs, J.M., and Faulkner, R.R. (1982) *Varieties of
Qualitative Research*, London: Sage.
MacBride, S. (1980) *Many Voices, One World. Towards a New More Just
and More Efficient World Information and Communication Order*,
London: Kogan Page.
McCall, G.J. and Simmons, J.L. (eds) (1969) *Issues in Participant Obser-
vation: a Text and Reader*, Reading, MA: Addison-Wesley.
McCombs, M. and Shaw, D.L. (1972) "The agenda-setting function of
mass media," *Public Opinion Quarterly* 36: 176–87.

McGerr, M. (1986) *The Decline of Popular Politics*, New York: Oxford University Press.

MacKenzie, J. (1984) *Propaganda and Empire*, Manchester: Manchester University Press.

McKinney, C. (1966) *Constructive Typology and Social Theory*, New York: Appleton-Century-Crofts.

McLoughlin, W.G. Jr (1960) *Billy Graham: Revivalist in a Secular Age*, New York: Ronald Press.

McLuhan, M. (1962) *The Gutenberg Galaxy*, Toronto: University of Toronto Press.

McLuhan, M. (1964) *Understanding Media*, New York: McGraw-Hill.

McNall, S.G. and Johnson, J.C. (1975) "The new conservatives: ethnomethodologists, phenomenologists, and symbolic interactionists," *Insurgent Sociologist* 5, 4: 49–65.

McQuail, D. (1987) *Mass Communication Theory: an Introduction*, 2nd edn, London: Sage.

McQuail, D. and Windahl, S. (1981) *Communication Models for the Study of Mass Communications*, London: Longman.

Madge, C. and Harrisson, T. (1939) *Britain by Mass-Observation*, Harmondsworth: Penguin.

Madge, J. (1953) *The Tools of Social Science*, London: Longmans, Green & Co.

Madge, J. (1962) *The Origins of Scientific Sociology*, New York: Free Press.

Mair, G. (1988) *Inside HBO: the Billion Dollar War Between HBO, Hollywood, and the Home Video Revolution*, New York: Dodd, Mead, & Co.

Malinowski, B. (1922) *Argonauts of the Western Pacific: an Account of Native Enterprise and Adventure in the Archipelagoes of Melanesian New Guinea*, London: Routledge & Kegan Paul.

Malinowski, B. (1967) *A Diary in the Strict Sense of the Term*, London: Routledge & Kegan Paul.

Manis, J.G. and Meltzer, B.N. (eds) (1967) *Symbolic Interaction: a Reader in Social Psychology*, Boston, MA: Allyn & Bacon.

Manning, P.K. (1977) *Police Work: the Social Organization of Policing*, Cambridge, MA: MIT Press.

Manning, P.K. (1982) "Analytic induction," in R.B. Smith and P.K. Manning (eds) *Qualitative Methods*, vol. II of *Handbook of Social Science Methods*, Cambridge, MA: Ballinger.

Marcus, G, and Fischer, M. (1986) *Anthropology as Cultural Critique*, Chicago: University of Chicago Press.

Marks, E. and de Courtivron, I. (eds) (1981) *New French Feminisms*, Brighton: Harvester.

Marvin, C. (1983) "Space, time, and captive communications history," in M. Mander (ed.) *Communications in Transition*, New York: Praeger.

Maso, I. (1987) *Kwalitatief Onderzoek* (Qualitative Research), Amsterdam: Boom.

Masterman, L. (1980) *Teaching about Television*, London: Macmillan.

Masterman, L. (1985) *Teaching the Media*, London: Comedia.

Masterman, L. (1988) *The Development of Media Education in Europe in the 1980s*, Strasbourg: Council of Europe.

Matta, F. (1981) "A model for democratic communication," *Development Dialogue* 2: 79–97.

Mayerle, J. (1989) "The most inconspicuous hit on television," *Journal of Popular Film and Television* 17, 3: 101–12.

Mead, G.H. (1934) *Mind, Self, and Society*, Chicago: University of Chicago Press.

Melody, W.H. and Mansell, R.E. (1983) "The debate over critical vs. administrative research: circularity or challenge," *Journal of Communication* 33, 3: 102–16.

Meltzer, B.N., Petras, J.W., and Reynolds, L.T. (1975) *Symbolic Interactionism. Genesis, Varieties and Criticism*, London: Routledge & Kegan Paul.

Messaris, P. (1988) "Barriers to pictorial comprehension by inexperienced viewers," paper, Speech Communication Association conference.

Metz, C. (1974) *Language and Cinema*, The Hague: Mouton.

Metz, C. (1982) *The Imaginary Signifier*, Bloomington, IN: Indiana University Press.

Metz, R. (1975) *CBS: Reflections in a Bloodshot Eye*, New York: New American Library.

Meyrowitz, J. (1985) *No Sense of Place*, New York: Oxford University Press.

Mies, M. (1979) *Towards a Methodology of Women's Studies*, The Hague: Institute of Social Studies.

Miles, M.B. (1979) "Qualitative data as an attractive nuisance: the problem of analysis," *Administrative Science Quarterly* 24: 590–601.

Miles, M.B. and Huberman, A.M. (1984) *Qualitative Data Analysis: a Sourcebook of New Methods*, London: Sage.

Mills, C.W. (1959) *The Sociological Imagination*, London: Oxford University Press.

Modleski, T. (1984) *Loving with a Vengeance*, New York: Routledge.

Moi, T. (1985) *Sexual/Textual Politics*, London: Methuen.

Molotch, H. and Lester, M. (1974) "News as purposive behavior: on the strategic use of routine events, accidents, and scandals," *American Sociological Review* 39, 1: 101–12.

Molotch, H. and Lester, M. (1975) "The great oil spill," *American Journal of Sociology* 81: 235–60.

Morgenstern, S. (ed.) (1979) *Inside the TV Business*, New York: Sterling.

Morley, D. (1980) *The "Nationwide" Audience*, London: British Film Institute.

Morley, D. (1981) "'The nationwide audience': a critical postscript," *Screen Education*, 39: 3–14.

Morley, D. (1986) *Family Television*, London: Comedia.

Morley, D. (1989) "Changing paradigms in audience studies," in E. Seiter, H. Borchers, G. Kreutzner, and E. Warth (eds) *Remote Control: Television, Audiences, and Cultural Power*, London: Routledge.

Morley, D. (1990) "Behind the ratings," in J. Willis and T. Wollen (eds) *Neglected Audiences*, London: British Film Institute.

Morley, D. and Silverstone, R. (1990) "Domestic communication," *Media, Culture and Society* 12: 31–55.

Morse, M. (1985) "Talk, talk, talk," *Screen* 26, 2: 2–17.

Mukerji, C. (1983) *From Graven Images*, New York: Columbia University Press.

Mulvey, L. (1986) "Visual pleasure and narrative cinema," (orig. publ. 1975), in P. Rosen (ed.) *Narrative, Apparatus, Ideology: a Film Reader*, New York: Columbia University Press.

Mulvey, L. (1989) *Visual and Other Pleasures*, London: Macmillan.

Naisbitt, J. (1982) *Megatrends*, New York: Warner.

Nash, W. (1990) *The Writing Scholar*, Newbury Park, CA: Sage.

Negt, O. (1968) *Soziologische Phantasie und Exemplarisches Lernen: zur Theorie der Arbeiterbildung* (Sociological Imagination and Exemplary Learning: toward a Theory of the Education of Workers), Frankfurt am Main: Europäische Verlagsanstalt.

Negt, O. (1980) "Mass media: tools of domination or instruments of emancipation?" in K. Woodward, *The Myths of Information*, London: Routledge & Kegan Paul.

Newcomb, H. and Alley, R. (1983) *The Producer's Medium: Conversations with Creators of American TV*, New York: Oxford.

Newcomb, H. and Hirsch, P. (1984) "Television as a cultural forum: implications for research," in W. Rowland and B. Watkins (eds) *Interpreting Television*, Beverly Hills, CA: Sage.

Nord, D. (1986) "Working-class readers: family, community, and reading in late nineteenth-century America," *Communication Research* 13: 156–81.

Oakley, A. (1981) "Interviewing women: a contradiction in terms," in H. Roberts (ed.) *Doing Feminist Research*, London: Routledge.

Ong, W. (1982) *Orality and Literacy*, London: Methuen.

O'Sullivan, T., Hartley, J., Saunders, D., and Fiske, J. (1983) *Key Concepts in Communication*, London: Routledge.

Park, R.E. (1922) *The Immigrant Press and Its Control*, New York: Harper.

Park, R.E. (1940) "News as a form of knowledge," *American Journal of Sociology* 45: 669–86.

Park, R.E., Burgess, E., and McKenzie, R.D. (1925) *The City*, Chicago: University of Chicago.

Partridge, S. (1982) *Not the BBC/IBA: the Case for Community Radio*, London: Comedia.

Pauly, J.J. (1991) "A beginner's guide to doing qualitative research in mass communication," *Journalism Monographs*, no. 125, February 1991.

Peirce, C.S. (1958) *Selected Writings*, Garden City, NJ: Doubleday.

Pekurny, R. (1980) "The production process and environment of NBC's 'Saturday Night Live'," *Journal of Broadcasting* 24, 1: 91–9.

Pelfrey, R. (1985) *Art and Mass Media*, New York: Harper & Row.

Peters, J.D. (1989) "John Locke, invididualism, and the origin of communication," *Quarterly Journal of Speech* 75, 4: 387–99.

Peters, V.A. and Wester, F.P. (1988) "De computer bij kwalitatief-inter-

preterend onderzoek: een onderzoeksnotitie" (The computer in qualitative interpretive research: a research memo), *Sociologische Gids*, 35:
332–45.

Peters, V.A. and Wester, F.P. (1990) *Qualitative Analysis in Practice*,
Nijmegen: Catholic University, Department of Research Methodology.

Pfaffenberger, B. (1988) *Microcomputer Applications in Qualitative Research*, London: Sage.

Phillips, D. (1971) *Knowledge From What? Theories and Methods in Social
Research*, Chicago: Rand McNally.

Phillips, D. (1973) *Abandoning Method. Sociological Studies in Methodology*, London: Jossey-Bass.

Piaget, J. and Inhelder, B. (1948) *The Child's Conception of Space*, New
York: Norton.

Pinard, M., Kirk, J.G., and Eschen, D. van (1969) "Processes of recruitment and commitment," *Public Opinion Quarterly* 33: 355–69.

Ploman, E.W. and Lewis, P.M. (1977) *The Financing of Community and
Public Access Channels on Cable Television Networks in Member Countries of the Council of Europe*, Strasbourg: Council of Europe.

Polkinghorne, D. (1988) *Narrative Knowing and the Human Sciences*,
Albany, NY: State University of New York Press.

Popper, K. (1952) *The Open Society and Its Enemies*, London: Routledge,
Kegan & Paul.

Postman, N. (1985) *Amusing Ourselves to Death*, New York: Viking.

Potter, J. and Wetherell, M. (1987) *Discourse and Social Psychology*,
London: Sage.

Prehn, O. (1986) "Community television in Denmark – three years of
experiments," *The Nordicom Review of Nordic Mass Communication
Research* 2: 6–14.

Propp, V. (1958) *Morphology of the Folktale* (orig. publ. 1928), The
Hague: Mouton.

Radcliffe-Brown, A.R. (1952) *Structure and Function in Primitive Society*,
New York: Free Press.

Radway, J.A. (1984) *Reading the Romance. Women, Patriarchy, and
Popular Literature*, London: Verso.

Radway, J.A. (1986) "Identifying ideological seams: mass culture, analytic
method, and political practice," *Communication* 9: 93–123.

Ravage, J. (1977) " 'Not in the quality business': a case study of contemporary television production," *Journal of Broadcasting* 21, 1: 47–60.

Ravage, J. (1978) *Television: the Director's Viewpoint*, Boulder, CO: West-
wood Press.

Reeves, J. (1988) "Rewriting 'Newhart': a dialogic analysis," *Wide Angle*
10, 1: 76–91.

Reinarman, C. and Levine, H.G. (1989) "Crack in context: politics and the
making of a drug scare," *Contemporary Drug Problems* (winter):
535–77.

Reiss, A.J. Jr (1971) *The Police and the Public*, New Haven, CT: Yale
University Press.

Richards, I.A. (1929) *Practical Criticism*, New York: Harcourt, Brace &
World.

Richards, J. and Sheridan, D. (eds) (1987) *Mass Observation at the Movies*, London: Routledge & Kegan Paul.

Roberts, H. (1981) *Doing Feminist Research*, London: Routledge & Kegan Paul.

Robinson, J.P. and Hirsch, P.M. (1969) "Teenage response to rock and roll music," paper, American Sociological Association.

Rock, P. (1979) *The Making of Symbolic Interactionism*, London: Macmillan.

Rorty, R. (ed.) (1967) *The Linguistic Turn*, Chicago: University of Chicago Press.

Rorty, R. (1989) *Contingency, Irony, and Solidarity*, Cambridge: Cambridge University Press.

Rosen, P. (ed.) (1986) *Narrative, Apparatus, Ideology: a Film Theory Reader*, New York: Columbia University Press.

Rosengren, K., Wenner, L., and Palmgreen, P. (eds) (1985) *Media Gratifications Research: Current Perspectives*, Beverly Hills, CA: Sage.

Said, E. (1978) *Orientalism*, Harmondsworth: Penguin.

Sampson, P. (ed.) (1987) *Qualitative Research: The "New", the "Old" and a Question Mark*, Amsterdam: ESOMAR.

Sanday, P.R. (1983) "The ethnographic paradigm(s)," in J. van Maanen (ed.) *Qualitative Methodology*, London: Sage.

Saussure, F. de (1959) *Course in General Linguistics*, London: Peter Owen.

Scannell, P. (1988) "Radio times: the temporal arrangements of broadcasting in the modern world," in P. Drummond and R. Paterson (eds) *Television and its Audience*, London: British Film Institute.

Schatz, T. (1981) *Hollywood Genres*, New York: Random House.

Schatzman, L. and Strauss, A.L. (1971) *Field Research: Strategies for a Natural Sociology*, Englewood Cliffs, NJ: Prentice-Hall.

Schlesinger, P. (1978) *Putting "Reality" Together*, London: Constable.

Schlesinger, P. (1987) "On national identity: some conceptions and misconceptions criticized," *Social Science Information* 26: 219–64.

Schmitz, U. (1990) *Postmoderne Concierge: die "Tagesschau"* (Postmodern Concierge: the "Tagesschau"), Opladen: Westdeutscher.

Schramm, W.L. (1957) "Twenty years of journalism research," *Public Opinion Quarterly* 21: 91–107.

Schramm, W.L. (ed.) (1960) *Mass Communications*, Urbana, IL: University of Illinois Press.

Schudson, M. (1978) *Discovering the News*, New York: Basic Books.

Schudson, M. (1982) "The politics of narrative form: the emergence of news conventions in print and television," *Daedalus* 111: 97–112.

Schudson, M. (1986) "Preface to the paperback edition," in M. Schudson *Advertising, the Uneasy Persuasion*, New York: Basic Books.

Schudson, M. (1987) "The new validation of popular culture: sense and sentimentality in academia," *Critical Studies in Mass Communication* 4, 1: 51–68.

Schudson, M. (1989) "The sociology of news production," *Media, Culture and Society* 11: 263–83.

Schulman, M. (1985) "Neighborhood radio as community communication," dissertation, Cincinnati, OH: Union Graduate School.

Schulman, M. (1988) "Community communication theory," paper, Union for Democratic Communication Conference, Ottawa.

Schutz, A. (1963) *Collected Papers*, vol. 1, The Hague: Martins Nijhoff.

Schutz, A. (1967) *The Phenomenology of the Social World*, Evanston, IL: Northwestern University Press.

Scribner, S. and Cole, M. (1981) *The Psychology of Literacy*, Cambridge, MA: Harvard University Press.

Searle, J. (1969) *Speech Acts*, London: Cambridge University Press.

Seidel, J.V. and Clark, J.A. (1984) "The ethnograph: a computer program for the analysis of qualitative data," *Qualitative Sociology* 7: 10–125.

Seiter, E., Borchers, H., Kreutzner, G., and Warth, E. (eds) (1989a) *Remote Control: Television, Audiences, and Cultural Power*, London: Routledge.

Seiter, E., Borchers, H., Kreutzner, G., and Warth, E. (1989b) " 'Don't treat us like we're so stupid and naive': towards an ethnography of soap opera viewers," in E. Seiter, H. Borchers, G. Kreutzner, and E. Warth (eds) *Remote Control: Television, Audiences, and Cultural Power*, London: Routledge.

Servaes, J. (1989) "The role and place of research in participatory communication projects," paper, World Association for Christian Communication (WACC), Manila.

Shamberg, M. (1971) *Guerilla Television*, Cincinnati, OH: Holt, Rinehart, & Winston.

Shanks, R. (1976) *The Cool Fire: How to Make It in Television*, New York: Norton.

Shanks, R. (1986) *The Primal Screen: How to Write, Sell, and Produce Movies for Television*, New York: Norton.

Shibutani, T. (1966) *Improvised News: a Sociological Study of Rumor*, New York: Bobbs-Merrill.

Short, J.F. (ed.) (1971) *The Social Fabric of the Metropolis. Contributions of the Chicago School of Urban Sociology*, Chicago: University of Chicago Press.

Silverman, D. (1985) *Qualitative Methodology and Sociology. Describing the Social World*, Brookfield, VT: Gower.

Silverstone, R. (1981) *The Message of Television: Myth and Narrative in Contemporary Culture*, London: Heinemann.

Silverstone, R. (1989) "Let us then return to the murmuring of everyday practices," *Media, Culture and Society* 6, 1: 77–94.

Silverstone, R. (1990) "Television and everyday life: towards an anthropology of the television audience," in M. Ferguson (ed.) *Public Communication: the New Imperatives*, London: Sage.

Silverstone, R., Morley, D., Dahlberg, A., and Livingstone, S. (1989) "Families, technologies and consumption," London: Centre for Research into Innovation, Culture, and Technology, Brunel University.

Silverstone, R., Hirsch, E., and Morley, D. (1990a) "Information and communication technologies and the moral economy of the household," paper, London: Centre for Research into Innovation, Culture, and Technology, Brunel University.

Silverstone, R., Hirsch, E., and Morley, D. (1990b) "Listening to a long conversation: an ethnographic approach to the study of information and communication technologies in the home," paper, London: Centre for Research into Innovation, Culture, and Technology, Brunel University.

Simmel, G. (1957) "Fashion," *American Journal of Sociology* 62: 541–58.

Simons, H.W. (ed.) (1989) *Rhetoric in the Human Sciences*, London: Sage.

Simpson, P. (1987) *Parents Talking Television: Television in the Home*, London: Comedia.

Sinclair, J. and Coulthard, M. (1975) *Towards an Analysis of Discourse*, London: Oxford University Press.

Singer, D. (1970) *Prelude to Revolution: France in May, 1968*, London: Jonathan Cape.

Sinha, A.K. (1985) *Mass Media and Rural Development: a Study of Village Communication in Bihar*, New Delhi: Concept.

Smith, R.B. and Manning, P.K. (eds) (1982) *Qualitative Methods*, vol. II of *Handbook of Social Science Methods*, Cambridge, MA: Ballinger.

Smythe, D. (1977) "Communication: blindspot of Western Marxism," *Canadian Journal of Political and Social Theory* 1: 1–27.

Snow, C.P. (1964) *The Two Cultures and a Second Look*, Cambridge: Cambridge University Press.

Splichal, S., Hochheimer, J., and Jakubowitz, K. (1990) *Democratization and the Media: an East-West Dialogue*, Trieste: Faculty of Sociology, Political Science and Journalism, University of Ljubljana.

Spradley, J.P. (1979) *The Ethnographic Interview*, New York: Holt, Rinehart & Winston.

Spradley, J.P. (1980) *Participant Observation*, New York: Holt, Rinehart, & Winston.

Stappers, J.G., Hollander, E., and Manders, H. (1976) *Onderzoeksprojekt Lokale Kabelomroep* (Research Project Local Cablecasting), research report, Nijmegen: Institute of Mass Communication.

Stappers, J.G., Hollander, E., and Manders, H. (1977) *Vier Experimenten met Lokale Omroep* (Four Experiments with Local Broadcasting), research report, Nijmegen: Institute of Mass Communication.

Stappers, J.G., Jankowski, N.W., and Olderaan, F.J. (1989) *Interactief op Inactief: een Onderzoek naar de Ontwikkeling van Experimenten met het Kabelnet in het kader van het Kabelkommunikatieprojekt in Zaltbommel* (A Research Project on Experimentation with the Cable System in Zaltbommel), Nijmegen: Institute of Mass Communication.

Steeves, L.H. (1987) "Feminist theories and media studies," *Critical Studies in Mass Communication*, 4: 95–135.

Stempel, G.H. and Westley, B.H. (1981) *Research Methods in Mass Communication*, Englewood Cliffs, NJ: Prentice-Hall.

Strassner, E. (ed.) (1975) *Nachrichten* (News), Munich: Fink.

Strassner, E. (1982) *Fernsehnachrichten* (Television News), Tübingen: Niemeyer.

Strauss, A.L. (1987) *Qualitative Analysis for Social Scientists*, Cambridge: Cambridge University Press.

Strauss, A.L. and Corbin, J. (1990) *Basics of Grounded Theory Methods*, Beverly Hills, CA: Sage.

Suleiman, S. and Crosman, I. (eds) (1980) *The Reader in the Text*, Princeton, NJ: Princeton University Press.

Sutherland, E. (1937) *The Professional Thief*, Chicago: University of Chicago Press.

Swidler, A. (1986) "Culture in action: symbols and strategies," *American Sociological Review* 51: 273–86.

Tesch, R. (1990) *Qualitative Research: Analysis Types and Software Tools*, Bristol, PA: Falmer Press.

Thayer, L. (ed.) (1982) "Communication and community," *Communication* 7, 1.

Thomas, R. (1989) *Oral Tradition and Written Record in Classical Athens*, Cambridge: Cambridge University Press.

Thomas, W.I. (1928) *The Unadjusted Girl*, New York: Harper & Row.

Thomas, W.I. and Znaniecki, F. (1918–20) *The Polish Peasant in Europe and America*, Chicago: University of Chicago Press.

Thompson, P. (1978) *The Voice of the Past*, London: Oxford University Press.

Thrasher, F.M. (1927) *The Gang: a Study of 1,313 Gangs in Chicago*, Chicago: University of Chicago Press.

Tilly, C. (1989) "How (and what) are historians doing?" *American Behavioral Scientist* 33: 685–711.

Todorov, T. (1968) "Le grammaire du récit" (The grammar of narrative), *Langages* 12: 94–102.

Tompkins, J. (ed.) (1980) *Reader-response Criticism: From Formalism to Poststructuralism*, Baltimore, MD: Johns Hopkins University Press.

Towler, R. (1986) Address to Royal Television Society, Cambridge.

Trow, M. (1957) "Comment on 'Participant observation and interviewing: a comparison'," *Human Organization* 16, 3: 33–5.

Tuchman, G. (1972) "Objectivity as strategic ritual: an examination of newsmen's notions of objectivity," *American Journal of Sociology* 77: 660–79.

Tuchman, G. (1977) "The exception proves in the rule: the study of routine news practices," in P. Hirsch, P. Miller, and G. Kline (eds) *Strategies for Communications Research: Annual Review of Communications Research*, vol. 6, Beverly Hills, CA: Sage.

Tuchman, G. (1978) *Making News: a Study in the Construction of Reality*, New York: Free Press.

Tuchman, G. (1980) "Facts of the moment: a theory of news," *Social Interaction* 3: 9–20.

Tulloch, J. and Alvarado, M. (1983) *Doctor Who: the Unfolding Text*, New York: St Martin's Press.

Turkle, S. (1984) *The Second Self: Computers and the Human Spirit*, New York: Simon & Schuster.

Turner, B.A. (1981) "Some practical aspects of qualitative data analysis," *Quality and Quantity* 15: 225–47.

Turner, R.M. and Surace, S.J. (1956) "Zoot-suiters and Mexicans: symbols in crowd behavior," *American Journal of Sociology* 63: 14–20.

Turow, J. (1989) *Playing Doctor: Television, Storytelling, and Medical Power*, New York: Oxford.

Umiker-Sebeok, J. (ed.) (1987) *Marketing Signs*, Berlin: Mouton de Gruyter.

UNESCO (1977) *Media Studies in Education*, Paris: UNESCO.

UNESCO (1982) "Declaration on media education," in L. Masterman (1985) *Teaching the Media*, London: Comedia.

UNESCO (1984) *Media Education*, Paris: UNESCO.

Vygotsky, L. (1962) *Thought and Language*, Cambridge, MA: MIT Press.

Wallas, G. (1915) *The Great Society: A Psychological Study*, New York: Macmillan.

Watson, J. and Hill, A. (1989) *A Dictionary of Communication and Media Studies*, 2nd edn, London: Edward Arnold.

Watt, I. (1957) *The Rise of the Novel*, London: Penguin; repr. 1961, Stanford, CA: Stanford University Press.

Wax, R.H. (1971) *Doing Field Work: Warnings and Advice*, Chicago: University of Chicago Press.

Webb, E., Campbell, D., and Schwartz, R. (1966) *Unobtrusive Measures: Nonreactive Research in the Social Sciences*, Chicago: Rand McNally.

Weber, M. (1918) "Politics as a vocation," repr. (1958) in H.H. Gerth and C. W. Mills (eds) *From Max Weber*, New York: Oxford University Press.

Weber, M. (1964) *The Theory of Social and Economic Organization*, New York: Free Press.

Wellman, B. and Berkowitz, S.D. (eds) (1988) *Social Structure: a Network Approach*, Cambridge: Cambridge University Press.

Wester, F.P. (1984) "De Gefundeerde Theorie-benadering: een Strategie voor Kwalitatief Onderzoek" (The "grounded theory" approach: a strategy for qualitative research), dissertation, Nijmegen: Catholic University.

Wester, F.P. (1987) *Strategieen voor Kwalitatief Onderzoek* (Strategies for Qualitative Research), Muiderberg: Coutinho.

Westley, W.A. (1951) *The Police: a Sociological Study of Law, Custom, and Morality*, Chicago: University of Chicago Press.

White, D.M. (1950) "The gatekeeper: a case study in the selection of news," *Journalism Quarterly* 27: 383–90.

White, R. (1984) "The need for new strategies of research on the democratisation of communication," paper, International Communication Association, San Francisco.

Williams, R. (1962) *Communications*, Harmondsworth: Penguin.

Williams, R. (1974) *Television: Technology and Cultural Form*, London: Fontana.

Williams, R. (1977) *Marxism and Literature*, London: Oxford University Press.

Williams, R. (1983a) "British film history: new perspectives," in J. Curran and V. Porter (eds) *British Cinema History*, Totowa, NJ: Barnes & Noble.

Williams, R. (1983b) *Keywords*, London: Fontana.

Wimmer, R.D. and Dommick, J.R. (1987) *Mass Media Research: an Introduction*, 2nd edn, Belmont, CA: Wadsworth.

Wimsatt, W. and Beardsley, M. (1954) "The intentional fallacy" and "The affective fallacy," in W. Wimsatt (ed.) *The Verbal Icon*, London: Methuen.

Wimsatt, W. and Brooks, C. (1957) *Literary Criticism: a Short History*, New York: Alfred A. Knopf.

Winch, P. (1958) *The Idea of a Social Science*, New York: Humanities Press.

Wittgenstein, L. (1958) *Philosophical Investigations*, London: Macmillan.

Wober, M. (1981) "Psychology in the future of broadcasting research," *Bulletin of the British Psychological Society* 34: 409–12.

Wodak, R., Nowak, P., Pelikan, J., Gruber, H., De Cillia, R., and Mitten, R. (1990) *"Wir sind unschuldige Täter": Studien zum antisemitischen Diskurs in Nachkriegsösterreich* ("We're innocent culprits": studies in the antisemitic discourse of postwar Austria), Frankfurt: Suhrkamp.

Wolcott, H. (1975) "Criteria for an ethnographic approach to research in schools," *Human Organization* 34, 2: 111–27.

Wolf, M., Meyer, T., and White, C. (1982) "A rules-based study of TV's role in the construction of social reality," *Journal of Broadcasting* 26, 4: 813–29.

Wright, A. (1979) *Local Radio and Local Democracy: a Study in Political Education*, London: Independent Broadcasting Authority.

Wright, W. (1975) *Six Guns and Society*, Berkeley, CA: University of California Press.

Young, I., Pye, R., and Thomas, H. (1979) *Evaluation of Channel 40 – Community Cable Television in Milton Keynes*, London: Communications Studies and Planning.

Zelditch, M. (1970) "Some methodological problems of field studies," in W.F. Filstead (ed.) *Qualitative Methodology: Firsthand Involvement with the Social World*, Chicago: Markham.

Index of names

Index of subjects